Classical Monologues

Women

Volume 4: From the Restoration to Bernard Shaw

CLASSICAL MONOLOGUES

Women

Volume 4: From the Restoration to Bernard Shaw

Edited with introductions by
Leon Katz

with the assistance of Georgi Iliev

APPLAUSE THEATRE & CINEMA BOOKS

NEW YORK

Classical Monologues: Women
Volume 4: From the Restoration to Bernard Shaw
edited with introductions by Leon Katz

ISBN 1-55783-615-9

Library of Congress Cataloging-in-Publication Data:
Classical monologues from Aeschylus to Bernard Shaw / edited with introductions by Leon Katz with the assistance of Georgi Iliev.
  p. cm.
  ISBN 1-55783-575-6
1. Monologues.
2. Drama—Collections.
3. Young men—Drama.
I. Katz, Leon, 1919–
  PN2080.C58 2002
808.82'45—dc21
2002004863

British Library Cataloging-in-Publication Data:
A catalog record of this book is available from the British Library

Applause Theatre & Cinema Books
151 West 46th Street, 8th Floor
New York, NY 10036
Phone: (212) 575-9265
Fax: (646) 562-5852
Email: info@applausepub.com
Internet: www.applausepub.com
Applause books are available through your local bookstore, or you may order at www.applausepub.com or call Music Dispatch at 800-637-2852.

SALES & DISTRIBUTION
North America: Europe:
Hal Leonard Corp.   Roundhouse Publishing Ltd.
7777 West Bluemound Road   Millstone, Limers Lane
P. O. Box 13819   Northam, North Devon EX39 2RG
Milwaukee, WI 53213   Phone: (0) 1237-474-474
Phone: (414) 774-3630   Fax: (0) 1237-474-774
Fax: (414) 774-3259   Email: roundhouse.group@ukgateway.net
Email: halinfo@halleonard.com
Internet: www.halleonard.com

CONTENTS

* Y=young, O=older; T=tragedy/drama, C=comedy

EIGHTEENTH-CENTURY FRENCH

EIGHTEENTH-CENTURY ENGLISH

EIGHTEENTH-CENTURY GERMAN

NINETEENTH-CENTURY FRENCH

NINETEENTH-CENTURY GERMAN

NINETEENTH-CENTURY ENGLISH

TWENTIETH-CENTURY ENGLISH

PRELIMINARY NOTE ON THE CHARACTERIZATION OF WOMEN IN WESTERN DRAMA

There's no getting away from it; most of it is damning testimony. The portrayals of women; the ideologies behind those portrayals; the characteristics attributed to them; the constrictions of situation in which they appear; the extraordinary psychology, morality, and causality, which are shown to govern their behavior; and the systematized rewards and punishments visited on them by the conventions of drama's structures might properly be said to belong to fantasy, if they were not reflections as in a partially shattered mirror of the same beliefs in reality. There's also no getting away from the fact that the portrayals of men suffer from the same fatalities. The difference, in effect, is enormous. There's implicit flattery in the portrayals of men even at their most "vicious": they're enlarged, after all, by manliness. There is implicit, at best, condescension and, at worst, condemnation in the portrayals of women even at their most "courageous" or "brilliant" or "virtuous": they're diminished, after all, by womanliness. For most of the development of Western drama, the basic assumption is that women are natively rudderless and that all of them—whether wise or foolish, virtuous or vicious, sane or insane—need guidance, constraint, and authority. Miraculously, with the exception of the most foolish and the most vicious, women characters themselves subscribe universally to that same set of beliefs.

To this extent: One of the extraordinary anomalies in our dramatic literature is the gusto with which women characters who are discovered to have committed moral transgressions volunteer to submit to or, if possible, anticipate the grimmest punishments of themselves they can imagine. They disgust themselves, verbally lash themselves, lay hands on themselves, starve themselves, and, if none of these are efficacious enough, they deliberately damn themselves to perdition with knives, swords, poisons, pistols, rivers, wells, or passing trains.

Or take the opposite case. There are the extraordinary number of women characters who take pride and pleasure in being models of servility, weakness, and helplessness. Listen to them carefully: they pride themselves on their abject surrender of themselves, their utter self-negation, and their proud admission that they don't have either the desire or the nature to exceed the handicap of womanhood; they flatter themselves on their perfect accommodations to subservience. The light they bathe in is shed by father, lover, or husband; the rule they live by is his, whether its substance is generous thought or private whim or worse. And the severity with which they live by this code is generally based on the demands father, lover, husband, or anyone makes on them. But that's the plus of the highest virtue: nobody asked and yet they give. Yet these apparent opposites are the same. Both are sworn to the principles of technical virtue and perfect obedience, and whether they are successful negotiators or fallen angels, they praise or blame themselves according to the same book of moral etiquette.

It's been observed before and it's observed here again that, as a consequence, the depiction of women as dramatic characters is made up of nothing but a small collection of cultural attributions. When we imagine we're discerning in that repository of fixed didacticisms characters' inner depth, meaning, or reality, we are not being blessed with unique powers of observation or intuition, but only with the delusionary comfort of self-flattery. Ingenuity can make anything of anything. It has recourse, after all, to a range of sophisticated vocabularies from the wisdom of street talk to the more formal packagings of words in professional psychology.

Sadly, apart from recreative pleasure, knowing all this helps not at all. No one—neither critics, dramaturgs, directors, spectators, nor (imagine) even playwrights—will voluntarily surrender their own moral and psychological idolatries for the small gain of admitting that, with respect to the realities of human beings, they're determinedly avoiding them and sticking to familiar pretense. Liars? No. We have no other filters for screening the truth of being, and the misfiltering of that truth is permanent. Characters—most particularly women characters as depicted in Western drama—are illusionary constructs, better or worse depending on the investment of illusionary perceptions with which the naked banality of their fixed didactic types is camouflaged and decorated.

The types are four—sometimes as is, sometimes qualified, sometimes mixed and matched: 1) helpless virtue (the patient Griselda); 2) sinister seductress (*la belle dame sans merci*); 3) Mother of Us All (Virgin Mary); 4) virago ("unwomanly" woman). Why these? For their implicit sermon, and for their fixity of reference, which is entirely toward their physical, moral, and psychological value to men. Two are "positive," two are "negative" models. The sermonizing may vary, as it does in our enlightened time, tolerating what was negative as positive and converting what was positive into negative; it makes no difference. The fundamental banality and unreality persist.

Then why bother? Why study to perform? Why pay attention at all? Habitually, it's done for the ingenuity of the construct. For the subtleties to be leeched out of the fixed pattern, for the game of intensifying a make-believe conviction, for the sheer force of, or the ingenious heaping of meaning onto, that make-believe. In fact, the only possible pleasure in all this:

creating artifice that exceeds the reach of banality. To be sure, the ingredients that go into the construction of that make-believe are themselves artificial constructs. Well, so it is in painting, so it is in music. And in those arts too the sheerest artifice can be converted into an illusion of representation. But when anyone wallows in that simple pleasure in those arts, we laugh, because we know better. We know that paint is paint and notes are notes, and that they refer more to themselves than to another referent. But in drama alone—well, in fiction too—we domesticate constructs and convert them into the real. As critics, we judge them, reason with them, correct their faults, and approve their good behavior; as audience, we fall in love with them, hate them, advise them, give up on them, and give them tenancy in the house next door. All of which is stupid, but relatively harmless. Real harm is done when constructs are divested of their decorative camouflage and revert to their original banality: to sermon, when we, their spectators, are asked to emulate artifice, the non-existent, and walk into a forest of mirrors in which the unreal reflects itself twice over and calls itself real. The illusion is costly; the emulation is impossible; the lunacy is rampant within the culture's ideological prisonhouse. That's where the defining nature of women characters is persistently lodged—within the confines of that ideological prisonhouse. Outside of which are real women.

In these pages—which catalogue a fair sampling of women characters in Western drama —something else becomes depressingly clear. With almost no exceptions, every woman depicted lives in only one relation: to men, and in only a very few postures toward them. In comedy, the push and pull of love, marriage, and adultery, with recourse to forgiveness and reconciliation; in tragedy, drama, and melodrama, the push and pull of love, hate, and adultery, with recourse to suicide and murder. The tempering of these relations and these recourses may be great or small, but until a slight modicum of fresh air was breathed into Western drama in the last hundred or so years, the fortunes of women in drama confronted almost nothing but the beneficence or the castigation of men. But make no mistake: as already pointed out above, reversing the moral understandings and preferences among these options opens no wide doors. The fundamental banality persists, and its unreality, and the tininess of the enclosure within which its morality has been renovated.

It's a depressing landscape. If you can find a way to adorn it with a bit of reality, a bit of truth, a bit of genuine conviction, more power to you. Of course, you'll only be decorating a corrupt body, but corrupt or not, illusionary or not, there is still the possibility in performance of that decoration bringing illusion and cliché closer to a semblance of reality, as close as transforming acting genius has done it many times over laboring in the lists of performance for the last more than two thousand years.

PREFACE

This anthology consists of more than five hundred entries in four volumes, the first two of men's monologues, the other two of women's.

The initial question is of course: what is "classic" and what is "classical?" "Classic" is more easily defined: every movie more than a year old. "Classical" as it pertains to plays is necessarily more difficult to pin down. For practical purposes, it involves some sort of separation from "modern," and the guidelines for that separation might be these: 1) texts that are "classical" are restricted by date to those that are roughly a century away (with a few exceptions which conscience did not permit to be excluded), and 2) texts that are recognizably at a distance from contemporary speech, and that demand a reasonable, sometimes considerable, stretch from an actor's normal rhetorical habits. Under these guidelines, it seems reasonable to include, for example, some nineteenth-century texts from farce and melodrama that have currently unfamiliar dialectal twists (see, for example, Sailor William in *Black-Ey'd Susan*, in Men's Volumes), as well as translations that though friendly to contemporary ears are still sufficiently distant from current speech to qualify. These demarcations may be a bit porous, but for practical purposes of audition and workshop, they should hold.

Similarly, the division between "younger" and "older" is also porous. What's young? Before our own age of lengthening longevity, right through the nineteenth century, it was more or less the rule that "young" hardly extended beyond the twenties—for men possibly to the very early thirties, for women at the very best to the early twenties. But not to be too harsh or doctrinaire, there is added here another, more malleable criterion: the weight of authority, the weight of experience, and the dignity of title. Between the two, the decision regarding the age of characters remains of course subjective, but the harm to characters' standing or reputation, in whatever category they find themselves, is at most, slight.

Emotion is the beginning, the wellspring, from which we naïvely suppose actors channel and shape their performances and bring them to life. Well, in a way, yes. But consider. A sequence of thoughts can conceivably be expressed with no particular emotion and be understood and accepted as rational communication. Try it the other way around—expressing emotion with no particular thought—and you'd be certifiable. Emotion is the ephemera of thought. And the actor's performance begins inside the line of logical—not emotional—connections of a text's moment to moment.

This anthology is devoted to the proposition that intelligent textual analysis is the primary instrument of performance, and it gives the occasion, in a large number of instances, for the actor to draw significantly on intellectual acuity preceding any emotional urges. To put it another way, a speech's emotional progression is its logical progression at a second remove. And the particularity and finesse of emotional performance corresponds precisely to the particularity and finesse of its intellectual perception.

With that proposition in mind, the headnotes preceding each of the monologues are of three kinds (sometimes featured individually, sometimes all in one): a description of the speech's strategy; a breakdown of its logical progression; a description of its context. Let's go over them one at a time:

STRATEGY

1. The speaker's strategy (his/her intention): Sometimes it's uniform throughout the speech, and in the labor of defining it, I've seen many actors stuck trying to articulate what that uniform intention might be. ("I want love"; no, says the mentor, that's not specific. All right, "I want to get her into bed"; no, says the mentor, that's not the motive behind the motive. Okay, "I want to dominate"; well, let's talk further about this.) But articulated precisely or not, it is as likely as not that initial intent may not stay fixed throughout the speech. When it doesn't, the vagaries of the character's mind may dance through a jungle of intents (see Lorenzaccio's remarkable speech when he's getting ready to murder de Medici in de Musset's *Lorenzaccio*) or the speaker taking cues from his listener's silent or spoken reaction, or his own, may alter its direction, qualify it, or change it altogether. The tendency in classically structured soliloquy is to stay doggedly on track, because the private conference with the self is usually intended to work toward the resolution of a dilemma, to process the likely obstacles to a plan of action, or—and these are the most interesting ones—to battle conscience whose fixed ideals and unspoken beliefs overwhelm practical intent. Whatever the case may be, the tracking of the "intent's" progress is one task assumed in these headnotes.

2. The playwright's strategies: They're not formulas but habits. Major speeches tend to fall into distinguishable kinds and tend to be shaped, by both habit and tradition, into certain formal patterns that have remained fairly fixed throughout the course of Western drama. Some of the most powerful speeches, in for example, Euripides, Seneca, Schiller, Büchner, or Shaw, are almost identical in their rhetorical structure. Some examples of the most usual ones (it might be helpful if we gave them names): the Speech of Justification (among the greatest, the Emperor Augustus in Corneille's *Cinna*); the Speech of Persuasion (among the most moving, Jocasta in Seneca's *Phoenician Women*); the Speech of Denunciation, in which the

decibels run from wrath (Theseus in Euripides' *Hippolytus*) to barely audible contempt (Mr. O'Connell's great speech in Granville-Barker's *Waste*); the formal narrative speech (messengers' recitations of offstage catastrophes in Greek tragedy, or Rodrigue's recounting of his battlefield triumph in *Le Cid*). All have formally shaped addresses, in which over and above their dramatic function and emotional investment (sometimes enormous and sometimes nil) the actor has also to catch the sheer display involved in the music and the epic scaling of their rhetoric. The playwright's strategy in these passages usually comes as close to aria as it does to flat speech, and not to honor that dimension is like muttering song lyrics under your breath instead of singing them out loud.

LOGICAL (SOMETIMES ALOGICAL) PROGRESSION
Whether rational or deranged, the mind is moving from one notion to the next in a chain of changing assertions that link. Figuring out the exact continuity of those links can be easy in narratives or in expositions that merely detail a sequence of ordered events. But when the connections are either muffled or random, the work of the actor begins. The headnotes try particularly hard to be helpful in this respect: at the risk of being accused of childishness, they sometimes enumerate unashamedly and naively the steps of these progressions, sometimes—can you believe it?—by the numbers. Why such silliness? Because it is precisely these progressions of linked-but-sometimes-difficult-to-grasp sense that provide the basis for the emotional progressions that then become the sustaining life of soliloquies.

CONTEXT
Obviously, there's the plot, the character, the situation just before, and the surrounding situation, that provide the immediate context for individual monologues. The headnotes provide necessary information concerning these facts. But there's the larger, enormously significant perspective—the mindset and the beliefs and assumptions which the plays inevitably reflect—that the headnotes dwell on too. It's within these structures of belief that plays and speeches harbor their ultimate meanings, and their exploration, certainly in the greatest performances I've been privileged to see, give the ultimate richness of meaning and effect to actors' interpretations.

On the question of translation, Voltaire still, I think, has the last word. It's discouraging. How close can translation get—to meaning, to tone, to deftness of statement, in translatorese? Voltaire in the eighteenth century had this to say, and nobody has yet spoken the bad news better:

> It is impossible to convey through any modern language, all
> the power of Greek expressions; they describe, with one
> stroke, what costs us a whole sentence... That language had
> not only the advantage of filling the imagination with a word,

but every word, we know, had its peculiar melody, which charmed the ear while it displayed the finest pictures to the mind; and for this reason all our translations from the Greek poets are weak, dry, and poor; it is imitating palaces of porphyry with bricks and pebbles.

What's true for Greek remains as true for modern language translation as well: no language can give up its peculiar music/sense to equivalents in another language. What Molière, for example, suffers in transit from French to English is possibly an exceptionally grim instance of bricks and pebbles making believe they're porphyry. When imitated precisely in English, his clarity, his ease, his perfect accommodation of plain sense to the straitjacket of hexameter couplets convert into deadly banality, insufferable in expression, and plainly laughable in sense. (Goethe, another victim, that this editor felt it best to sidestep altogether. *Faust* in English sometimes marches to the tune and sense of Jack and Jill.)

What to do? Without hoping for true equivalence, for the purposes of actors speaking texts intended to stand in for some of the greatest dramatic passages in other languages, the uneasy solution is simply to avoid the unspeakable, in both senses. No rigid policy was followed: for example, of using only up-to-date, "relevant"—and sometimes hopelessly removed from the original—translations on the one hand, or scrupulously "faithful"—and sometimes hopelessly unspeakable—versions on the other. Compromises, of course, abound—some for reasons of availability, others in the interest of sampling different tacks to a single author's texts when multiple selections from the same author are included. The criterion was roughly this: how comfortably can the text sit on the actor's tongue, and how far can it reach toward the overall effect, admittedly very approximate, of the original? And admittedly, you can't win.

RESTORATION

135.
CLEOPATRA, WITH ROYAL CEREMONY, JOINS ANTONY IN DEATH (UI)

(1671) JOHN DRYDEN, *ALL FOR LOVE*, ACT V, SC. 1

"Give me my robe," commands Cleopatra in Shakespeare's tragedy, "put on my crown; I have Immortal longings in me"; and later, "I am fire and air; my other elements I give to baser life."

But unlike Shakespeare's, Dryden's Cleopatra doesn't aspire to such elevation; she remains entirely terrestrial. Still, deriving *All for Love* from *Antony and Cleopatra,* and in Cleopatra's death following much of Shakespeare's patterning of the scene, eventually Dryden's queen in those last moments aspires to a dignity undetected in the earlier action of the play. In her suicide beside the body of Antony, she puts aside the meaner woman in evidence before, and as she takes the asp to her breast and puts on the robes of majesty, she becomes, if not transcendent, certainly noble, majestic.

With their defeat at the battle of Actium, both Antony and Cleopatra are at the mercy of the victorious Octavius Caesar, and have the alternatives of being dragged through the streets of Rome in triumph or dying a "Roman" death by suicide. At the sight of the body of Antony, Cleopatra instantly takes her cue. She rejects the thought of Caesar's mercy, and relishes the thought of closing life with Antony and leaving Octavia, his wife, with nothing but the ceremony of mourning after. She sends her women off, and for a moment—Dryden's invention—is alone with Antony. "We're now alone in secrecy and silence; And is not this like lovers?" And is it not another triumph over Octavia? But the moment contracts the large event to a quiet, human scale. When the women return, Cleopatra sets the stage for death: her robes, her crown, the asps—and, seated beside the corpse of Antony ("See how the lovers sit in state together, As they were giving laws to half mankind"), she's ready for her death. But—again, Dryden's addition—a momentary lapse into fear quickly overcome, and dying, reaches toward the Antony waiting after death, and the body beside her. [See, in Men's vols.: "Antony Mourns His Fallen State" and "Antony Accuses Cleopatra of Being the Instrument of His Dounfall."]

CLEOPATRA

My lord, my lord! speak, if you yet have being;
Sigh to me, if you can not speak; or cast
One look! Do anything that shows you live.
Too far to hear,
A lump of senseless clay.
He charged me not to grieve.
And I'll obey him.
I have not loved a Roman not to know
What should become his wife—his wife, my Charmion!
For 'tis to that high title I aspire,
And now I'll not die less. Let dull Octavia
Survive to mourn him, dead. My nobler fate
Shall knit our spousals with a tie too strong
For Roman laws to break.
Caesar is merciful,
To those that want his mercy. My poor lord
Made no covenant with him to spare me
When he was dead. Yield me to Caesar's pride?
What! to be led in triumph through the streets,
A spectacle to base plebeian eyes,
While some dejected friend of Antony's,
Close in a corner, shakes his head, and mutters
A secret curse on her who ruined him?
I'll none of that.
Quick, my friends,
Despatch. 'Ere this, the town's in Caesar's hands.
My lord looks down concerned, and fears my stay,
Lest I should be surprised.
Keep him not waiting for his love too long.
You, Charmion, bring my crown and richest jewels;
With them, the wreath of victory I made
(Vain augury!) for him who now lies dead.

2

You, Iras, bring the cure of all our ills.
The aspics,
Must I bid you twice?

(Exit Charmion and Iras)
'Tis sweet to die when they would force life on me,
To rush into the dark abode of death,
And seize him first. If he be like my love,
He is not frightful, sure.
We're now alone in secrecy and silence;
And is not this like lovers? I may kiss
These pale, cold lips; Octavia does not see me.
And oh! 'tis better far to have him thus
Than see him in her arms.—Oh, welcome,
Short ceremony, friends,
But yet it must be decent. First, this laurel
Shall crown my hero's head: he fell not basely,
Nor left his shield behind him.—Only thou
Couldst triumph o'er thyself; and thou alone
Wert worthy so to triumph.
These ensigns of pomp and royalty to meet my love
As when I saw him first on Cydnus' bank,
All sparkling, like a goddess; so adorned,
I'll find him once again. My second spousals
Shall match my first in glory. Haste, haste; both,
And dress the bride of Antony.
—'Tis done.
Now seat me by my lord. I claim this place,
For I must conquer Caesar, too, like him,
And win my share of the world.—Hail, you dear relics
Of my immortal love!
O let no impious hand remove you hence,
But rest for ever here! Let Egypt give
His death that peace which it denied his life.—
Reach me the casket.
Underneath the fruit
The aspic lies.
Welcome, thou kind deceiver!

(Putting aside the leaves)
Thou best of thieves, who, with an easy key,
Dost open life and, unperceived by us,
Even steal us from ourselves, discharging so
Death's dreadful office better than himself,
Touching our limbs so gently into slumber

3

That Death stands by, deceived by his own image,
And thinks himself but sleep.
Haste, bare my arm, and rouse the serpent's fury.

(Holds out her arm, and draws it back)
Coward flesh,
Wouldst thou conspire with Caesar to betray me
As thou wert none of mine? I'll force thee to it,
And not be sent by him,
But bring, myself, my soul to Antony.

*(Turns aside, and then shows her arm
bloody)*
Take hence. The work is done.
Already, death, I feel thee in my veins.
I go with such a will to find my lord
That we shall quickly meet.
A heavy numbness creeps through every limb,
And now 'tis at my head. My eyelids fall,
And my dear love is vanished in a mist.—
Where shall I find him—where? O turn me to him,
And lay me on his breast!—Caesar, thy worst.
Now part us, if thou canst.

(Dies)

AUGURY: an omen, prophecy. ASPICS: asps, or Egyptian cobras. CYDNUS: a river in
southeastern Asia Minor.

136.

MRS. PINCHWIFE, FORCED BY HER HUSBAND TO WRITE TO HORNER REJECTING HIS ADVANCES, SUBSTITUTES ANOTHER LETTER (YC)

(1675) WILLIAM WYCHERLEY, *THE COUNTRY WIFE*, ACT IV, SC. 2

[Quoting from entry in Men's vols.: "Pinchwife Apprehends His Wife

Authoring a Letter of Her Own Invention"] "Pinchwife, to cheat the town's cuckold-makers, has gone into the country to buy a wife ignorant of men's uses of women and equally of women's wiles toward men. His aim is to keep her close, in fact imprisoned at home, out of reach of the town's seductions. Unhappily for him, his sister Alithea introduces wife Margery to the theater, where at her first visit she exchanges glances with Horner [for whom see, in Men's vols.: "Horner Explains to His Doctor the Advantages of Pretending to Be a Eunuch"], she instantly falls in love with him, and he is instantly determined to have her.... Determined to be finally rid of Horner's attentions to his wife, Pinchwife dictates the letter Margery is to send to Horner repulsing him. In his absence, she writes another more to her taste."

Beneath the comic wit in the writing of this famous letter-writing scene, there is an assumption concerning human nature, whose outlook toward sustained civilized decorum is bleak. Just as Horner is the quintessential representative of Restoration libertinism in his working principle that only the thinnest veneer of propriety conceals the universal appetite for sexual animality, Margery Pinchwife is the proof of his thesis. She, who is quintessentially innocent of even the thinnest of social veneers, matches perfectly in impulse what he has experimentally determined. Loving is rutting, and the supreme experimental intelligence of Horner has merely learned what Margery cannot conceivably formulate, but only perfectly and mindlessly exemplify.

The writing of the letter is part of Margery's process of self-education, in which she learns, one logical step after the other, the self-protective strategies for getting around the obstacles of that "veneer." The portrait of Margery is the portrait of pure, sure instinct that cannot, given human nature unspoiled, help but thread its way through the mire of prohibition to arrive at its natural object.

MRS. PINCHWIFE

(Beginning her letter)
"For Mr. Horner"—So, I am glad he has told me his name;
Dear Mr. Horner, but why should I send thee such a letter, that
will vex thee, and make thee angry with me;—well I will not
send it—Ay but then my husband will kill me—for I see
plainly, he won't let me love Mr. Horner—but what care I for
my husband—I won't so I won't send poor Mr. Horner such a
letter—but then my husband—But oh—what if I writ at

bottom, my husband made me write it—Ay but then my husband wou'd see't—Can one have no shift, ah, a *London* woman wou'd have had a hundred presently; stay—what if I shou'd write a letter, and wrap it up like this, and write upon't too; ay but then my husband wou'd see't—I don't know what to do—But yet evads I'll try, so I will—for I will not send this letter to poor Mr. Horner, come what will on't.

"Dear, Sweet Mr. Horner—*so—(She writes, and repeats what she hath writ.)* my husband wou'd have me send you a base, rude, unmannerly letter—but I won't—*so*—and wou'd have me forbid you loving me—but I won't—*so*—and wou'd have me say to you, I hate you poor Mr. Horner—but I won't tell a lie for him—*there*—for I'm sure if you and I were in the country at cards together,—*so*—I cou'd not help treading on your toe under the table—*so*—or rubbing knees with you, and staring in your face, 'till you saw me—*very well*—and then looking down, and blushing for an hour together—*so*—but I must make haste before my husband come; and now he has taught me to write letters: You shall have longer ones from me, who am, dear, dear, poor dear Mr. Horner, your most humble friend, and servant to command 'till death, Margery Pinchwife."

Stay—I must give him a hint at bottom—*so*—now wrap it up just like t'other—*so*—now write for Mr. Horner,—But oh now what shall I do with it? for here comes my husband.

(Enter Pinchwife)
Here.—No I must not give him that,

(He opens, and reads the first letter.)
so I had been served if I had given him this.
(Aside) Lord, what shall I do now? Nay then I have it—
Pray let me see't. Lord, you think me so arrant a fool, I cannot seal a letter, I will do't, so I will.

(Snatches the letter from him, changes it for the other, seals it, and delivers it to him)
So, han't I done it curiously? I think I have, there's my letter going to Mr. Horner; since he'll needs have me send letters to folks.

SHIFT: stratagem. EVADS: a corruption of "egad;" in turn a corruption of "ye gods."

137.

OLIVIA MOCKS THE PLAIN DEALER, AND DISMISSES HIM (YC)

(1676) WILLIAM WYCHERLEY, *THE PLAIN DEALER*, ACT II, SC. 1

Captain Manly, like the Alceste of Moliere's *The Misanthrope* (from whom he derives) [see, in Men's vols.: "Alceste Condemning Celimene's Falseness, Also Confesses His Love"], is inflexible in his hatred of the insincerities and hypocrisies of humankind, and invests his whole love in one who is its prime example. While away at sea, he entrusted her with his whole fortune for safe-keeping, and entrusted her care to his bosom friend Vernish. Returning, he discovers that they've married, and that Olivia has taken his wealth.

Slowly, he learns the whole truth of his betrayal. "Like the rest of the cheats of the world," Olivia confesses to herself during Manly's first visit to her, when he sees her entertaining fashionable fools and over-hears her railing at reputations, including his own, "when our cullies or creditors have found us out, and will or can trust us no longer... we are forced to use our lovers like cards, when we can get no more by 'em—throw 'em up in a pet, upon the first dispute." It is her only recourse, but a safe one. She at once turns her railing directly on Manly, and with the assurance of possessing his fortune (of which he at first knows nothing), her raillery sings out ingeniously, wittily, and terminally. From this exercise in mockery, there's clearly no turning back. But there's nothing to lose. As she expends her credit with him at one blow, she airs all the resentments toward him and malicious judgments of him she harbored during the time of his infatuation. As she does so, her pleasure and invention grow. Best for last: casually slipped into her railing is the news that not only has she married while he was gone, but the wealth he left with her can't be wrested again from her husband, whose "honor" would reckon that only her dishonor could have made Manly's fortune hers, and so there is no asking for its return.

> OLIVIA
>
> Noble captain, you cannot, sure, think anything could take me more than that heroic title of yours, captain; for you know we women love honor inordinately. Then, that noble lion-like mien of yours, that soldier-like, weather-beaten complexion,

and that manly roughness of your voice; how can they otherwise than charm us women, who hate effeminacy!

And then, that captain-like carelessness in your dress, but especially your scarf; 'twas just such another, only a little higher tied, made me in love with my tailor as he passed by my window the last training-day; for we women adore a martial man, and you have nothing wanting to make you more one, or more agreeable, but a wooden leg.

I go on then to your humor. Is there anything more agreeable than the pretty sullenness of that? than the greatness of your courage? which most of all appears in your spirit of contradiction, for you dare give all mankind the lie; and your opinion is your only mistress, for you renounce that too, when it becomes another man's.

Turn hither your rage, good Captain Swagger-huff, and be saucy with your mistress, like a true captain; but be civil to your rivals and betters; and do not threaten anything but me here, no, not so much as my windows, nor do not think yourself in the lodgings of one of your suburb mistresses beyond the Tower.

(Hark you a little, for I dare trust you with the secret: you are a man of so much honor, I'm sure)—I say, then, not expecting your return, or hoping ever to see you again, I have delivered your jewels to—My husband.

Ay, my husband; for since you could leave me, I am lately and privately married to one, who is a man of so much honor and experience in the world, that I dare not ask him for your jewels again, to restore 'em to you, lest he should conclude you never would have parted with 'em to me on any other score but the exchange of my honor: which rather than you'd let me lose, you'd lose, I'm sure, yourself those trifles of yours.

Oh, speak not! My servants know it not: I am married; there's no resisting one's destiny or love, you know. Nay, love him though I have married him, and he me: which mutual love I hope you are too good, too generous a man to disturb, by any future claim, or visits, to me. 'Tis true, he is now absent in the country, but returns shortly; therefore I beg of you, for your own ease and quiet, and my honor, you will never see me more.

But if you should ever have anything to say to me hereafter, let that young gentleman there be your messenger. Alas, his youth would keep my husband from suspicions, and his visits from scandal; for we women may have pity for such as he, but no love: and I already think you do not well to spirit him away to sea; and the sea is already but too rich with the spoils of the shore.

(Enter Lettice)
Well, Lettice, are the cards and all ready within? I come, then.—Captain, I beg your pardon: if you would have me thrive, curse me; for that you'll do heartily, I suppose. And, to requite all your curses, may the curse of loving me still fall upon your proud, hard heart, that could be so cruel to me in these horrid curses! but heaven forgive you!

(Exit Olivia)

SUBURBAN WOMEN BEYOND THE TOWER: loose women from the countryside.

138.

THE DUCHESS OF EBOLI, FRUSTRATED IN HER AMBITION, DETERMINES TO SETTLE FOR ADULTEROUS LOVE (YT)

(1676) THOMAS OTWAY, *DON CARLOS*, ACT I, SC. 1 AND ACT II, SC.1

The Duchess of Eboli is blunt in her motive and her strategy: if she can't have royalty, at least she can have better sex. She had hoped for union with King Philip of Spain himself, and then with his son Don Carlos, with not a glimmer of hope, and has to suffer marriage with old Ruy-Gomez, an "imperfect feeble dotard" who plots and spies for the King. But she has little trouble carrying out her intention with Prince John of Austria, the randy brother of the King who has the moral outlook of his counterparts in Restoration comedy. In comedy, the two might have fared well, playing coy at first, succumbing soon, quarreling over mutual jealousy, reconciling—all of which is later accomplished here—but in tragedy, there's a considerable price to pay—for her, of course; not for him. The Duchess at the end is killed by the jealous husband who, ironically, himself plotted falsely the King's becoming jealous of his wife and son. At the beginning, though, clear-eyed and unavailable to conscience, the Duchess plots her court career.

DUCHESS OF EBOLI

In thy fond policy, blind fool, go on,
And make what haste then canst to be undone,
Whilst I have nobler business of my own.
Was I bred up in greatness; have I been
Nurtured with glorious hopes to be a queen;
Made love my study, and with practised charms
Prepared myself to meet a monarch's arms;
At last to be condemned to the embrace
Of one whom nature made to her disgrace,
An old, imperfect, feeble dotard, who
Can only tell (alas!) what he would do?
On him to throw away my youth and bloom
As jewels that are lost to enrich a tomb?
No, though all hopes are in a husband dead,
Another path to happiness I'll tread;
Elsewhere find joys which I'm in him denied:
Yet, while he can, let the slave serve my pride.
Still I'll in pleasure live, in glory shine;
The gallant, youthful Austria shall be mine;
To him with all my force of charms I'll move;
Let others toil for greatness, whilst I love.
O Heaven! What charms in youth and vigor are!
Yet he in conquest has not gone too far;
Too easily I'll not myself resign;
Ere I am his, I'll make him surely mine;
Draw him by subtle baits into the trap,
Till he's too far got in to make escape;
About him swiftly the soft snare I'll cast,
And when I have him there, I'll hold him fast.

THY FOND POLICY...TO BE UNDONE: her husband, who has just shared with her his plot to undo the Prince Don Carlos, and gain succession to the throne. THE GALLANT, YOUTHFUL AUSTRIA: Don John of Austria, the King's brother.

139.

STATIRA'S RAGE AGAINST ALEXANDER IS UNDERMINED BY HER INFATUATION FOR HIM (YT)

(1677) NATHANIEL LEE, *THE RIVAL QUEENS, OR THE DEATH OF ALEXANDER THE GREAT*, ACT I, SC. 1

"We only warm the head," wrote Dryden about Lee's tragedies, "but you the heart." The master of the heroic play was, in effect, passing on the mantle to a new mastery: Otway's and Lee's tragedies of pity and passion. Whose passion, and pity for what?

Whether it was honored, believed, mocked, or insulted, there had been in both the tragedy and comedy of the Restoration an assumption by women that they were equal in worth to men. An attack or casual humiliation or being ignored evoked rhetorical flights of bitter, sustained rage. Some of the most memorable passages in Restoration comedy are the diatribes of women suddenly fallen from the pedestal of adoration to find themselves "scorned." But the suddenness of their fall, and their consequent rage, was no accident; it was the result of the intruding recognition that their claim had had at best only a tenuous reality.

Statira in this, her initial speech in the tragedy, makes that very discovery, and exhibits that very passion. She, the wife of Alexander the Great, learns, during his time of courtly ease in Babylon, that he's asked his first wife, Roxana, to return. The news inflames Statira, who screams, "Give me a knife, a draught of poison," to kill herself. Her passion runs its course, but then it's supplanted. The very claim she is making by her rage is gradually undercut: she remembers her love; she remembers her love's nurturing his wounds; she remembers his jessamine breath, his sweet breast, his talk, his passion, his grace, his very falseness which was "a kind of heaven." It was a Love that, like a crippling injury or illness, surrendered to its own helplessness, and falling in love with that very condition, ended by giving helplessness enthusiastically willing consent. And helplessness confronting "scorn" or any other abuse wrung pity.

This was not generally the practice of the "scorned" in Restoration comedy, but in Restoration tragedy, females became more and more "softened," and what in the comedies was the mark of their unabashed self-valuation became more and more in the tragedies the mark of their unabashed self-abasement. After the briefest intermission of a few years in Restoration drama, Virtue once again hugged its own abasement with pride, which posture became once again synonymous with the purity of female character.

The gradual softening of Statira's determination to kill herself in rage ends a bit later in her deciding instead merely to see no more of Alexander, ever, and retire to isolated seclusion. She of course does not. The hot passion of the confrontations between Statira and Roxana later in the play kept *The Rival Queens* popular with actresses and audiences well into the eighteenth century.

STATIRA

Give me a knife, a draught of poison, flames;
Swell, heart; break, break, thou stubborn thing.
Now, by the sacred fire, I'll not be held;
Why do you wish me life, yet stifle me
For want of air? Pray give me leave to walk.
He hates,
He loathes the beauties which he has enjoyed.
O, he is false, that great, that glorious man
Is tyrant midst of his triumphant spoils,
Is bravely false to all the gods, forsworn.
Yet who would think it? No, it cannot be,
It cannot. What, that dear, protesting man!
He that has warmed my feet with thousand sighs,
Then cooled 'em with his tears, died on my knees,
Outwept the morning with his dewy eyes,
And groaned and swore the wond'ring stars away?
O, 'tis my fondness, and my easy nature
That would excuse him; but I know he's false,
'Tis now the common talk, the news o' th' world,
False to Statira, false to her that loved him.
That loved him, cruel Victor as he was,
And took him bathed all o'er in Persian blood,
Kissed the dear, cruel wounds, and washed 'em o'er
And o'er in tears; then bound 'em with my hair,
Laid him all night upon my panting bosom,
Lulled like a child, and hushed him with my songs.

My Parisatis,
Thus with thy hand held up, thus let me swear thee.
By the eternal body of the sun,

Whose body, O, forgive the blasphemy,
I loved not half so well as the least part
Of my dear, precious, faithless Alexander;
For I will tell thee, and to warn thee of him,
Not the spring's mouth, nor breath of jessamine,
Nor violets' infant sweets, nor opening buds
Are half so sweet as Alexander's breast;
From every pore of him a perfume falls,
He kisses softer than a southern wind,
Curls like a vine, and touches like a god.
Then he will talk, good gods, how he will talk!
Even when the joy he sighed for is possessed,
He speaks the kindest words and looks such things,
Vows with such passion, swears with so much grace,
That 'tis a kind of heaven to be deluded by him.
But what was it that I would have you swear?
Alas, I had forgot. Let me walk by
And weep awhile, and I shall soon remember.

PARISATIS: Statira's sister. JESSAMINE: jasmine.

140.
LADY KNOWELL PRETENDS TO CLASSICAL LEARNING AND VISITS SCORN ON EVERYTHING LESS (OC)

(1678) APHRA BEHN, *SIR PATIENT FANCY*, ACT I, SC. 1

Almost concurrent with Moliere's attack on ladies' learning [see Vol. 3, No. 130] is Aphra Behn's similar jeer in London. But Mrs. Behn's portrait takes pleasure in the delight her Lady Knowell takes in her own pretension, not merely in a sober recitation of inadvertent absurdities. A bubbling enthusiast for the ancients, Lady Knowell's joy in them happens to proceed her knowledge of them: though that's only half true, since she's attained a half, though flawed, knowledge. Unlike Moliere's Philaminte, whom we are to take to be a reprehensible instance of both social and intellectual unreason, Lady Knowell's bouncing liveliness, for its delightful grin, invites forgiveness for so small a lapse as her pretension to learning. She might even prove that the pleasure in pretension is at least as pleasurable—possibly more so—as the pleasure of actual learning.

Lady Knowell arrives at her home with the young Leander Fancy in tow, and meets the two young ladies—Lucretia, her daughter, and Isabella, Leander's true fancy, who is visiting. Lady Knowell bubbles happily about the ancients while Leander, whom she is too old to fancy but does, is in torture to get away from her. Not a possibility. Lady Knowell, suspecting Leander's preference for Isabella, keeps him tightly at her side, and, inviting him to the pleasures of reading Martial with her in her own chamber, spirits him out of the room and away from temptation.

LADY KNOWELL

Oh, fy upon't. See, Mr. Fancy, where your cousin and my Lucretia are idling. *Dii boni*, what an insupportable loss of time's this? Which might be better employed, Mr. Fancy, in consultation with the ancients.—Oh, the delight of books! when I was of their age, I always employed my looser hours in reading—if serious, 'twas Tacitus, Seneca, Plutarch's *Morals*, or some such useful author; if in an humor gay, I was for poetry, Virgil, Homer, or Tasso. Oh, that love between Rinaldo and Armida, Mr. Fancy! Ah, the caresses that fair Corcereis gave, and received from the young warrior; ah, how soft, delicate, and tender! Upon my honor, I cannot read them in the excellence of their original language, without I know not what emotions. But oh! faugh, Mr. Fancy. Can any thing that's great or moving be expressed in filthy English?—I'll give you an energetical proof, Mr. Fancy; observe but divine Homer in the Grecian language—*Ton d'apamibominous prosiphe podas ocbus Achilleus!* Ah, how it sounds! which English'd dwindles into the most grating stuff:—Then the swift-foot Achilles made reply. Oh faugh.

Come, Mr. Fancy, we'll pursue our first design of retiring into my cabinet, and reading a leaf or two in Martial; I am a little dull, and would fain laugh. Our discourse will be so much better than with these young ladies. Oh, how I hate the impertinence of women, who for the generality have no other knowledge than that of dressing; I am uneasy with the unthinking creatures. No, I am for the substantial pleasure of an author. *Philosophemur!* is my motto,—I'm strangely fond of you, Mr. Fancy, for being a scholar. Well, then, Mr. Fancy, let's to my cabinet—your hand.

MARTIAL (ca. AD 38–102): Roman author, famous for his epigrams. DII BONI: "dei boni," "good gods." [PUBLIUS CORNELIUS] TACITUS (ca. AD 55–120): Roman historian. [LUCIUS ANNAEUS] SENECA (ca. 4 BC–AD 65): Roman philosopher and playwright. PLUTARCH (ca. 46–120): Greek biographer. VIRGIL [PUBLIUS VERGILIUS MARO] (70–19 BC): Roman poet, author of *The Aeneid*. HOMER (tenth century BC): Greek epic poet, author of *The Iliad* and *The Odyssey*. [TORQUATO] TASSO (1544–95): Italian poet. RINALDO AND ARMINDA: the lovers in Tasso's poem, *Rinaldo*. *TON D'APAMIBOMINOUS PROSIPHE PODAS OCBUS ACHILLEUS*: from the *Iliad;* a Homeric "formula," meaning essentially, "thus said Achilles," but literally, "thus answering back, spoke the swift-footed Achilles." *PHILOSOPHEMUR*: Latin, "let's philosophise."

141.

LADY FANCY COMPLAINS TO HER NEW LOVER OF HER UNABATINGLY ATTENTIVE HUSBAND (YC)

(1678) APHRA BEHN, *SIR PATIENT FANCY*, ACT II, SC. 1

Sir Patient Fancy, an old hypochondriac, has taken a second wife, Lucia, who is young and beautiful; and though she pretends the greatest affection and strictest marital virtue toward her husband, has never abandoned her lover Wittmore, whom she would have married but for that they shared not only their love but their poverty. It's Lady Fancy's torment now that her doting old husband gives her no leisure from his sight, or time for her lover. They've escaped for a moment into the garden, where Lady Fancy hopes to remove Wittmore's doubts of her fidelity by confessing her helplessness in escaping her husband's attentions. But even this stolen moment is to be interrupted by the jealous old man's prying. His sudden appearance will force them to invent a story [see, in Men's vols.: "Wittmore, Under Instructions from Lucia, Must 'Feign a Courtship' to Isabella"]: that Wittmore is in fact the suitor of Sir Fancy's daughter, and then, forced to prove it, he will provoke Lady Fancy's jealousy.

But before she suffers that annoyance, she reviews for Wittmore the ones she suffers now: not only does Sir Patience cling to her at home, but he brings her everywhere he goes abroad, most terribly to his meetings with the other religious of his (obviously puritanical) sect who "sneer at me, pat [her] breasts, and cry fie, fie upon this fashion of tempting nakedness." Not even her pretending sickness like his will give them opportunity; he'll plague her "with continual physic and extempore prayer till I were sick indeed." No way out.

Lady Fancy

Sir Patient is now asleep, and 'tis to those few minutes we are obliged for this enjoyment, which should love make us transgress, and he should wake and surprise us, we are undone forever. No, let us employ this little time we have in consulting how we may be often happy; and securely so: Oh, how I languish for the dear opportunity! For though I am yet unsuspected by my husband, I am eternally plagued with his company; he's so fond of me, he scarce gives me time to write to thee, he waits on me from room to room, hands me in the garden, shoulders me in the balcony, nay, does the office of my women, dresses and undresses me, and does so smirk at his handywork. In fine, dear Wittmore, I am impatient till I can have less of his company, and more of thine.

Does he never go out of town? Never without me. Nor to church? To a meeting-house and then too carries me, and is as vainly proud of me as of his rebellious opinion, for his religion means nothing but that, and contradiction; which I seem to like too, since 'tis the best cloak I can put on to cheat him with.

But, dear Wittmore, there's nothing so comical as to hear me cant, and even cheat those knaves, the preachers themselves, that delude the ignorant rabble. Judge what a fine life I lead the while, to be set up with an old, formal, doting, sick husband, and a herd of sniveling, grinning hypocrites, that call themselves the teaching saints; who, under pretence of securing me to the number of their flock, do so sneer upon me, pat my breasts, and cry fie, fie upon this fashion of tempting nakedness. *(Through the nose)*

Think, dear Wittmore, think, I have thought over all our devices to no purpose. He has no mutinous cabal, nor coffee-houses, where he goes religiously to consult the welfare of the nation. His imagined sickness has made this their rendezvous. Ah, perhaps when he goes to his blind devotion, I can pretend to be sick? That may give us at least two or three opportunities to begin with. Oh! No! Then I should be plagued with continual physic and extempore prayer till I were sick indeed.

Damn the humorous coxcomb and all his family; what shall we do?

"REBELLIOUS OPINION...CONTRADICTION": dissenting from Church of England doctrine. CANT: to pretend religiousness or piety. THE TEACHING SAINTS: what the Puritans called themselves. CABAL: a circle of conspirators.

142.

APHRA BEHN SEES NO HINDRANCE TO WOMEN WRITING AS WELL AS MEN (OC)

(1678) APHRA BEHN, *SIR PATIENT FANCY*, EPILOGUE

Aphra Behn, almost as though responding to Moliere's denigration of women's learned ambitions [see Vol. 3, No. 130], asks: "What has poor woman done, that she should be Debarred from sense and sacred poetry?" and makes her case. But after enumerating the ways in which women are not credited and yet are not equal to, and are actually superior to males in knowing, observing, and being able to bear fops and country fools and city fools and punks and cuckolds; in having sensibilities in love and subtleties in manipulating pleasure unequaled by men; and because of these virtues are peculiarly fit for writing plays as plays are currently liked. There is one—surprising—brag that is not so much for women writers in general as for Aphra Behn in particular: that it's time for the three unities (of time, place, action) and for traditional "method and rule" in writing plays to give way to—what Mrs. Behn particularly prides herself on, and for which she was both applauded and berated—writing "unlabored farce." The uncorseting of the unities and of the other critical strictures was turned to hilarious advantage in her farces, and earned her the right to ask again at her argument's end: "pray tell me then Why women should not write as well as men."

BEHN

I here and there o'erheard a coxcomb cry, *(Looking about)*
Ah, rot it—'tis a woman's comedy.
One, who because she lately chanced to please us,
With her damned stuff, will never cease to tease us.

What has poor woman done, that she must be
Debarred from sense and sacred poetry?
Why in this age has Heaven allowed you more,
And women less of wit than heretofore?
We once were famed in story, and could write
Equal to men; could govern, nay, could fight.
We still have passive valor and can show,
Would Custom give us leave, the active too,
Since we no provocations want from you.
For who but we could your dull fopperies bear,
Your saucy love and your brisk nonsense hear;
Endure your worse than womanish affectation,
Which renders you the nuisance of the nation;
Scorned even by all the misses of the Town,
A jest to vizard mask, the pit-buffoon;
A glass by which the admiring country fool
May learn to dress himself *en ridicule:*
Both striving who shall most ingenious grow
In lewdness, foppery, nonsense, noise, and show.
And yet to these fine things we must submit
Our reason, arms, our laurels, and our wit:
Because we do not laugh at you, when lewd,
And scorn and cudgel ye when you are rude.
That we have nobler souls than you, we prove,
By how much more we're sensible of love;
Quickest in finding all the subtlest ways
To make your joys, why not to make you plays?
We best can find your foibles, know our own,
And jilts and cuckolds now best please the Town;
Your way of writing's out of fashion grown.
Method and rule—you only understand;
Pursue that way of fooling, and be damned.
Your learned cant of action, time, and place,
Must all give way to the unlabored farce.
To all the men of wit we will subscribe
But for your half wits, you unthinking tribe,
We'll let you see, whate'er besides we do,
How artfully we copy some of you:
And if you're drawn to th' life, pray tell me then
Why women should not write as well as men.

VIZARD MASK: masked women in audience. PIT-BUFFOON: clownish wits in the "pit"
(i.e., "orchestra" level). JILTS: a woman who jilts a lover.

143.

CORNELIA REMINDS HER SISTER OF THE DULLNESS OF MARRIAGE COMPARED TO PLAYING AT "COURTEZANSHIP" (YC)

(1679) APHRA BEHN, *THE FEIGNED COURTEZANS*, ACT II, SC. 1

Cornelia's the sprightly one; Marcella the more timid. So that Marcella might escape a detestable marriage to Count Octavio, both have secretly left Viterbo, their home, and, accompanied by their servants Petro and Phillipa, have come to Rome, where, under the tutelage of Cornelia, they are to pass for courtesans. Cornelia persuades the reluctant Marcella to pretend the life of a courtesan, recommending to her sister "the thousand satisfactions to be found" in it over "a dull virtuous life." Honoring her sister's timidity, Cornelia agrees to go no further than pretending behind a visor, but her inclination, she confesses, might otherwise be to "advance in this same glorious profession." Petro was wondering, though, whether their offering nothing but nods and smiles to potential lovers is making the lovers suspect that they are "honest," "which by some is accounted much the lewder scandal of the two," and so Cornelia urges her sister that they "be kind a little to redeem their reputations."

But rather than for Marcella to return to the embraces of Octavio, and for herself, Cornelia, to "whistle through the grate" of St. Teresa's convent, she thinks it might be better, when they have sold all their jewels, to contemplate the possibility of then selling their remaining jewel.

Aphra Behn in her comedies, like Cornelia in her masquerade, loves the entertainment of deftly skirting the very edge of scandal, and when necessity demands, going over.

CORNELIA

Hang the malicious world—There's charms in wealth and honour, but none half so powerful as love, in my opinion; 'slife, sister, thou art beautiful, and hast a fortune too, which before I wou'd lay out upon so shameful a purchase as such a bedfellow for life as Octavio, I wou'd turn errant keeping curtezan, and buy my better fortune. That word startles thee? Why, 'tis a noble title, and has more votaries than religion;

there's no merchandize like ours, that of love, my sister:—and can you be frighted with the vizor, which you your self put on? A little impertinent honour, we may chance to lose, 'tis true; but our downright honesty I perceive you are resolv'd we shall maintain through all the dangers of love and gallantry; though to say truth, I find enough to do, to defend my heart against some of those members that nightly serenade us, and daily show themselves before our window gay as young bridegrooms, and as full of expectation. Why, if all these come to pass, we have no more to do than to advance in this same glorious profession, of which now we only seem to be—in which, to give it its due, there are a thousand satisfactions to be found, more than in a dull virtuous life: Oh, the world of dark-lanthorn-men we should have! the serenades, the songs, the sighs, the vows, the presents, the quarrels, and all for a look or a smile, which you have been hitherto so covetous of, that *Petro* swears our lovers begin to suspect us for some honest jilts; which by some is accounted much the leuder scandal of the two:—therefore I think, faith, we must e'en be kind a little to redeem our reputations. And faith, sister, if 'twere but as easy to satisfy the nice scruples of religion and honour, I should find no great difficulty in the rest—besides, another argument I have, our money's all gone, and without a miracle can hold out no longer honestly. We must sell our jewels. And when they are gone, what jewel will you part with next?—Ah, no! Go home to Viterbo, ask the old gentleman pardon, and be receiv'd to grace again, you to the embraces of the amiable Octavio, and I to St. Teresa's, to whistle through a grate like a bird in a cage?—for I shall have little heart to sing.—But come, let's leave this sad talk, here's men—let's walk and gain new conquest, I love it dearly.

ERRANT: corruption of *arrant*, downright, notorious. VIZOR: mask. DARK-LAN-THORN-MEN: men with lanterns serenading women in the night. JILTS: women who cast off men after having encouraged them. LEUDER: lewder. ST. TERESA'S: nunnery.

144.

CLEOMENA BANISHES PITY FOR HER DEAD LOVER, VOWING REVENGE INSTEAD (YT)

(1679) APHRA BEHN, *THE YOUNG KING*, ACT III, SC. 5

The Warrior-Woman Cleomena is the "Virago he-daughter" of the Queen of Dacia, who, to raise Cleomena as her successor, gave her an "Amazonian education," so that "if it were not for her beauty," one of the courtiers remarks, "one would swear [she] were no woman, she's so given to noise and fighting." Cleomena derives from a long line of Amazons in the French Romances from which Aphra Behn adapted her plot: the warrior queen or princess who, covered in armor or simply in male disguise, finds herself fighting her own lover, one of them usually dying or at least wounded before the discovery is made of her, or sometimes his, identity. The gender game is played in earnest in the Romances, and it adapts beautifully—allowing for its fantasy exaggeration—to Restoration representations of the ideal of woman: she has both the warrior's prowess on the one hand—her male equivalence—which only "veils the face of nature" since it "does not see what hides within," and on the other hand, hidden within is of course "a woman's heart." That "softness" combined with beauty vies forever with the toughness of the trained warrior, the tension and balance defining her, in more moderate versions certainly, in Restoration comedy as well as tragedy.

Life is too short, many readers and spectators feel, to disentangle the plots of the Romances. In this one thread of many—the story of Cleomena and Thersander—the entanglements are sufficiently bewildering. When the lovers meet, they mistake one another for Gods, so perfect is their beauty, and both are equally struck dumb. He, Thersander, the Prince of Scythia, is already in disguise—he's come to Dacia to rescue his dear friend Amintos from captivity, pretending, for that mission, to be a Dacian warrior. While there, he inadvertently becomes a battlefield hero, and though the sworn enemy of Dacia, he falls in love with its princess, who knows him only in his disguise as "Clemanthis." Several mind-numbing turns of plot produce the situation—not uncommon in Romance—of the disguised Thersander (as the Dacian "Clemanthis") scheduled to do

one-on-one battle with the real (Scythian) Thersander—and since
this is a patent impossibility, he requisitions his rescued friend
Amintos to disguise himself as the disguised "Clemanthis" so that
they can stage a mock battle, and no one will be the wiser. But enemies
of "Clemanthis" intervene before the scheduled battle, and kill him
(or think they do). Cleomena, coming on the apparently dead
"Clemanthis" and supposing mistakenly that her enemy Thersander
killed him, in this scene makes her vows: no tears, no pity; nothing
must be in mind or heart but revenge against Thersander.

The ensuing events have Cleomena in disguise as "Clemanthis"
actually fighting a duel with and being overcome by Thersander, who
wonders, with reason, who this might be in his disguise. Solutions
and explanations of this and other plot threads use up Act V.

CLEOMENA

Remove me to the body of my love—

> *(They lead her to Amintor [disguised as*
> *Clemanthis], who lies wounded; she*
> *gazes on him a while, his face being all*
> *bloody.)*

—I will not now deplore as women use,
But call up all my vengeance to my aid.
Expect not so much imbecility—
From her whose love nor courage was made known
Sufficiently to thee. Oh, my Clemanthis!
I wou'd not now survive thee,
Were it not weak and cowardly to die,
And leave thee unreveng'd.
—Be calm, my eyes, and let my soul supply ye;
A silent broken heart must be his sacrifice:
Ev'ry indifferent sorrow claims our tears,
Mine do require blood, and 'tis with that
These must be washt away—

> *(Rises, wipes her eyes)*

Whatever I design to execute,
Pimante, and Semiris, I conjure ye,
Go not about to hinder, but be silent,
Or I will send my dagger to this heart.
Remove this body further into the wood,
And strip it of these glittering ornaments,
And let me personate this dear dead prince.

Obey, and dress me strait without reply.
There is not far from hence a druid's cell,
A man for piety and knowledge famous:
Thither convey the breathless sacred corps,
Laid gently in my chariot,
There to be kept conceal'd till further orders.
But haste to do as I command ye:
Haste, haste, the time and my revenge require it.
If thou wou'dst give me proofs of thy esteem,
Forget all words, all language, but revenge.
Let me not see so much of woman in thee
To shed one tear, but dress thy eyes with fierceness,
And send me forth to meet my love, as gay,
As if intended for my nuptial day.
That soul that sighs in pity of my fate,
Shall meet returns of my extremest hate:
Pity with my revenge must find no room;
I'll bury all but rage within thy tomb.

PIMANTE: follower of Cleomena. SEMERIS: woman to Cleomena.

145.

THE PRINCESS OF CLEVES, MOURNING HER HUSBAND'S DEATH, BIDS FAREWELL TO HER LOVER AND THEIR UNCONSUMMATED LOVE (YT)

(1681) NATHANIEL LEE, *THE PRINCESS OF CLEVES*, ACT V, SC. 3

There's a rare sensitivity and dignity in Lee's writing of the last scene of *The Princess of Cleves* that is owed not to him but to his source, the French novel of the same name by Mme. De Lafayette—a rare moment in his adaptation that does not altogether vulgarize its source by throwing its tragic story into the world of English Restoration comedy. What is casually taken for granted in Restoration comedy concerning sexual morality is the subject of tortured consideration in the French original.

The novel, a masterpiece of psychological analysis, studies the

Princess' becoming inflamed with sexual desire for an amoral libertine, which subtly causes the death of her husband. Both husband and wife have so internalized the moral code concerning sex, love, and marriage that they, with so much mutual accord in understanding, are deeply attuned to one another's sensibility. The tragedy of the husband's death is oddly enough a tribute to the depth of his understanding of his wife's emotional torment. As for the wife, she is one of the great studies in the literature of love in which the internalization of the moral code is so profoundly invested that her suffering is wholly within the province of her own heart—no external force or circumstance need weigh on her feelings or conduct. She is wholly at one with the encoded system of virtue, so much so that she is wholly and uniquely its victim as well.

In the play, there's a finely tuned *lack* of understanding, too, between the rake, Nemours, and the woman. His reading of her feelings and her intentions is consistently off the mark—but only by a hair. That hair, of course, is the difference between a sensitive reading of the Princess' sexual longing and a vulgarized one. Symptomatically, there's little difference between the two; more profoundly, and compassionately, one recognizes the component of suffering that reminds one of the Racinian torments occasioned by the seductions of "the passions."

Nemours, in the play, learning of the death of the Prince of Cleves, hurries to the Princess with the expectation that with the marriage difficulty out of the way, she'll be ripe for plucking. He finds her on her knees before the sarcophagus of her husband, swearing penance, and begging to join him in death. She turns to Nemours, and with perfect honesty describes her burning passion for him, its growth to enormity, its likely prognosis if she had succumbed to him, and her vow that "you shall never see me more."

PRINCESS

Dear lord,
If anything on earth be worth thy view,
Look down and hear me, hear my sighs and vows,
Till death has made me cold and wax like thee.
Water shall be my drink and herbs my food,
The marble of my chapel be my bed,
The altar's steps my pillows, while all night,
Stretched out, I groaning lie upon the floor,
Beat my swollen breasts and thy dear loss deplore.
Take, take me then

From this bad world. Quench these rebellious thoughts.
For, O, I have a pang, a longing wish
To see the luckless face of loved Nemours,
To gaze a while and take one last farewell,
Like one that is to lose a limb. 'Tis gone.
It was corrupt, a gangrene to my honour.
Yet I methinks would view the bleeding part,
Shudder a little, weep, and grudge at parting.
But by the soul of my triumphant saint
I swear this longing is without a guilt,
Nor shall it ever be by my appointment.

      (Enter Nemours)
Ha, but he's here!
Is't possible, my lord?
Is this a time for love,
In tears and blacks, the livery of death?
We'll talk of murdered love, and you shall hear,
From this abandoned part of him that was,
How much you have been loved.

Yes,
Sighing I speak it, sir. You have inspired me
With something which I never felt before,
That pleased and pained, the quickenings of first love;
Nor feared him then, when with his infant beams
He dawned upon my chill and senseless blood.
But, O, when he had reached his fierce meridian,
How different was his form! That angel face,
With his short rays, shot to a glaring god.
I grew inflamed, burnt inward, and the breath
Of the grown tyrant parched my heart to ashes.
Nor need I blush to make you this confession,
Because, my lord, 'tis done without a crime.

Rise, I conjure you, rise. I've told you nothing
But what you knew, my lord, too well before;
Not but I always vowed to keep those rules
My duty should prescribe.
'Tis duty's charge,
The voice of honour and the cry of love,
That I should fly from Paris as a pest,
That I should wear these rags of life away
In sunless caves, in dungeons of despair,
Where I should never think of man again—

But more particularly that of you,
For 'tis but too, too true, you were the cause
Of Cleves' untimely death, I swear I think
No less than if you had stabbed him through the heart.

Hear then my bosom thought. 'Tis the last time
I e'er shall see you, and 'tis a poor reward
For such a love. Yet, sir, 'tis all I have,
And you must ask no more.
Silence, silence, I command you.
No, no, Nemours; I know the world too well.
You have a sense too nice for long enjoyment.
Cleves was the man that only could love long.
Nor can I think his passion would have lasted,
But that he found I could have none for him.
'Tis obstacle, ascent, and lets and bars,
That whet the appetite of love and glory.
These are the fuel for that fiery passion;
But when the flashy stubble we remove,
The god goes out and there's an end of love.
But, O, when once satiety has palled
You sicken at each view, and every glance
Betrays your guilty soul and says you loathe.
I know it, sir. You have the well-bred cast
Of gallantry and parts to gain success;
And do but think, when various forms have charmed you,
How I should bear the cross returns of love?
For this I brave your noblest qualities.
I'll keep your form at distance, curb my soul,
Despair of smiles and tears, and prayers and oaths,
And all the blandishments of perjured love.
I will, I must, I shall, nay, now I can
Defy to death the lovely traitor, man.
Farewell. 'Tis past.
Why must it be
That I should charge you with the death of Cleves?
Alas, why met we not ere I engaged
To my dead lord? And why did fate divide us?
Let go. Believe, no other man
Could thus have wrought me, but yourself, to love.
Believe that I shall love you to my death.
Believe this parting wounds me like the fate
Of Cleves or worse. Believe—but, O, farewell.
Believe that you shall never see me more.

APPOINTMENT: decision. LIVERY (of death): characteristic dress (here, of mourning).
MERIDIAN: highest point. PEST: plague.

146.

QUEEN ELIZABETH RAGES AT HER COUNCILORS' CONDEMNING ESSEX FOR HIGH TREASON (OT)

(1681) JOHN BANKS, *THE UNHAPPY FAVORITE, OR THE EARL OF ESSEX*, ACT I, SC. 1

[Quoting from Men's vols.: "Essex, Abject, Begs the Queen for a Return to Favor...":] "Banks was one of the [Restoration] playwrights who engaged in gently disassembling the lofty scaffolding of heroic tragedy, and bringing dramatic sentiment within the range of more modest and more common feeling. Love in its more heartfelt modes, friendship, pity—what were called the 'softer' passions, hence, 'she-tragedies'—were displacing the male-oriented Heroic tragedies with their 'Honor'-driven, battlefield-beset, male heroes." Elizabeth, in Banks' play, "loves Essex in the she-tragedy mode—as a 'woman'—but is obliged to maintain her royal authority—the public figure torn by unrevealable private emotion." But Elizabeth, unlike the run of she-tragedy pitiable heroines, is hardly pitiable; her tender love remains within; without, she's powerful virago.

The Earl of Essex's enemies in the Queen's council, notably Burleigh, are plotting to undo him, and offer for Elizabeth's signature a warrant for his arrest. The rhetoric of rage rarely explodes at such a frenzied pitch as in Elizabeth's ranting howl against her councilors who, without her knowledge, have condemned her favorite, the Earl of Essex, for high treason. The power, the authority with which she "rams [their] impudent petition down their throats" is charged with sufficient scorn to flatten the pretensions of any minister, even one with the stamina and sagacity of Burleigh; ironically, Elizabeth's complaint that she is merely a woman, and so lacking the strength and spirit of her royal father Henry VIII, in the very act of so complaining exhibits a strength and spirit her father might well have envied.

Ultimately, it is Essex who condemns himself. In their several scenes of confrontation, Elizabeth cannot show the real degree of her love since, given the queen's station, she cannot so much as intimate so much compromising feeling toward a subject. Essex, baffled by the Queen's cold and judgmental discourse at their meetings in open court, reaches a level of rage against her that eventually almost exceeds the Queen's against her councilors, giving Elizabeth, so demeaned, no alternative but to assent to his doom. [For more on Essex and Elizabeth, see the four Essex monologues in the Men's vols.]

ELIZABETH

For the impeaching Robert Earl of Essex
Of several misdemeanours of high treason.
Ha!
—Say, my Nottingham,
And Rutland, did you ever hear the like!
But are you well assured I am awake?
Bless me, and say it is a horrid vision,
That I am not upon the throne—
Ha! Is't not so?—Yes, traitors, I'll obey you.—

(She rises in a rage.)
Here, sit you in my place; take Burleigh's staff,
The Chancellor's seal, and Essex's valiant head,
And leave me none but such as are yourselves,
Knaves for my council, fools for magistrates,
And cowards for commanders.—
Ingrateful people! Take away my life
'Tis that you'd have; for I have reigned too long.—
You too well know that I'm a woman, else
You durst not use me thus.—Had you but feared
Your Queen as you did once my royal father,
Or had I but the spirit of that monarch,
With one short syllable I should have rammed
Your impudent petitions down your throats,
And made four hundred of your factious crew
Tremble, and grovel on the earth for fear.
No more.—Attend me in the House tomorrow.
Ha! I suspect that Cecil too is envious;
And Essex is too great for thee to grow—

A shrub that never shall be looked upon
Whilst Essex, that's a cedar, stands so nigh.—
Tell me, why was not I acquainted with
This close design; for I am sure thou know'st it.
Be dumb; I will hear no excuses.—
I could turn cynic, and outrage the wind,
Fly from all courts, from business, and mankind,
Leave all like Chaos in confusion hurled;
For 'tis not reason now that rules the world:
There's order in all states but man below,
And all things else do to superiors bow;
Trees, plants and fruits rejoice beneath the sun,
Rivers and seas are guided by the moon;
The lion rules through shades and ev'ry green,
And fishes own the dolphin for their queen;
But man, the verier monster, worships still
No god but lust, no monarch but his will.

FACTIOUS: biased by party politics. THE HOUSE of Lords. VERIER: utmost.

147.

BELVEDERA VENTS RAGE AT HER HUSBAND FOR EXPOSING HER TO AN OLD LECHER'S ASSAULT (YT)

(1682) THOMAS OTWAY, *VENICE PRESERV'D*, ACT III, SC. 2

Belvedera rages against Jaffeir, her husband. He bears for the moment the weight of the suffering they both share and both unwittingly engendered. They're without means; Senator Priuli, her father, suffering his own rage at their marriage, which he reviles, has cut them off entirely, and Jaffeir, himself enraged at such treatment, joins his friend Pierre in plotting rebellion against the corrupt state of Venice, of which Priuli is for him the very symbol.

　　The play depicts both the cynical corruption of the state as well as the equally sick corruptions of the rebels. To gain their trust, Jaffeir is forced to give them a binding pledge of his loyalty. He offers—and is not alone among men of high integrity in Western drama in making such a morally blind offer—what he values most: his wife as hostage. And should he betray them—he stipulates—he gives one of its elders, Renault, who will be her guardian, a dagger with which to take Belvedera's life. Belvedera, bewildered, trembling at the prospect of this strange imprisonment but not fully comprehending what's at stake, is led away. In his attempt to find an honorable course of action to counter the victimization of his wife and children by Priuli, Jaffeir ends up victimizing his wife.

As Belvedera describes here, Renault, during the night, with Jaffeir's dagger in hand, attempts to rape her; her screams prevent him, but confronting Jaffeir now, she accuses him of betraying her by abandoning her to these rebels, and begins the conversion of her husband from a supporter of the rebels to their eventual betrayer. Morally, there is little to choose between state and conspirators, but Jaffeir, caught between the two, in making his choices loses "honor" either way. Choosing cautiously and with anguish, step by step he inevitably betrays himself and his friend Pierre, bringing about both their deaths and the bereft Belvedera's madness. The depiction of the political world of this Venice is almost a complete reversion to the corruptions depicted in Jacobean tragedy.

BELVEDERA

I'm sacrificed! I am sold! betrayed to shame!
Inevitable ruin has inclosed me!
No sooner was I to my bed repaired,
To weigh, and (weeping) ponder my condition,
But the old hoary wretch to whose false care
My peace and honor were entrusted, came
(Like Tarquin) ghastly with infernal lust.
O thou Roman Lucrece! thou couldst find friends to vindicate
thy wrong!
I never had but one, and he's proved false;
He that should guard my virtue has betrayed it—
Left me! undone me! Oh, that I could hate him!
Where shall I go? Whither, whither wander?

There was a time
When Belvedera's tears, her cries, and sorrows
Were not despised; when if she chanced to sigh
Or look but sad—there was indeed a time
When Jaffeir would have ta'en her in his arms,
Eased her declining head upon his breast,
And never left her till he found the cause.

But let her now weep seas,
Cry till she rend the earth, sigh till she burst
Her heart asunder: still he bears it all,
Deaf as the wind, and as the rocks unshaken.

What's he to whose curs'd hands last night thou gavs't me?
Was that well done? Oh! I could tell a story
Would rouse thy lion heart out of its den,
And make it rage with terrifying fury.
Remove me from this place! Last night, last night!
No sooner wert thou gone, and I alone,
Left in the power of that old son of mischief,
No sooner was I lain on my sad bed,
But that vile wretch approached me; loose, unbuttoned,
Ready for violation. Then my heart
Throbbed with its fears. Oh, how I wept and sighed,
And shrunk, and trembled; wished in vain for him
That should protect me. Thou, alas, wert gone!
He drew the hideous dagger forth thou gav'st him,
And with upbraiding smiles, he said "Behold it;
This is the pledge of a false husband's love."
And in my arms then pressed, and would have clasped me;
But with my cries I scared his coward's heart,
Till he withdrew and muttered vows to hell.
These are thy friends! with these, thy life, thy honor,
Thy love—all staked, and all will go to ruin.

TARQUIN...LUCRECE: when Lucrece, the wife of King Tarquin of Rome in the 6th century BC, renowned for her beauty and virtue, was raped by his son, also called Tarquin, she informed her father and her husband, and having exacted an oath of vengeance from them, stabbed herself to death. (When the Tarquins were expelled from Rome, the monarchy ended, and was followed by the establishment of the Republic.) STAKED: put at risk.

148.

LANDLADY GAMMER GIME, DESPERATE, BEGS HER RENT FROM WASTEALL (OC)

(1686) APHRA BEHN, *THE LUCKY CHANCE*, ACT II, SC. 1

Restoration libertines, even those with a measure of sexual scruple, have no scruples at all in dealing with tradesmen, innkeepers, landlords, "Israelite" lenders, all dunners except their own kind who hold their gambling chits. Their ingenuity in holding the dunning rabble from their door is on a par with their strategy for getting unwilling women through that door. Wit, prowess, and an equally starving servant are the means; Mr. Wasteall, his remaining belongings in pawn, must resort to them.

"Mr. Wasteall" is in fact Gayman, abandoned by fortune, living in decayed lodgings, needing for tonight his suit, his wig, his cravat, "and so forth," all in pawn, and with no one to turn to for rescue, as his equally starving footman Rag explains to him, but his landlady, Gammer Gime, on whom he's worked magic before, but at terrible cost. "Oh! name her not, the thought on't turns my stomach. A sight of her is a vomit, but he's a bold hero that dares venture on her for a kiss, and all beyond that, sure, is hell itself." But she's his "last, last refuge," and Rag runs to get her, and Gayman, to stave off the moment of a kiss, plies her instead with wine. But Gammer Gime will have none of his dodges. She has only one thing in mind: the rent he owes her, for which she's desperate. It's her desperation he must overcome. It's his simple guile—the wine—that wins her from an entirely determined dunner to an entirely willing benefactress.

> LANDLADY
>
> More of your money and less of your civility, good Mr. Wasteall. Dear me no dears, Sir, but let me have my money, eight weeks' rent last Friday; besides taverns, ale-houses, chandlers, laundresses' scores, and ready money out of my purse, you know it, Sir.
>
> Is this all the thanks I have for my kindness, for patching, borrowing and shifting for you? 'Twas but last week I pawned my best petticoat, as I hope to wear it again, it cost me six and twenty shillings besides making, then this morning my new

Norwich mantua followed, and two postle spoons, I had the whole dozen when you came first, but they dropped, and dropped, till I had only Judas left for my husband. Then I've passed my word at the George Tavern for forty shillings for you, ten shillings at my neighbour Squabs for ale, besides seven shillings to mother Suds for washing, and do you fob me off? Come, come, pay me quickly, or old Gregory Gime's house shall be too hot to hold you.

You had good clothes when you came first, but they dwindled daily, till they dwindled to this old campaign, with tanned coloured lining, once red, but now all colours of the rainbow, a cloak to skulk in a-nights, and a pair of piss-burned shammy breeches. Nay, your very badge of manhood's gone too. Your silver sword I mean, transmogrified to this two-handed basket hilt, this old Sir Guy of Warwick, which will sell for nothing but old iron. In fine, I'll have my money, Sir, or i'faith Alsatia shall not shelter you. Rot your wine, d'ye think to pacify me with wine, Sir?

> *(She refuses to drink. He holds open her*
> *jaws and throws a glass of wine into her*
> *mouth.)*

What, will you force me? No, give me another glass, I scorn to be so uncivil to be forced. My service to you, Sir. This shan't do, Sir.

> *(She drinks)*

Well Sir, you have no reason to complain of my eyes, nor my tongue neither, if rightly understood.

> *(Weeps)*

I am a little hasty sometimes, but you know my good nature. *(She drinks)* Would this wine might ne'er go through me if I would not go, as they say, through fire and water, by night or by day for you.

> *(She drinks)*

Well, you have no money in your pocket now, I'll warrant you; here, here's ten shillings for you old Gregory knows not of.

> *(She opens a great greasy purse.)*

I own I was to blame. Here Sir, you shall take it. Why, is there no way to redeem one of your suits? Let me see, hum, what does it lie for? Well, say no more, I'll lay about me. Let me see,

the caudle cup that Molly's grandmother left her will pawn—
I'll sneak it out. Well, Sir, you shall have your things presently,
trouble not your head, but expect me.

(Exeunt Landlady)

CHANDLERS: candle makers. MANTUA: a loose coat of silk woven in Norwich. [A]POS-
TLE SPOONS: with the images of the twelve apostles on the handles. FOB OFF: to put
off. PISS-BURNED SHAMMY BREECHES: soiled goat-skin-leather breeches. TWO-HAN-
DLED BASKET HILT, THIS OLD SIR GUY OF WARWICK: nickname for an old-fashioned
sword, a heavy sword with a basket-shaped cover over the hand. ALSATIA: a district in
central London, once a sanctuary for debtors and lawbreakers. CAUDLE: a small cup
for warm cordial drinks.

149.
LADY TOUCHWOOD CRIES
MALEDICTION ON MASKWELL, HER
UNGRATEFUL, FORGETFUL SEDUCER (oc)

(1694) WILLIAM CONGREVE, *THE DOUBLE DEALER*, ACT I, SC. 6

Lady Touchwood is raging against the villainies of a man with whom
she herself collaborated in accomplishing those villainies. She accuses him of betraying his friend Mellefont—a betrayal she herself insti-
gated. She accuses him further of "dishonoring" herself—a dishonor
she invited to make him confederate against her enemy, Mellefont.
Further, she accuses him of betrayal against her husband, whom
Maskwell has, obviously with her complicity, cuckolded. Worst of all,
he is insulting her passion by the very indifferent face he is putting on
those betrayals while she rages.

The secret of his calm and her passion is that both are aware that
the reason for their liaison had nothing to do with love for each other,
but only with this: that Lady Touchwood, who was madly in love with
Mellefont and who had been utterly spurned by him, engaged
Maskwell to undo Mellefont to satisfy her revenge, and, to bind him
to that intention, surrendered her favors to him. [As noted in Men's
vols. entry: "Mellefont Recounts How Lady Touchwood Invaded His
Bedchamber and Wooed with Fury":] "The play's...interest is not at all
in tracking the scorned woman's or the endangered lover's emotion-

al 'journeys,' but...exclusively in their game-maneuvers, one to destroy, the other to forestall. The means? Diplomatic alliances." All the characters—even bound lovers—operate like rival nations on the fixed principle of private interest, involving a tireless courting of alliances, and as occasion demands, dissolving and restructuring them according to that principle.

It is almost as though emotion is not personal but political. Lady Touchwood is raging at her erstwhile lover Maskwell with no feeling for him, but for Mellefont, and the betrayal she feels is not of Maskwell as her lover, but that he has not accomplished the only commission she genuinely had for him: to break up Mellefont's match with the young Cynthia. Worn out in her diatribe, Lady Touchwood at last breaks out of pretense and confesses bluntly: "In vain I do disguise myself to thee, thou knowest the very inmost windings...of my soul." He does indeed. Her rage is little more than the outward show of despair that Mellefont is to be married tomorrow, and that Maskwell has not yet moved to prevent it. She recalls Maskwell to his mission: help make Mellefont mine, "and next[,] immediate ruin seize him." The intent of the woman is absolute. So great is her passion for Mellefont that it's provoked her equal hatred; she wants to win him again to destroy him instantly. Her ally, already remunerated by her "favors," must tell her how.

(Enter Lady Touchwood and Maskwell)

LADY TOUCHWOOD

I'll hear no more.—Y'are false and ungrateful; come, I know you false. That I should trust a man, whom I had known betray his friend! Your fond friend Mellefont, and to me; can you deny it? Have you not wronged my lord, who has been a father to you in your wants, and given you being? Have you not wronged him in the highest manner, in his bed?

Oh, what's more is most my shame,—have you not dishonoured me? Insolent devil! But have a care,—provoke me not; for by the eternal fire, you shall not 'scape my vengeance.—Calm villain! How unconcerned he stands, confessing treachery and ingratitude! Is there a vice more black!—Oh I have excuses, thousands, for my faults: fire in my temper, passions in my soul, apt to every provocation; oppressed at once with love and with despair. But a sedate, a thinking villain, whose black blood runs temperately bad, what excuse can clear? One who is no more moved with the reflection of his crimes than of his face; but walks unstartled from the mirror, and straight forgets the hideous form. Can no gratitude incline you, no obligations touch you? Have not my fortune and my person been subjected to your pleasure? Were you not in the nature of a servant, and have not I in effect made you lord of all, of me, and of my lord? Where is that humble love, the languishing, that adoration, which once was paid me, and everlastingly engaged?

And have I not met your love with forward fire? Do you wind me like a larum, only to rouse my own stilled soul for your diversion? Confusion! Oh Maskwell, in vain I do disguise me from thee, thou knowest me, knowest the very inmost windings and recesses of my soul.—Oh Mellefont! I burn; married tomorrow! Despair strikes me. Yet my soul knows I hate him too: let him but once be mine, and next immediate ruin seize him. How, how? Thou dear, thou precious villain, how?

LARUM: alarum, a mechanical alarm.

150.

LADY PLIANT LOUDLY REJECTS, THEN SOFTLY INVITES, THE LOVE SHE IMAGINES IN MELLEFONT (OC)

(1694) WILLIAM CONGREVE, *THE DOUBLE DEALER*, ACT II, SC. 5

[Continues No. 149, above.] The scheme by the jealous Lady Touchwood to undo Mellefont's courtship to Cynthia works wonders. It's not Cynthia he's after, her story went, but her stepmother, Lady Pliant; his intent was to marry Cynthia only to have standing opportunities with Lady Pliant. Lady Pliant, learning of this iniquity, was horrified; also delighted. Now she accuses Mellefont of planning incest. She refuses to allow him his defense. She warns him of expecting illicit opportunities. She wonders if her defenses will hold firm.

And she excuses his passion, since neither he nor she can help it if she has charms.

All this is addressed to the nonplussed Mellefont, who surmises how this rumor came about. But not for a moment does he have the opportunity to disabuse the excited Lady Pliant, who, as Congreve has it, is "insolent to her husband, but easy to any pretender." Had the tale been true, and had Mellefont indeed been infatuated with her, the instructions within her adamant condemnation of his lewd plans would have been easy enough to follow.

LADY PLIANT

Fiddle, faddle, don't tell me of this and that, and everything in the world, but give me mathemacular demonstration, answer me directly—but I have not patience—oh! The impiety of it, and the unparalleled wickedness! Oh merciful Father! How could you think to reverse nature so, to make the daughter the means of procuring the mother? Ay, for though I am not Cynthia's own mother; I am her father's wife; and that's near enough to make it incest.

Oh reflect upon the horror of that, and then the guilt of deceiving everybody; marrying the daughter, only to make a cuckold of the father; and then seducing me, debauching my purity, and perverting me from the road of virtue, in which I have trod thus long, and never made one trip, not one *faux pas*; oh consider it, what would you have to answer for, if you should provoke me to frailty? Alas! Humanity is feeble, heaven knows! Very feeble, and unable to support itself.

And nobody knows how circumstances may happen together,—to my thinking, now I could resist the strongest temptation,—but yet I know, 'tis impossible for me to know whether I could or not, there's no certainty in the things of this life.

Oh Lord, ask me the question! I'll swear I'll refuse it: I swear I'll deny it—therefore don't ask me, nay you shan't ask me, I swear I'll deny it. Oh Gemini, you have brought all the blood into my face, I warrant, I am as red as a turkey-cock; oh fie, cousin Mellefont!

I'll deny you first, and hear you afterwards: For one does not know how one's mind may change upon hearing—hearing is one of the senses, and all the senses are fallible; I won't trust my honour, I assure you; my honour is infallible and un-come-at-able. Maybe you don't think it a sin,—they say some of you gentlemen don't think it a sin,—maybe it is no sin to them that don't think it so; indeed, if I did not think it a sin,—but still my honour, if it were no sin,—but then, to marry my daughter, for the conveniency of frequent opportunities,—I'll never consent to that, as sure as can be. I'll break the match.

Nay, nay, rise up, come you shall see my good nature. I know love is powerful, and nobody can help his passion: 'tis not your fault; nor I swear it is not mine.—How can I help it, if I have charms? And how can you help it, if you are made a captive; I swear it's pity it should be a fault,—but my honour,—well, but your honour too—but the sin!—Well but the necessity—oh Lord, here's somebody coming, I dare not stay. Well, you must consider of your crime; and strive as much as can be against it,—strive to be sure—but don't be melancholy, don't despair, but never think that I'll grant you anything; oh Lord, no;—but be sure you lay aside all thoughts of the marriage, for though I know you don't love Cynthia, only as a blind for your passion to me; yet it will make me jealous,—oh Lord, what did I say? Jealous! No, no, I can't be jealous, for I must not love you, therefore don't hope, but don't despair neither,—oh, they're coming, I must fly.

(Exit)

MATHEMACULAR: mathematical, scientific. *FAUX PAS*: wrong step.

151.

AMANDA CONSIDERS, BUT HER VIRTUE QUESTIONS, SEDUCING HER HUSBAND INCOGNITO TO RECLAIM HIM (YC)

(1696) COLLEY CIBBER, *LOVE'S LAST SHIFT*, ACT III, SC. 1

"Can I justify," asks Amanda, "my intended design upon my husband?" It's a nice question, and a particularly difficult one to answer in 1696. The play *Love's Last Shift* was itself a harbinger of a new state of affairs for the apologetics of virtue, and what Amanda wants to know is whether her old-fashioned notions of a woman's virtue can tolerate the trick she is contemplating playing on her husband. He hasn't seen her since he abandoned her when she was sixteen, and since she is certainly no longer recognizable to him, is it decent for this forgotten wife to seduce him as though she were a stranger, and after a night's session, will she, as she anticipates, win back his love by her anonymous but hopefully convincing performance?

We remember that in Elizabethan and Italian Renaissance comedy, this disguising-for-bed-sport was a standard ploy, and in Restoration comedy, of which *Love's Last Shift* is an instance, it has no other connotation but that of verve, inventiveness, and charm. Then why is Amanda, in the midst of this gay permissiveness, raising old-fashioned questions about moral propriety? [For more on *Love's Last Shift*, see entries on Loveless and Sir Novelty Fashion in Men's vols.]

She is asking her question at the moment when a seismic shift is just beginning in English social morality, when the libertinism of the Restoration is succumbing to angry sermonizings from the pulpit and to the dormant middle class morality, which had not been visible on the stage since the return to the throne of Charles II.

Consulting her friend Hillaria, an unreconstructed Restoration lady of fashion, Amanda is rewarded with the familiar libertine posture: "If he doesn't intrigue with you, he will with somebody else in the meantime, and I think you have as much right to his remains as any one." Opposing this easy flippancy is Amanda's "To me, the rules of virtue have been ever sacred, and I am loath to break them." And striking this new-old note, Amanda becomes the harbinger of the heroines of the succeeding century whose deliberations on this very matter of unsullied virtue become the very center of their dramatic being.

Nevertheless, in this early stage of change, Amanda settles for the practical question of the likelihood of her getting away with it, and with the encouragement of Hillaria, she does the deed. That it will succeed goes without saying, but that it will provoke in her husband a powerfully sentimental conversion to virtue will become justification enough for Amanda's lapse from virtue for virtue's sake.

AMANDA

Dear Hillaria, help me, for I am at a loss. Can I justify, think you, my intended design upon my husband?

Why if I court and conquer him as a mistress am I not accessory to his violating the bonds of marriage? For, though I am his wife, yet while he loves me not as such, I encourage an unlawful passion, and though the act be safe, yet his intent is criminal.

I am assured the love he will pretend to me is vicious, and it is uncertain that I shall prevent his doing worse elsewhere. To say truth, I find no argument yet strong enough to conquer my inclination to it. But is there no danger of his knowing me? Well, no. Not the least in my opinion. In the first place, he confidently believes me to be dead; then he has not seen me these eight or ten years; besides, I was not above sixteen when he left: this, with the alteration the smallpox have made— though not for the worse—I think are sufficient disguises to secure me from his knowledge. And to this I may add the considerable amendment of my fortune, for when he left me I had only my bare jointure for a subsistence—besides my strange manner of receiving him.

I can't help a little concern in a business of such moment, for though my reason tells me my design must prosper, yet my fears say it were happiness too great. Oh, to reclaim the man I'm bound by heaven to love, to expose the folly of a roving mind in pleasing him with what he seemed to loathe were such a sweet revenge for slighted love, so vast a triumph of rewarded constancy as might persuade the looser part of womankind even to forsake themselves and fall in love with virtue.

ALTERATION THE SMALLPOX HAVE MADE: an epidemic at the time that caused disfigurement. JOINTURE: an estate or property settled on a woman in consideration of marriage, and to be enjoyed by her after her husband's death.

152.

MRS. FLAREIT, SCORNED, FURIOUS, RAVING, TRIES TO RUN HER MOCKING LOVER THROUGH WITH A SWORD (oc)

(1696) COLLEY CIBBER, *LOVE'S LAST SHIFT*, ACT IV, SC. 1

Among the raging, thrown-over, elderly, and no longer ravishing ladies in Restoration comedy, of whom there is a sizable contingent, perhaps none is so definitively thrown-over, so significantly elderly, and so abusively raging as Mrs. Flareit. The Mrs. Flareits are shown little mercy by either their playwrights or their lovers, who move them to emotions, actions, and words of such injudicious violence as to bring shame and scorn upon them even in their own eyes. Given so anticipatable a situation in Restoration comedy for women who are ancient and scorned, Mrs. Flareit is a sad study in helpless ineptitude, although it must be admitted that against the insulting barbarism of such disengaged lovers as Sir Novelty Fashion, there is no adequate retaliation that is civilized.

Mrs. Flareit, the kept mistress of Sir Novelty, loathes him, but is jealous at the thought that he is pursuing the young fortune, Narcissa. Having written, as Narcissa, an invitation to him to meet her, masked, in the fashionable walks of St. James' Park, she tests his fidelity with questions such as: "Will you never see that common creature Flareit more?" and "You must hate her," and (as Narcissa) "Will you love me forever?" to which he answers that he hated Flareit long ago for her stinking breath, that even though he was "led away" before, he detests a strumpet, and that he's sworn to Narcissa forever. At which information, Mrs. Flareit unmasks, boxes his ear, and begins her rant, to the shocked amusement of the folk strolling in the Park.

Her ineptitude: Imagining for a delusionary moment that he really loves her, she switches suddenly to the opposite tack, and tries "Woman": genteel, of a fine dignity, she understands his change of heart, asks the return of letters, bids him a soft and tearful farewell, and leaving, asks not to be impeded in her going. Pleased, he makes no attempt to do so, at which her rage redoubles, and with play-acting decidedly out of the way, she reaches for rhetoric, for sword, for anything that will appease her fury.

Mrs. Flareit

What, will nothing but a maidenhead go down with you!
Thou miserable, conceited wretch! Foh, my breath stinks, does
it! I'm a homely puss, a strumpet not worth your notice!
Devil, I'll be revenged. What, no pretense, no evasion, now!
Come, come, swear you knew me all this while. Furies and
hell! This is beyond all sufferance. Thou wretch, thou thing,
thou animal, that I—to the everlasting forfeiture of my sense
and understanding—have made a man! For till thou knewest
me, it was doubted if thou wert of human kind. And dost thou
think I'll suffer such a worm as thee to turn against me? No!
When I do, may I be cursed to thy embraces all my life and
never know a joy beyond thee.

(Aside) His bravery's affected. I know he loves me, and I'll
pierce him to the quick. I have yet a surer way to fool him.
(With tears in her eyes) Now, woman.

—Sir Novelty, pray, sir, let me speak with you. Before we
part—for I find I have irrecoverably lost your love—let me
beg of you that from this hour you ne'er will see me more or
make any new attempts to deceive my easy temper, for I find
my nature's such I shall believe you, though to my utter ruin.
One thing more, sir. Since our first acquaintance you have
received several letters from me. I hope you will be so much a
gentleman as to let me have 'em again. Those I have of yours
shall be returned tomorrow morning. And now, sir, wishing
you as much happiness in her you love as you once pretended
I could give you, I take of you my everlasting leave. Farewell,
and may your next mistress love you till I hate you.

(She is going)
Pray, sir, give me leave to pass; I can't bear to stay. *(Crying)*
What is it that frightens me? Your barbarous usage. Pray, let
me go.

(Mrs. Flareit looks back)
(Aside) Ha, not move to call me back! So unconcerned! Oh, I
could tear my flesh, stab every feature in this dull, decaying
face that wants a charm to hold him. Damn him! I loathe him
too! But shall my pride now fall from such an height and bear
the torture unrevenged? No! My very soul's on fire, and
nothing but the villain's blood shall quench it. Devil, have at
thee.

*(Snatches Young Worthy's sword and
runs at him. He draws and stands upon
his guard. Young Worthy takes the
sword from her and holds her.)*

Prevented! Oh, I shall choke with boiling gall. Oh, oh, umh!
Let me go! I'll have his blood, his blood, his blood! *(Raving)*
Death and vengeance, am I become his sport? He's pleased,
and smiles to see me rage the more! But he shall find no fiend
in hell can match the fury of a disappointed woman! Scorned,
slighted, dismissed without a parting pang! Oh, torturing
thought! May all the racks mankind e'er gave our easy sex,
neglected love, decaying beauty, and hot raging lust light on
me if e'er I cease to be the eternal plague of his remaining life,
nay, after death, when his black soul lies howling in despair, I'll
plunge to hell and be his torment there.

(Exit in a fury)

153.

AMANDA, OF TWO MINDS, CONSIDERS HER HUSBAND'S JUSTIFICATIONS FOR INFIDELITY, AND HER OWN FOR REVENGE (YC)

(1696) SIR JOHN VANBRUGH, *THE RELAPSE*, ACT V, SC. 4

[On *The Relapse*, see also entries on Loveless in Men's vols.] After his
conversion, Loveless, Amanda's husband, lives with equanimity
under the eye of virtue until he is dogged by old urges. Vanbrugh's
skepticism about the likelihood of a libertine's instant and permanent regeneration produced his sequel to *Love's Last Shift*, called,
precisely, *The Relapse*.

Beginning marriage with Amanda with "the raging flame of wild
destructive lust Reduced to a warm pleasing fire of lawful love," the
flames shoot up again when Amanda's young, desirable cousin,
Berinthia, comes to live with them, and Loveless hopelessly succumbs to appetite. Berinthia, playing both secret rival to Amanda and

ostensible friend, arranges for Amanda to witness, at a safe distance, her own (masked) assignation with Loveless—but she does so to test Amanda, whose protestations of virtue Berinthia finds hard to bear. On the supposition that Amanda, after witnessing her husband's betrayal, will be an easy mark for the seducer Worthy (Berinthia's revenge against wifely virtue), she arranges for Amanda's witnessing and also for Worthy's lying in wait for a certainly vengeful and so newly willing Amanda.

After witnessing her husband's betrayal, Amanda arrives home in a jealous rage: proof positive is hers. It's she who now will be tested: will she respond to betrayal with betrayal? Her woman gives her news of visitors—the Ladies Fiddle, Faddle, and so on. Amanda, without patience and without civility, gets rid of the woman, and settles to grimly contemplating her next move. First, she explores its logic: yes, Loveless in youth had excuse enough; now, after "reason...has pointed out the course he ought to run," he's beyond pardon. But then, the fault might be hers: no longer sixteen, no longer (she confessed earlier to a legacy of smallpox) beautiful; but still—and the desire for revenge mounts once more, and she stands ready, at the end of her brief, to be revenged—by herself taking a lover.

But Vanbrugh, cynical enough concerning Loveless, respects Colley Cibber's original version of Amanda, to whom virtue was "sacred." When the lover approaches, her rejection of him is so high-minded that he too is reduced to heeding example, and becomes in no time a converted libertine. (For unexplained reason, the resolution of Loveless and Amanda is unexplored; we catch a glimpse of them amongst the crowd of characters gathered for the final scene. They're already reconciled. How? Why?)

(Enter Amanda, as just returned, her
Woman following her)

AMANDA

Prithee what care I who has been here? My Lady Bridle and my Lady Tiptoe? My Lady Fiddle and my Lady Faddle! What dost stand troubling me with the visits of a parcel of impertinent women? When they are well seamed with the smallpox, they won't be so fond of showing their faces.— There are more coquettes about this town—Would the world were on fire, and you in the middle on't! Begone! leave me!— *(Exit Woman)* At last I am convinced. My eyes are testimonies of his falsehood. The base, ungrateful, perjured villain!—

—Good gods! what slippery stuff are men compos'd of!
Sure the account of their creation's false,
And 'twas the woman's rib that they were form'd of.
But why am I thus angry?
This poor relapse should only move my scorn.
'Tis true,
The roving flights of his unfinished youth
Had strong excuses from the plea of nature;
Reason had thrown the reins loose on his neck,
And slipped him to unlimited desire.
If therefore he went wrong, he had a claim
To my forgiveness, and I did him right.
But since the years of manhood rein him in,
And reason, well digested into thought,
Has pointed out the course he ought to run;
If now he strays,
'Twould be as weak and mean in me to pardon,
As it had been in him t'offend. But hold:
'Tis an ill cause indeed, where nothing's to be said for't.
My beauty possibly is in the wane;
Perhaps sixteen has greater charms for him:
Yes, there's the secret. But let him know,
My quiver's not entirely emptied yet,
I still have darts, and I can shoot 'em too;
They're not so blunt, but they can enter still:
The want's not in my power, but in my will.
Virtue's his friend; or, through another's heart,
I yet could find the way to make his smart.

       (*Going off, she meets Worthy*)
Ha! he here!
Protect me, Heaven! for this looks ominous.

SEAMED: disfigured.

45

154.

BELLINDA STRUGGLES HEROICALLY AND SUCCEEDS IN DOWNING HER PASSION FOR THE MARRIED SIR CHARLES (YC)

(1697) MARY PIX, *THE INNOCENT MISTRESS*,
ACT IV, SC. 7, AND ACT V, SC. 1

So elevated, so refined is the love of Bellinda and Sir Charles that it transcends the barest hint of sexuality; it is entirely and proudly platonic. But, to her dismay, Bellinda, after having surrendered her soul to this love, discovers that Sir Charles is married. The peculiar circumstance of his marriage exculpates him from any serious charge of deceit or viciousness, but the barrier of marriage is so sacred to Bellinda that she resolves at once to break the connection, leave the city, retire to a life of isolation, and "chase from [her] struggling soul all this fond tenderness."

But there's a peculiar brand of tenderness against which she is to struggle—the one derived from the French romances of La Calprenede and of Mme. de Scudery, under the spell of whose *carte de tendre*, or guide to love's tenderness, a significant portion of English heroines were to fall. A significant portion of English readers as well; from 1645 to 1670, translations and imitations of the French heroic romances were read to the exclusion of every other kind of prose fiction. "Leave this soft melancholy poetry," her friend Mrs. Beauclair urges Bellinda. "It nurses your disease"—the same disease that afflicted the young girls in Moliere's *Les Precieuses Ridicules* [see Vol. 3, No. 114]. But Moliere's Madelon was a cartoonish parody; Bellinda is the real thing. Only in her opening scenes is playwright Pix a bit ironic about Bellinda's fantasy feeling and fantasy language, but quickly they become the truth of feeling, leaving neither Pix nor her character Bellinda guilty of any vestige of parody, insisting entirely on the truth of *precieuse* emotion and language, which translates the fantasies of chivalric heroism into the psychology and morality of love.

Bellinda, the paragon of *precieuse* sensibility, is packing in a hurry. Her will demands that she "remove" from the city at once, but she debates. Her language is *precieuse*, but her quandary is real. She longs to rid herself of the "tenderness" to which she is genuinely captive, but she can't bear its loss. The battle between Honor and Love—

between Virtue and "Tenderness"—would hardly matter, she reasons, if—and here is the implicit arrogance and vanity of preciosity—like lesser women of lesser capacity for this almost-holy commitment, she could abandon a lover, if not for Honor's sake, at least for another lover. But for votaries of tenderness of Bellinda's stature, even "racks, gibbets and dungeons" are as nothing compared to the torture of lovers parting.

Intensified to such a degree, this commitment to love returns it—after the ravages the Restoration visited on the very idea of love—to the level of religious devotion. And so, at Sir Charles' reappearance, Bellinda's language moves closer to the rhetoric of religious vows—removing from the world, denigrating worldly love as ephemeral, and ending in "indifferency"—and then with a terminal struggle not to succumb once again, because of his presence, to her former devotion, Bellinda shuts the door on worldly hope for their future together, and prays that Heaven may "set seas and earth and worlds of fire between us" to satisfy the stern demand of "virtue, fate and honor." Strenuously committed heroines of this dimension, though they've not been behindhand in tragedy, are newly revived here in English comedy.

BELLINDA

The little hurry of my quick remove has took up all my
thoughts, and I have not considered what I am about. See him
no more, him whom I could not live a day, an hour without!
No more behold his eyeballs tremble with respectful passion!
Hear no more the soft falling accents of his charming tongue!
View him dying at my feet no more! O virtue! Take me to
thee, chase from my struggling soul all this fond tenderness,
secure me now, and I'm thy votary forever.

Honour and love. Oh, the torture to think they are domestic
foes that must destroy the heart that harbours 'em. Had my
glass but been my idol, my mind loose, unconstant, wavering,
like my sex, then I might have 'scaped these pangs. Love, as
passing meteors, with several fires just warms their breasts and
vanishes, leaving no killing pain behind. 'Tis only foolish. I
have made a god of my desire greater than ever the poets
feigned. My eyes received no pleasure but what his sight gave
me. No music charmed my ears but his dear voice. Racks,
gibbets and dungeons, can they equal losing all my soul
admires? Why named I them? Can there be greater racks
Than what despairing, parting lovers find,
To part, when both are true, both would be kind?

He comes! Keep back, full eyes, the springing tears, and thou, poor trembling heart, now be manned with all thy strongest stoutest resolutions! There will be need.

(Enter Sir Charles)
Sir Charles, we have both been punished with unwarrantable love. You interrupt me when I just begin. Grant it true; we might have lived till weary grown of one another, till you, perhaps, might coldly say "I had a mistress..." Now to part, when at the mention of each other's names our hearts will rise, our eyes run o'er, 'tis better much than living to indifferency, which time and age would certainly have brought.

In remote and unfrequented shades I'll pass my solitary hours, and like a recluse waste the remainder of my wretched days. That sad, silent look discovers such inward worlds of woe it strikes me through, staggers my best resolves, removes the props I have been raising for my sinking fame, and, blind with passion, I could reel into thy arms. Tell me, on what are thy thoughts employed?

On the curse of life, imposed on us without our choice, and almost always attended with tormenting plagues? Yet we may meet again in peace and joy, when this gigantic honour appears no bugbear, and our desires lawfully be crowned. It is a guilty thought, nor shall I ever dare to form it a wish.

Mark me, Sir, you know I do not use to break my word. If, by letters, messages, or the least appearance, though cautiously as treasons plotted against the state, you approach me, I'll fly the kingdom, or, if that is too little, the world. Away, away! Divide him, heaven, from my fond, guilty eyes. Set seas and earth and worlds of fire between us, for virtue, fate and honour, with an united cry, have doomed that we must meet no more.

(Exit)

GLASS: mirror. RACK: a medieval device for torture. GIBBET: gallows with a projecting arm at the top, from which the bodies of criminals were hung in chains, and left suspended after execution.

155.

LADY BRUTE EXPLORES ARGUMENTS FOR ASSENTING TO A LOVER AS REVENGE AGAINST A HUSBAND (YC)

(1697) SIR JOHN VANBRUGH, *THE PROVOK'D WIFE*, ACT I, SC. 1

"Two years married!" groans Lord Brute. Following Restoration husband protocol, he has scrupulously instructed himself to hate his wife for the incontrovertible reason that she is a wife, and his. And to confirm his utter distaste for his married state, he scrupulously responds to her every question and every word with studied provocation. And yet she, for all her youth, for all her beauty, for all her total absence of love for him, has remained always faithful, always obliging, always indulgent, even toward his acid tongue. But now, she bethinks herself: it may be time for revenge, and that revenge must of course be a lover. Yet Lady Brute, wishing to be reasonably scrupulous in taking such a step, hunts for principled justifications. The most delicious would be that she is being punished [by a just Providence?] in a cruel husband because of her cruelty to a lover. What arguments, she asks, can bolster such a convenient supposition? She finds two, possibly two and a half, and is comforted by the thought that if she were to continue to explore in those directions, she would end up with more than enough sound reason. And then the scales fall from her eyes: What is wrong with seeking for guidance within the confines of the idea of virtue is the very notion of virtue itself. Conclusion: "virtue's an ass, and a gallant's worth forty on't."

Treated as a joke or not, the buzzing in the ear of conscience was already [see No. 151, above] in these latter years of the Restoration, taking its toll on the casuistical hedonism of the earlier years, and Lady Brute, for all her easy tossing over her shoulder of the very idea of virtue, had still, however breezily, to find her way around it.

LADY BRUTE

The devil's in the fellow I think—I was told before I married him, that thus 'twould be; but I thought I had charms enough to govern him; and that where there was an estate, a woman must needs be happy; so my vanity has deceived me, and my ambition has made me uneasy. But some comfort still; if one would be revenged of him, these are good times; a woman may have a gallant, and a separate maintenance too—The surly puppy—yet he's a fool for't: for hitherto he has been no monster: but who knows how far he may provoke me. I never loved him, yet I have been ever true to him; and that, in spite of all the attacks of art and nature upon a poor weak woman's heart, in favour of a tempting lover. Methinks so noble a defence as I have made, should be rewarded with a better usage—or who can tell—perhaps a good part of what I suffer from my husband may be a judgement upon me for my cruelty to my lover. Lord with what pleasure could I indulge that thought, were there but a possibility of finding arguments to make it good.—And how do I know but there may—Let me see—What opposes?—My matrimonial vow?—Why, what did I vow: I think I promised to be true to my husband. Well; and he promised to be kind to me. But he han't kept his word— Why then I'm absolved from mine—aye, that seems clear to me. The argument's good between the King and the people, why not between the husband and the wife? Oh, but that condition was not expressed.—No matter, 'twas understood. Well, by all I see, if I argue the matter a little longer with myself, I shan't find so many bugbears in the way, as I thought I should. Lord what fine notions of virtue do we women take up upon the credit of old foolish philosophers. Virtue's its own reward, virtue's this, virtue's that;—virtue's an ass, and a gallant's worth forty on't.

156.

LADY LUREWELL REVEALS THE CAUSE FOR HER HATRED OF MEN: HER FIRST BETRAYER (OC)

(1699) GEORGE FARQUHAR, *THE CONSTANT COUPLE*, ACT III, SC. 4

About men: "I hate all that don't love me, and slight all that do." Lady Lurewell lives by a determined cynicism that leaves her free of entanglement, even when she is tempted to succumb. Whimsically, with easy malice, she plays for fools all the men who swarm, turning them for her own amusement, and for her confirmation, into liars, cheats, and batterers of and toward one another. But at this moment, when her maid Parly broaches the question of her hatred of men—"the injuries you have suffered by men must be very great, to raise such heavy resentments against the whole sex"—Lady Lurewell puts aside mockery, and recalls soberly the origin of her hatred, the confession of her shame. In Farquhar, and in Restoration comedy, that confession has not yet taken on the pious or sentimental morbidity that infuses later and similar recollections, confessionals, and accusations of the same crime, but even in Lady Lurewell, the moral imperative is already moving close to the surface of her narrative, and produces, at the critical moment, her tears.

Lady Lurewell

Injuries, indeed. They robbed me of that jewel, which preserved, exalts our sex almost to angels, but, destroyed, debases us below the worst of brutes, mankind.

'Tis a subject that always sours my temper; but since by thy faithful service I have some reason to confide in your secrecy, hear the strange relation. Some twelve years ago I lived at my father's house in Oxfordshire, blest with innocence, the ornamental, but weak guard of blooming beauty. I was then just fifteen, an age oft fatal to the female sex; our youth is tempting, our innocence credulous, romances moving, love powerful, and men are villains. Then it happened that three young gentlemen from the university coming into the country, and being benighted, and strangers, called at my father's. He was very glad of their company, and offered them the entertainment of his house. They had some private frolic or design in their heads, as appeared by their not naming one another, which my father perceiving, out of civility, made no inquiry into their affairs. Two of them had a heavy, pedantic, university air, a sort of disagreeable scholastic-boorishness in their behaviour—but the third!

He was—but in short, nature cut him out for my undoing; he seemed to be about eighteen. He had a genteel sweetness in his face, a graceful comeliness in his person, and his tongue was fit to soothe soft innocence to ruin. His very looks were witty, and his expressive eyes spoke softer prettier things than words could frame.

His discourse was directed to my father, but his looks to me. After supper I went to my chamber, and read *Cassandra*, then went to bed, and dreamt of him all night, rose in the morning, and made verses; so fell desperately in love. My father was so pleased with his conversation, that he begged their company next day; they consented, and next night, Parly—he bribed my maid with his gold out of her honesty, and me with his rhetoric out of my honour: she admitted him to my chamber, and there he vowed, and swore, and wept, and sighed—and conquered.

(Weeps)

He swore that he would come down from Oxford in a fortnight, and marry me. Alas! what wit had innocence like mine? He told me that he was under an obligation to his companions of concealing himself then, but that he would write to me in two days, and let me know his name and quality. After all the binding oaths of constancy, joining hands, exchanging hearts, I gave him a ring with this motto, "Love and Honour"—then we parted; but I never saw the dear deceiver more.

I need not tell my griefs, which my father's death made a fair pretence for; he left me sole heiress and executrix to three thousand pounds a year. At last my love for this single dissembler turned to a hatred of the whole sex, and resolving to divert my melancholy, and make my large fortune subservient to my pleasure and revenge, I went to travel, where in most Courts of Europe I have done some execution. Here I will play my last scene; then retire to my country house, live solitary, and die a penitent.

But still love this dear dissembler? Most certainly. 'Tis love of him that keeps my anger warm, representing the baseness of mankind full in view; and makes my resentments work.

"CASSANDRA": a French heroic romance in ten volumes by La Calprenede, which appeared serially between 1642 and 1645.

157.

ANGELICA PASSIONATELY DEFENDS HER HONOR AGAINST THE DRUNKEN SIR HARRY (YC)

(1699) GEORGE FARQUHAR, *THE CONSTANT COUPLE*, ACT V, SC. 1

Speaking one language and meaning another, or speaking one language immoderately and meaning it only moderately, is standard for witty women in comedy pretending to spurn "loose desire." But Angelica means what she says, and Sir Harry can't believe it—and has no reason to believe it—supposing that she negotiates, as he does, through the understood, not the spoken. Sir Harry is habituated to the old game—his name is Sir Harry Wildair—but Angelica is one of the new breed of chaste maidens who, unlike even very chaste maidens of genuine Restoration vintage, really does suffer outrage at naked suggestion and naked talk. She's not haughtily pretending, she's damned angry, and determined to hold off Sir Harry's drunken propositions. But she does it in language that will encroach more and more in the coming century on dramatic discourse, a language that begins its flaying of vice from such a height of virtue that comedy will gradually lose patience with it, and before the end of the next century, it will be understood once again as Sir Harry, with his low mind, understands it here.

Angelica, even at this juncture in 1699, is obviously in great danger of being understood in just such comic terms. Not only her language, but her argument is exceptionally high-minded. And it is the high-mindedness that issues from a new assumption concerning human vice: that it does not come from an evil heart, but from a good one that is temporarily off-track. Angelica, like the comic playwrights soon to come, is turning her back on the doctrinal Puritanism that condemned characters like Master Wendoll in *A Woman Killed with Kindness* [see, in Men's vols.: "Wendoll Battles with His Conscience"] to moral helplessness because of his soul's inherent sinfulness. Now the soul, soon to be more usually known as the heart, is understood to be inherently benevolent, but sometimes frail. "Your very self is guard against yourself. I'm sure," she warns Sir Harry, "there's something generous in your soul. My words shall search it out." Both words and deeds will be searching out that "generosity" from the late

1690s on, and dozens of old-style libertines like Sir Harry will be reduced to tears and elevated to serious blank verse when, as Angelica does here, virtue "fires" what is "generous" in such souls "for [its] own defense." [A further example, in Men's vols.: "Loveless Embraces Love of Virtue...."] And to touch that heart, she holds up one mirror to the "tender flower" of her own honor and reputation, and a contrasting one to "the foulness of [his] own thought" in which to study his behavior.

But then, while her argument from virtue is still struggling to win over the reprobate, an older principle of comedy takes over, and Angelica's conversion of Sir Harry is done not really by virtue's persuasion, but by a letter, which reveals that the villain Vizard has fooled Sir Harry into supposing that he's come to a bawdy house, and that Angelica has been making difficulties only about her price. Disabused, he falls to his knees, and speaks the *de rigeur* blank verse which is both apology and reassurance to Angelica of his dormant but suddenly rediscovered love of virtue.

ANGELICA

I conjure you, sir, by the sacred name of honour, by your dead
father's name, and the fair reputation of your mother's
chastity, that you offer not the least offence. Already you have
wronged me past redress.

What madness, Sir Harry, what wild dream of loose desire
could prompt you to attempt this baseness? View me well. The
brightness of my mind, methinks, should lighten outwards,
and let you see your mistake in my behaviour. I think it shines
with so much innocence in my face; that it should dazzle all
your vicious thoughts. Think not I am defenceless 'cause
alone. Your very self is guard against yourself. I'm sure, there's
something generous in your soul. My words shall search it out,
and eyes fire it for my own defence.

View me well. Consider me with a sober thought, free from
those fumes of wine that cast a mist before your sight; and you
shall find that every glance from my reproaching eye is armed
with sharp resentment, and with repelling rays that look
dishonour dead.

If my beauty has power to raise a flame, be sure it is a virtuous
one; if otherwise, 'tis owing to the foulness of your own
thought, which throwing this mean affront upon my honour,

has alarmed my soul, and fires it with a brave disdain.
Were I a man, you durst not use me thus. But the mean poor
abuse you cast on me, reflects upon yourself. Our sex still
strikes an awe upon the brave, and only cowards dare affront a
woman.

Think, sir, that my blood, for many generations, has run in the
purest channel of unsullied honour. Consider what a tender
flower is woman's reputation, which the least air of foul
detraction blasts. Call then to mind your rude and scandalous
behaviour. Remember the base price you offered: then think
that Vizard, villain Vizard, caused all this, yet lives. That's all.
Farewell!—And promise me, Sir Harry, to have a care of
burgundy henceforth.

CONJURE: implore. REDRESS: remedy, righting. UNSULLIED: unstained.

158.

MILLAMANT, FOR HER PLEASURE, VEXES HER LOVER MIRABELL (YC)

(1700) WILLIAM CONGREVE, *THE WAY OF THE WORLD*, ACT II, SC. 1

It was George Meredith who pointed out that high comedy, or comedy of manners, can flourish only in a society that has achieved equality of the sexes. The wit combat, which is the essence of high comedy,
can't occur unless neither is under any subservience to the other.
Whether Millamant has such equality, she asserts it, in fact demands
it, exploits it, and tests it to the very verge of exceeding its proprieties.
But independence of constraint is the battle-cry of Millamant; her
understanding of her value has nothing to do with "attainment," or
"character," or "favor." Her having value at all for herself means only
that she possesses infinite liberty.

It is a supposition that can only be supported in a society that has
not only the benefit of infinite leisure and infinite subservience, but
also a mastery of its real and only and infinitely pleasurable constraints: the code of its proprieties. It is, in fact, apart from the pursuit
of money, love, and marriage, a society's only way of filling time—

learning the code and all its codicils, performing them with grace and diffidence. And for Millamant, dancing within those wide yet precise constraints at the edge of excess.

But Millamant finds little satisfaction in the one constraint that can painfully limit her liberty: the subservience to which the lover automatically submits, first in her private feeling, then in its gross exposure. Attuned to that danger, she'll have none of it. But the lover's vulnerability, instead of being a liability against oneself, can be used as a weapon against the other: it is Millamant's technique for holding Mirabell in bondage. She does it gaily and masterfully, driving him to desperation, but still keeping him in check. Note her technique. Pretending none or casual feeling of her own, she exposes his vulnerability, mocks it, gives it no deference. Laughing outright, she ventures: "What would you give that you could help loving me?" Shamed by this mockery and gross exposure, his response is dour, but carefully tempered; nevertheless, she drags even that into the light, mocking his response to her mockery. Worse, she play-acts sympathy for his "melancholy," ventures to share it, but to signal clearly her uncontrollable indifference to his plight, she laughs at it outright.

This is Millamant at the edge of propriety: pretending uncontrollable foolishness, she is testing the limit of his willing bondage. Her tally? He remains secured, she remains free.

MILLAMANT

Long! Lord, have I not made violent haste! I have asked every living thing I met for you; I have enquired after you, as after a new fashion. Oh, but then I had—Mincing, what had I? Why was I so long?

Oh, ay, letters—I had letters—I am persecuted with letters—I hate letters. Nobody knows how to write letters; and yet one has 'em, one does not know why. They serve one to pin up one's hair. Only with those in verse, I never pin up my hair with prose. I fancy one's hair would not curl if it were pinned up with prose. I think I tried once.

Ay, poor Mincing tift and tift all the morning. Mirabell, did not you take exceptions last night? Oh, ay; and went away. Now I think on't I'm angry.—No, now I think on't I'm pleased—for I believe I gave you some pain.

Does that please me? Infinitely; I love to give pain. One's

cruelty is one's power, and when one parts with one's cruelty, one parts with one's power; and when one has parted with that; I fancy one's old and ugly.

I think I must resolve, after all, not to have you. We shan't agree. And yet our distemper in all likelihood will be the same; for we shall be sick of one another. I shan't endure to be reprimanded, nor instructed; 'tis so dull to act always by advice, and so tedious to be told of one's faults—I can't bear it. Well, I won't have you, Mirabell—I'm resolved—I think— you may go—ha, ha, ha! What would you give, that you could help loving me?

Come, don't look grave then. Well, what do you say to me? Prithee, don't look with that violent and inflexible wise face; like Solomon at the dividing of the child in an old tapestry hanging. No, if you keep your countenance, 'tis impossible I should hold mine. Well, after all, there is something very moving in a lovesick face. Ha, ha, ha!—well, I won't laugh, don't be peevish—heigho! Now I'll be melancholy, as melancholy as a watch-light. Well, Mirabell, if ever you will win me, [woo] me now.—Nay, if you are so tedious, fare you well.

TIFT: arranged. WATCH-LIGHT: a small candle in a sick room.

159.

LADY WISHFORT DEFIES MIRABELL'S SLANDERS CONCERNING HER AGE, AND PREPARES FOR THE SURPRISE OF AN UNKNOWN SUITOR (OC)

(1700) WILLIAM CONGREVE, *THE WAY OF THE WORLD*, ACT III, SC. 1

Along with Sheridan's Mrs. Malaprop, the most famous of English comedy's superannuated termagants is Congreve's Lady Wishfort, whose function in the plot is to stand in the way of Mirabell's marriage to her niece, Millamant. To conceal his suit to Millamant,

Mirabell had once had the temerity to pretend, and Lady Wishfort had the vanity to suppose, that the young man was paying court to her in earnest. Her disillusion has made her his violent enemy, and she is eager now, in revenge, to marry so that (and here, the roundaboutness of Congreve's plot made difficulties even for his first-night audience) she can dispossess her niece of her fortune and make Mirabell's suit profitless. She's awaiting a Sir Rowland now, who, she's told, has been infatuated with her picture, and is ready, she prays, to marry her at once. (Mirabell has forestalled her there too. Sir Rowland is only Mirabell's servant Waitwell in disguise; Mirabell will have only to expose the fraudulence of the marriage to bring Lady Wishfort to shame and surrender.)

But at the moment, Lady Wishfort is on tenterhooks. She's at her dressing table preparing for Sir Rowland's visit, but more to the immediate point, waiting to learn from her delayed maid Foible's secret mission to Sir Rowland whether he is in fact coming. Her suspicions are aroused when she learns from a visitor, Marwood (who has motives of her own for opposing Mirabell's marital plans), that she's seen Foible a moment before in the park chatting with Mirabell. Foible, at last arriving, has quickly to reinvent her conversation with Mirabell: it was nothing, she lies, but his satires and lampoons against Lady Wishfort.

And so Lady Wishfort is to undo Mirabell by imminent marriage. Turning to her mirror, she is horrified to recognize that her anger has cracked the (egg-white-based) plaster covering her face—which had been smoothed into immobility—and begins repair. While doing so—one of the famous moments in Congreve's comedy—she studies possible angles and postures for receiving her expected suitor. But her primary fear is that she, and not he, will be called upon to make significant overtures. Her modesty, her terror of "offending against decorums," focuses all her speculation on Sir Rowland's potential for being importunate enough to overcome her fear of "breaking with form."

(Enter Foible)

LADY WISHFORT

O Foible, where hast thou been? What hast thou been doing? Hast thou not betrayed me, Foible? Hast thou not detected me to that faithless Mirabell? What hadst thou to do with him in the Park? What did the filthy fellow say? Superannuated! Ods my life, I'll have him—I'll have him murdered. I'll have him poisoned. Where does he eat? I'll marry a drawer to have him poisoned in his wine. Audacious villain!

"Frippery? old frippery!" Was there ever such a foul-mouthed fellow? I'll be married tomorrow, I'll be contracted tonight. "Frippery? superannuated frippery!" I'll frippery the villain; I'll reduce him to frippery and rags. A tatterdemalion!—I hope to see him hung with tatters, like a Long Lane pent-house, or a gibbet-thief: A slander-mouthed railer: I warrant the spendthrift prodigal's in debt as much as the million lottery, or the whole court upon a birthday. I'll spoil his credit with his tailor. Yes, he shall have my niece with her fortune, he shall.

Ay, dear Foible; thank thee dear Foible. He has put me out of all patience. I shall never recompose my features to receive Sir Rowland with any economy of face. This wretch has fretted me that I am absolutely decayed. Let me see the glass.—Cracks, say'st thou? Why, I am arrantly flayed; I look like an old peeled wall. Thou must repair me, Foible, before Sir Rowland comes; or I shall never keep up to my picture.

But art thou sure Sir Rowland will not fail to come? Or will I not fail when he does come? Will he be importunate, Foible, and push? For if he should not be importunate—I shall never break decorums—I shall die with confusion, if I am forced to advance—oh no, I can never advance—I shall swoon if he should expect advances. No, I hope Sir Rowland is better bred, than to put a lady to the necessity of breaking her forms. I won't be too coy neither. I won't give him despair—but a little disdain is not amiss; a little scorn is alluring.

Yes, but tenderness becomes me best—a sort of a dyingness.—You see that picture has a sort of a—ha, Foible? A swimminess in the eyes. Yes, I'll look so. My niece affects it; but she wants features. Is Sir Rowland handsome? Let my toilet be removed—I'll dress above. I'll receive Sir Rowland here. Is he handsome? Don't answer me. I won't know: I'll be surprised. I'll be taken by surprise. A brisk man, is he! Oh, then he'll importune, if he's a brisk man. I shall save decorums if Sir Rowland importunes. I have a mortal terror at the apprehension of offending against decorums. Nothing but importunity can surmount decorums. Oh, I'm glad he's a brisk man! Let my things be removed, good Foible.

(Exit)

DRAWER: a bartender. TATTERDEMALION: one in ragged clothes. LONG LANE was given over to old-clothes dealers. A PENT-HOUSE: a shed with an overhanging roof. GIBBET-THIEF: a felon who escaped hanging. MILLION LOTTERY: in 1694 the government raised a loan of 1,000,000 pounds by means of a lottery, the prizes being annuities for sixteen years—apparently these annuities were in arrears. ROYAL BIRTHDAY: which is celebrated like a national holiday with parade, fireworks, etc.

160.

LADY WISHFORT REHEARSES AGREEABLE POSTURES FOR RECEIVING HER LOVER (oc)

(1700) WILLIAM CONGREVE, *THE WAY OF THE WORLD*, ACT IV, SC. 1

[Continues No. 159, above.] When the moment of his expected arrival is upon her, Lady Wishfort makes final preparation for his entrance: her posture once again, her languor, her whatever that will induce the critical first impression, the one that will astonish and persuade.

The ridiculous character in Congreve is one who has no suspicion of what or who one is. Stumbling repeatedly on the reality occasions the strenuous effort of burying those moments of hideous recognition. The particular ridiculousness of Lady Wishfort lies in the distance she's erected between the image of dainty beauty she has of herself and what age, vanity, and frustration have irrevocably made of her.

(Lady Wishfort and Foible)

LADY WISHFORT

Is Sir Rowland coming, say'st thou, Foible? and are things in order? Have you pulvilled the coachman and postilion, that they may not stink of the stable, when Sir Rowland comes by? And are the dancers and the music ready, that he may be entertained in all points with correspondence to his passion? And—well—and how do I look, Foible? Well, and how shall I receive him? In what figure shall I give his heart the first impression? There is a great deal in the first impression. Shall I

sit?—No, I won't sit—I'll walk—ay, I'll walk from the door
upon his entrance; and then turn full upon him.—No, that
will be too sudden. I'll lie—ay, I'll lie down—I'll receive him
in my little dressing-room; there's a couch—yes, yes, I'll give
the first impression on a couch.—I won't lie neither, but loll
and lean upon one elbow, with one foot a little dangling off,
jogging in a thoughtful way—yes—and then as soon as he
appears, start, ay, start and be surprised, and rise to meet him
in a pretty disorder—yes—oh, nothing is more alluring than a
levee from a couch in some confusion.—It shows the foot to
advantage, and furnishes with blushes, and recomposing airs
beyond comparison. Hark! There's a coach.

PULVILLED: powdered with a scented powder. POSTILION: the one who rides the near
horse of a carriage. LEVEE: rising.

161.

MILLAMANT OFFERS HER CONDITIONS FOR MARRIAGE TO MIRABELL (YC)

(1700) WILLIAM CONGREVE, *THE WAY OF THE WORLD*, ACT IV, SC. 1

[Quoting from Men's vols.: "Mirabell Offers His Conditions for
Marriage to Millamant":] "When the paragons of Restoration lovers,
Mirabell and Millamant, contracted on the one hand to become 'a
tractable and compliant husband,' and on the other to 'dwindle into a
wife,' Restoration comedy, as one critic mourned, was over. Their surrender goes far beyond the range of other marital succumbings in
other Restoration comedy's endings. Those acknowledge giving up
their sexual independence. These surrender a great deal more.

"What had been developing in Congreve's comedies and in their
society's moment was an extraordinary sense of private worth, the
value of the self as such. Not the 'self' in its native state, as a given; but
in its subsequent refinement: self-cultivation aimed at achieving the
exquisite—a state of personal perfection which has no value or use
beyond itself. Rooted in diffidence toward outward show [see, in
Men's vols.: "Sir Fopling Flutter Displays on His Person the French
Mode"], it also forbids invasion of its inward privacy. Its most cruel

betrayal is by 'the world's' defining it, diminishing it to a function, a role, a name. 'Painter,' for example, or 'Poet,' is bad; 'Tradesman' or 'Fool' is even worse; they're functions, roles. The 'liberty' whose passing Millamant laments, a lamentation in which Mirabell concurs, is also her freedom from circumscription, from the imprisonment of definition: 'Wife.'

"But there were contingencies; the private condition had to be attained at a price. It depended on both the easy assurance of love, and the equally comfortable assurance of money. The delicacy of the balance between the maintenance of their self-reflective self-image and the necessity of their stooping to its supportive needs (Mirabell's plotting all through the comedy for the guarantee that money will accompany marriage, and Millamant's walking backwards all through the comedy into the coils of marriage), is for both of them the desperate reason for their contract. It will guarantee their 'world's' gross needs (marriage; money; possibly—'Name it not!' says Millamant—offspring) without compromising, not to speak of violating, their very being.

"The overriding irony of their endeavor is that for each the provisos of the other are trivial, irrelevant, of small note; their own, on the other hand, are the binding assurances of their self-preservation."

Millamant, knowing the dreaded moment approaches when Mirabell will come like a soon-to-be-husband thing to "ask for her hand," mourning the fact that the liberty she relished more than marriage is over, waits his entry with a copy of Suckling in her hand. She reads aloud the comforting lines that express almost adequately her feeling of the moment: "Press me no more for that slight toy," and awaits the dooming declaration, retreating as long as possible and as far as possible from its imprisoning certainty. Her acceptance is finally uttered in the context of refusal, the refusal of anything to do with a marital concord that impinges too damningly on her being, her liberty.

MILLAMANT

(Reading aloud)
"I prithee, spare me, gentle boy,
Press me no more for that slight toy,—
That foolish trifle of a heart—
I swear it will not do its part,
Though thou dost thine, employ'st thy power and art."

Natural, easy Suckling!—I'll fly and be followed to the last moment. Though I am upon the very verge of matrimony, I expect you should solicit me as much as if I were wavering at the grate of a monastery, with one foot over the threshold. I'll be solicited to the very last, nay, and afterwards.

Oh, I should think I was poor and had nothing to bestow, if I were reduced to an in-glorious ease, and freed from the agreeable fatigues of solicitation. Oh, I hate a lover that can dare to think he draws a moment's air, independent on the bounty of his mistress. There is not so impudent a thing in nature as the saucy look of an assured man, confident of success. The pedantic arrogance of a very husband has not so pragmatical an air. Ah! I'll never marry, unless I am first made sure of my will and pleasure.

My dear liberty, shall I leave thee? My faithful solitude, my darling contemplation, must I bid you then adieu? Ay, adieu—my morning thoughts, agreeable wakings, indolent slumbers, all ye *douceurs*, ye *sommails du matin*, adieu?—I can't do't, 'tis more than impossible. Positively, Mirabell, I'll lie abed in a morning as long as I please: And d'ee hear, I won't be called names after I'm married; positively I won't be called names. Ay, as wife, spouse, my dear, joy, jewel, love, sweetheart, and the rest of that nauseous cant, in which men and their wives are so fulsomely familiar—I shall never bear that.

Good Mirabell; don't let us be familiar or fond, nor kiss before folks, like my Lady Fadler and Sir Francis: nor go to Hyde Park together the first Sunday in a new chariot to provoke eyes and whispers; and then never to be seen there together again; as if we were proud of one another the first week, and ashamed of one another for ever after. Let us never visit together, nor go to a play together, but let us be very strange and well bred: let us be as strange as if we had been married a great while; and as well bred as if were not married at all.

Have I more conditions to offer? Trifles,—as liberty to pay and receive visits to and from whom I please; to write and receive letters, without interrogatories or wry faces on your part. To wear what I please; and choose conversation with regard only to my own taste; to have no obligation upon me to converse with wits that I don't like, because they are your acquaintance; or to be intimate with fools, because they may be your relations. Come to dinner when I please, dine in my dressing-room when I'm out of humor, without giving a reason. To have my closet inviolate; to be sole empress of my tea-table, which you must never presume to approach without first asking leave. And lastly, wherever I am, you shall always knock at the door before you come in. These articles subscribed, if I continue to endure you a little longer, I may by degrees dwindle into a wife.

[SIR JOHN] SUCKLING (1609–42): a British poet. PRAGMATICAL: officious. *DOUCEURS*: sweetnesses. *SOMMEILS DU MATIN*: morning naps, i.e., "beauty sleep." CANT: insincere statements.

162.

LADY WISHFORT DISCOVERS MIRABELL'S PLOT TO UNDO HER (OC)

(1700) WILLIAM CONGREVE, *THE WAY OF THE WORLD*, ACT V, SC. 1

[Continues Nos. 159 and 160, above] The fat is in the fire for faithful Foible when Lady Wishfort discovers that she has been plotting in collusion with Mirabell all the while. Worse—Mirabell bound Foible to his cause by wedding her in secret to his servant Waitwell, who, disguised as Sir Rowland, married Lady Wishfort. She's been the ridiculous butt, she now discovers, of Mirabell's conniving. In her wrath, Lady Wishfort rages at Foible, relieving her humiliation by a torrent of abuse that does credit to her familiarity with the stews and prisons and byways of London's underside, to which Hell she's consigning Foible.

(Lady Wishfort and Foible)

LADY WISHFORT

Out of my house, out of my house, thou viper, thou serpent, that I have fostered! thou bosom traitress, that I raised from nothing!—begone, begone, begone, go, go!—that I took from washing of old gauze and weaving of dead hair, with a bleak blue nose, over a chafing-dish of starved embers, and dining behind a traverse rag, in a shop no bigger than a bird-cage,— go, go, starve again, do, do!

Away, out, out; go set up for yourself again!—do, drive a trade, do, with your three-penny worth of small ware, flaunting upon a pack-thread, under a brandy-seller's bulk, or against a dead wall by a ballad-monger! Go, hang out an old prisoner gorget, with a yard of yellow colberteen again! do! an old gnawed mask, two rows of pins, and a child's fiddle; a glass necklace with the beads broken, and a quilted nightcap with one ear! Go, go, drive a trade!—These were your commodities, you treacherous trull, this was your merchandise you dealt in, when I took you into my house, placed you next myself, and made you governante of my whole family! You have forgot this, have you, now you have feathered your nest?

To betray me, to marry me to a cast servingman; to make me a receptacle, an hospital for a decayed pimp? No damage? O thou frontless impudence, more than, a big-bellied actress! I have been your property, have I? I have been convenient to you, it seems, while you were catering for Mirabell, I have been broker for you? What, have you made a passive bawd of me?—This exceeds all precedent; I am brought to fine uses, to become a botcher of second-hand marriages between Abigails and Andrews! I'll couple you! Yes, I'll baste you together, you and your Philander! I'll Duke's Place you, as I'm a person. Your turtle is in custody already; you shall coo in the same cage, if there be constable or warrant in the parish.

(Exit)

WASHING OF OLD GAUZE AND WEAVING OF DEAD HAIR: for making wigs. CHAFING-DISH: an apparatus consisting of a metal dish with a heating lamp beneath it, for cooking food or keeping it hot. PACK-THREAD: strong twine for sewing or tying packages. TRAVERSE RAG: a ragged curtain hung up as a screen. BULK: stall. GORGET: a woolen kerchief worn over the bosom. COLBERTEEN: cheap lace. TRULL: a prostitute, strumpet. GOVERNANTE: housekeeper. CAST: cast-off, discharged. FRONTLESS: shameless. BIG-BELLIED ACTRESS: an obviously pregnant actress appearing on stage. BOTCHER: mending tailor. ABIGAILS AND ANDREWS: ladies' maids and gentlemen's servants. PHILANDER: lover. DUKE'S PLACE: where St. James' Church was situated—there irregular or "Fleet street" marriages were performed. TURTLE: turtle-dove, sweetheart. WARRANT: for arrest.

163.

MIRANDA EXPLAINS TO HER FIANCE HOW THE LOVER BEFORE MARRIAGE CAN MAKE THE HUSBAND AFTERWARD MORE INVITING (YC)

(1700) CATHERINE TROTTER, *LOVE AT A LOSS*, ACT II, SC. 2

Her friend Lucilia wonders how Miranda can be loved by a man like Constant—his very name is, after all, a strong argument—and not have in mind to marry him. But Miranda, more of the mind of Congreve's Millamant [see No. 158, above], explains: "I don't love him so well, but that I had rather torment him, than he should torment me.... I like...an obsequious humble Servant, better than a surly Lord and Master." The motives that justify Millamant are the same as those that explain Miranda: her tormenting her lover, her inability to "compose [her] face for the wedding day," the ceremony being "so unreasonable a thing as taking for better or for worse," are, like Millamant's, strategies of deferment of the dark day and its dark consequence.

Miranda, in this same vein, proposes to her betrothed Constant—a proposal that more or less caps his torment—that he second her taking a lover—Beaumine [see Beaumine's monologues in Men's vols.]—in advance of that day. Her reason? Constant has already proved a way of curing love by "being perpetually with her." A lover, even though as gay and witty as Constant is earnest, once grown familiar and dull "as a book I have already read," will make Constant seem new again, and she'll return to him with new pleasure.

The strongest urgency of the moment for the Mirandas and Millamants is to distance themselves from eager pliancy and eager surrender to expectation, and to demand of both the time of love and the time of marriage no diminution of their sense of their own stature. As with Millamant's Mirabell, when Constant is pushed to the limits of his patience and leaves his tormenting mistress in anger, Miranda exhibits no qualm. The lover, already secured by "passion," will in the end comply.

Miranda

Well, seriously, I have been trying this month to compose my face for the wedding day; for I fancy if one has not a most reverend countenance, one will never be thought in earnest at so unreasonable a thing as taking for better or for worse. It looks so like a jest or stark madness.

Ay, but that surly [countenance] of yours, Constant, has such a husbandly air, 'twill spoil the jest; I never look upon it but I'm afraid I'm married already.

Nay, those laughing eyes bring to my thoughts that charming fellow that danced and sung himself into my heart. I must have some time to drive him out again, and then, Constant— O such a grace, such an air, such a humour; if you knew him you must be fond of him for love of me, he's just my counterpart.

Nay, don't be jealous. It's in concern for your life I would delay this marriage. For, if in the height of my passion, the tempter shou'd come my way—he makes an attack; duty opposes; inclination assists him; prohibition strengthens it. Nature prevails, runs away with me. You pursue and cut his throat; I break my heart; you can do no less than stab yourself to complete the tragedy, and prevent all this mischief—

You have a better way of curing a woman's love, being perpetually with her. And since you have found it so effectual an experiment, I'm resolved to try it upon my new inclination, till he has said all the fine things he can, show'd all his humours, played over all his tricks, left nothing farther for imagination to work on; but grown as dull to me as a book I have just read. Then you'll be new again, like one that has been long out of print! And I am always fond of the second edition, revised, corrected, and amended. (But be sure you take care never to let me peruse it thro'; reserve something for my curiosity, Constant. For you know the best books, when we have studied 'em perfectly, are thrown aside, or only kept for show, and any trifling novel that we never met with before, entertains us better.)

What, is it 'nangry now? And what would it do? Can it break its cage? Flutter about, tire itself, and hurt its wings; and to what purpose? Well, I am good-natured, and since you are so

impatient—I am resolved—as soon as possible—to engage my
charmer, grow weary of him as fast as I can, return to you
with new pleasure, then here's my hand on it.

EIGHTEENTH-CENTURY FRENCH

164.

MARINE IMPLORES MADAME TO ACCEPT THE SAFETY OF THE FINANCIER TURCARET RATHER THAN THE PLEASURE OF THE GAMBLING KNIGHT (YC)

(1709) Alain-René Le Sage, *Turcaret*, tr. Richard Aldington, Act I

Under the protection of contracts awarded by the government of
Louis XIV, "revenue farmers," or tax-collectors, gouged the citizens of
France, keeping half the revenue for themselves, impoverishing the
country, and bankrupting the crown. Turcaret is one of these especially blessed—the wealthiest and most unscrupulous class in France.
The Baroness, an impoverished widow, has the extraordinary good
fortune to have attracted Turcaret as an admirer, and thrives on his
attentions, his gifts, and his promise of marriage. But improvident
and weak-willed as she is, she puts all this good fortune in jeopardy
by favoring a young Knight, as impoverished as herself, whom she
supports out of the largesse she harvests from her benefactor.

It is Marine, the familiar maidservant of neo-classical comedy
whose tongue is traditionally licensed to chastise her masters, who

calls the foolish Baroness to account. Is she mad? Get rid of the Knight, she demands, "attach yourself to M. Turcaret, to marry or to ruin him."

Given the financial and moral condition of France at the time, Marine's advice is not reprehensible, but merely sound. The only motive in their world is money, none other, and the play of love, of friendship, of duty, even of charity, is entirely in the service of that appetite alone. Le Sage in this grim portrait of his country anticipates by more than two hundred years the equally practical and equally grim descriptions in Balzac of nineteenth-century France, with only one pursuit flourishing there as well.

Marine is blunt. She lays out the facts—she speaks, after all, the play's exposition—so logically, so incontrovertibly, that the Baroness has no alternative but to agree: she will give up her Knight for the gross but copiously generous Turcaret. The vacillating woman of course betrays her decision at almost the next moment, but by play's end, that hardly matters. She, the Knight, and Turcaret himself, are each in turn bilked, usually by a most trusted ally, until—at the play's famous ending—Frontin, the valet of the irresponsible Knight, with greater cunning than all of them, has garnered all the available loot for himself.

MARINE

No, Madam, I cannot be silent; your behaviour is unendurable. You exhaust my patience. You are the widow of a foreign colonel killed in Flanders last year; you have already spent the small dower he left you when he went away, and you had nothing left but your furniture which you would have been obliged to sell if Fortune had not permitted you to make a conquest of M. Turcaret, the financier. Is this not true, Madam? Well, this M. Turcaret who is not a very lovable man and whom you do not love although you have decided to marry him as he has promised you marriage; M. Turcaret, I say, is in no hurry to keep his word to you and you wait patiently for him to carry out his promise because every day he makes you some valuable present; I have nothing to say against that; but what I cannot endure is that you should have saddled yourself with a little gambling Knight who will gamble away the spoils of the financier. Eh! What do you propose to do with the Knight? Keep him as a friend? Of course, and especially friends who can be used as a last resource. For example, this one might very well marry you in case M. Turcaret fails you; he is not one of these Knights who are vowed to celibacy and forced to run off to the help of Malta; he is a Parisian Knight; he fights his campagnes at lansquenet. With his impassioned air, his sugary tones, his smirking face, he seems to me a positive comedian; and what confirms me in this opinion is that Frontin, his good valet Frontin, says nothing to me against him. And from that I conclude that the master and the valet are two rogues in league to dupe you; and you allow yourself to be deceived by their tricks, although you have known them for some time. It is true that he was the first during your widowhood to offer you his hand point-blank; and this appearance of fidelity has so set him up in your good graces that he uses your purse as if it were his own.

If this goes on, do you know what will happen? M. Turcaret will find out that you want to keep the Knight as a friend, and he will not think it permissible for you to keep friends. He will not marry you; and if you are reduced to marrying the Knight it will be a very bad marriage for both of you.
Madam, the future must be foreseen. From this time on keep in mind a solid establishment; profit by M. Turcaret's prodigalities, while you wait for him to marry you. If he fails to do so, there will indeed be a little talking in the world; but to make up for it you will have good furniture, ready money, jewels, good banknotes and shares; and then you will find some capricious or needy gentleman who will restore your reputation by a good marriage. Listen to reason. You must attach yourself to M. Turcaret, to marry or to ruin him. You will snatch from the wreck of his fortune at least enough to set up a coach and to support a brilliant figure in the world; and, whatever they may say, you will tire out the chatterers, weary gossip, and gradually they will grow accustomed to ranking you with the women of quality.

His valet is coming; greet him icily; begin at once the great work you meditate.

RUN OFF TO THE HELP OF MALTA: in the Middle Ages Christian orders of knights defended the isle of Malta against the Turks. HE FIGHTS HIS CAMPAGNES AT LANSQUENET: at games of cards.

165.

THE BARONESS, LYING, WINS BACK THE CONFIDENCE AND LOVE OF TURCARET (OC)

(1709) ALAIN-RENÉ LE SAGE, *TURCARET*,
TR. RICHARD ALDINGTON, ACT II

[Continues No. 164, above] The Baroness has had the folly to dismiss her maidservant Marine because of her too-blunt advice to rid herself of her larcenous but attractive Knight, and vengefully, Marine has informed Turcaret of the Baroness' duplicity in keeping and rewarding the Knight with his gifts. In a rage, Turcaret comes to denounce the Baroness and break off all ties. But the Baroness—like all the characters in the play—is an accomplished liar, and easily wins back not only his confidence and devotion but also his largesse.

BARONESS

Listen to me... All the extravagances you have just committed are founded on a false report with Marine... Sir, do not swear and do not interrupt me; remember you are calm.
Do you know why I have just dismissed Marine? It was because she was constantly reproaching me with the inclination I have for you. "Is there anything so ridiculous," she would say to me continuously, "as for a colonel's widow to think of a M. Turcaret, a man without birth, without wit, of the lowest appearance... While you could choose a husband from any twenty men of the first quality; when you refuse your consent even to the pressing instances of the whole family, of a marquess by whom you are adored and whom you are weak enough to sacrifice to this M. Turcaret."

I do not pretend to make a merit of it, sir. This young marquess is a young nobleman of very agreeable person, but his morals and conduct do not please me. He comes here sometimes with my cousin the Knight, his friend. I found out he had won Marine to his interests and for that reason I dismissed her. She has come and poured out a thousand impossibilities to you to avenge herself, and you were credulous enough to believe her. Ought you not at the time to have reflected that a servant in a passion was speaking to you, that had I had anything to reproach myself with I should not have been so imprudent as to dismiss a girl whose indiscretion I had to fear? Did not this thought present itself spontaneously to your mind? Did she not tell you among other things that I no longer had the large diamond you put on my finger playfully the other day and forced me to accept? And if I were to show you the diamond at this moment, what would you say?

Here it is, sir; do you recognize it? You see what reliance is to be placed on the gossip of servants. No, your furious behaviour is inexcusable; why, you are unworthy of forgiveness. Should you have allowed yourself to be so easily prejudiced against a woman who loves you but too tenderly? Admit that you are a very weak man. A complete dupe.

166.

ZAIRE PLEADS HER LOVE OF THE SULTAN OSMAN AGAINST CHRISTIAN CONVERSION (YT)

(1732) VOLTAIRE, *ZAIRE*, TR. WILLIAM F. FLEMING, ACT I, SC. 1.

Voltaire, the great exponent of eighteenth-century Enlightenment, makes a case in *Zaire*, his most famous tragedy, against religious intolerance. Zaire, unbeknownst to herself, was born a Christian, but, raised in captivity in the Sultan Osman's palace, is for all she knows a Muslim; and captive or no, she is deeply in love with Osman, and he with her. A Christian knight, Nerestan, has brought ransom money from the West to free another longtime captive Lusignan, who is one of the descendants of the once-Christian rulers of Jerusalem. By signs and portents known only to drama, it's discovered that both Zaire and the young Knight Nerestan are both the long-lost children of Lusignan. The issue of Zaire's religious commitment is, of course, now engaged, and Lusignan, with the newfound authority of a father, enforces on her a vow of Christian faith and practice.

It's the implication of Volataire's scenario that the tragedy to follow is initiated by this heavy-handed imposition on Zaire of religion's exclusionary intolerance by the single-mindedness of the near-fanatic, Lusignan. In the course of her wavering between fidelity to Osman and commitment to her new religious cohorts, Osman learns of a planned meeting of Zaire and her brother, and unaware of their relation, he succumbs to raging jealousy, and kills her. The consequence is a standard eighteenth-century tragic conclusion: murder, suicide, and forgiveness all around. But though Sultan Osman's story leans heavily on *Othello*, Zaire's leans heavily on Voltaire's own excoriating hatred—spelled out voluminously in a lifetime of pamphleteering—of fanaticism.

Zaire in this speech argues against her fellow-slave Fatima's assertion that she is, and should accept that she is, a Christian. Zaire argues first, her utter lack of assurance of that fact; second, the happenstance of geography for one's religious faith—the essence of Voltaire's argument; and third, her love for Osman. But peeping through her arguments is the suggestion—one from which even Voltaire was apparently not immune—that the pull of the Christian faith is somehow in her blood.

ZAIRE

Alas, I know not who or what I am,
Not even who gave me birth.
Nerestan has often said
I am the daughter of a Christian;
But I've no other proof;
Should that alone persuade me to embrace
A faith detested by the man I love?
Our thoughts, our manners, our religion, all
Are formed by custom, and the powerful bent
Of early years: born on the banks of Ganges
I worshipped pagan deities;
Born in Paris, I would have been a Christian; here
I am a happy Muslim: we know
Only what we learn; the instructing parent's hand
Engraves onto our feeble hearts those characters
Which time retouches, and fixes deeply in our minds
Examples that noone but God
Can ever erase. But you were brought
A captive here at an age when reason, joined
To wise experience, informed your soul,
And well confirmed its faith. For me, who was a slave
To Saracens even from my cradle,

The light of Christian faith broke in too late.
Yet far from wishing harm to laws so pure,
Spite of myself, I do admit, the cross,
Whenever I look upon it, fills my soul
With reverent awe, and often I invoked
Its heavenly aid in secret, before my heart
Was Osman's. Yours is a noble faith;
I honor all its charitable laws
Which old Nerestan many times has told me
Would wipe away men's tears, and make mankind
One great united family of love.
A Christian must be happy. But would you
Have me refuse a gift so pure
As Osman's heart? No: I will confess my weakness.
But for the Sultan, I would have long ago
Embraced your faith, and been like you, a Christian.
But Osman loves me, and my every thought,
My every hope is fixed
On him alone, and my enraptured soul
Can dwell on nothing but on him.
Think on his lovely form, my friend,
And graceful mind, his noble deeds,
His glory and renown.
The crown he offers is not worth my care;
My poor return of gratitude would ill
Repay his passion; love would spurn his gift.
It is not Osman's throne, but Osman's self
That I adore. Perhaps I am to blame,
But trust me, Fatima, if heaven had doomed him
To Zaire's state, if he were now, like me,
A wretched slave, and I on Syria's throne,
Either love deceives me much, or I should stoop
With joy, and raise him up to me and empire.

SARACENS: a designation among Christians in the Middle Ages of their Muslim enemies. CHARITABLE LAWS: one of the five main postulates of Islam is charitable donation.

167.

LISE CONFESSES THAT SHE LOOKS TOWARD HER COMING MARRIAGE WITH GRIEF AND DISCONTENT (YC)

(1736) VOLTAIRE, *THE PRODIGAL*, TR. WILLIAM F. FLEMING, ACT II, SC. 1

It's small wonder that the comedies of Voltaire have no audience any more. In them, the great and deadly satirist disappears behind a facade of pious respectability, leaving little chance of observing the tiniest lash of his wit. But if we're ever to listen to such a respectable, neutralized voice at all, it's just as well to hear it from the chastened tongue of the otherwise acidic Voltaire.

His comedy, *The Prodigal*, repeats the familiar tale of the virtuous but priggish younger son and the profligate but good-hearted elder son to the near advantage of the former and the ultimate advantage of the latter. In Voltaire's play, not for the first time and hardly for the last, the elder prodigal (the young Euphemon) has been gone for years, and now returns incognito. But the maiden, Lise, has meantime been promised to the second son (Fierenfat), and is clearly in misery. The plot waits for the elder son to reveal himself, Lise to rediscover his true qualities and her reawakening love for him, and for a last-minute switch of the betrothed.

Lise confides to the chambermaid Martha her deep distress. She still "retains a passion" for the absent son whom she "ought to abhor," and laments that her marriage to the younger son will disinherit him. The reputation of marriage itself underwent a considerable upgrading in comedy in the early years of the eighteenth century, and Lise, like the more respectable maidens of her time, neither despises nor fears the institution itself, but only its "tyranny" when one like herself is unwillingly yoked to "an arbitrary tyrant." "Such a marriage is the hell of this world."

LISE

The noise and bustle of this preparation for marriage has something terrible in it. The more I think on the weight of this yoke, the more this heart of mine trembles at it. Marriage, in my opinion, is the greatest good, or the greatest evil; there is no such thing as a medium in it: where hearts are united, where harmony of sentiment, taste and humor strengthen the bonds of nature, where love forms the tie, and honor gives a sanction to it, it is surely the happiest state which mortals can enjoy. What pleasure must it be to own your passion publicly, to bear the name of the dear beloved object of your wishes! your house, your servants, your livery, everything carrying with it some pleasing remembrance of the man you love; and then to see your children, those dear pledges of mutual affection, that form, as it were, another union: O such a marriage is a heaven upon earth: but to make a vile contract, to sell our name, our fortune, and our liberty, and submit them to the will of an arbitrary tyrant, and be only his first slave, an upper servant in his family; to be eternally jarring, or running away from one another, the day without joy, and the night without love; to be always afraid of doing what we should not do; to give way to our own bad inclinations, or to be continually opposing them; to be under the necessity either of deceiving an imperious husband or dragging out life in a languid state of troublesome duty and obedience; to mutter, and fret, and pine away with grief and discontent; O such a marriage is the hell of this world. But I am resolved to shut my eyes and see nothing. I would not wish to know whether I am still weak enough to retain a passion for a wretch whom I ought to abhor, nor would I increase my disgust for one man by regretting the charms of another. No: let the false Euphemon live happy and content, if he can be so; but let him not be disinherited; never will I be so cruel and inhuman as to make myself his sister on purpose to ruin and destroy him. Now you know my heart, search into it no further, unless you mean to tear it in pieces.

168.

LISE PERSUADES THE PRODIGAL'S FATHER OF HIS SON'S REPENTANCE (YC)

(1736) VOLTAIRE, *THE PRODIGAL*,
TR. WILLIAM F. FLEMING, ACT III, SC. 4–5

[Continues No. 167, above] The plot moves to its obligatory scene, the rehabilitation of the young Euphemon before his father, which is accomplished by a sudden shift from the classical to the newer sentimental model. The familiar reversal of feeling of the irascible old father is accomplished not by the conventional devices of classical comedy, but by the conversion of the father in a scene steeped in the devices of sentimental persuasion. Its appeal becomes the standard for the eighteenth century: the heart as the primary, and only, terrain of dramatically convincing reversal. The nature and function of the heart in this process is demonstrated in Lise's appeal to the old father:

1) Her overall intent is, as she puts it, to "melt the good Euphemon [senior]'s" heart while her own "flutters and leaps" at the prospect.

2) She recapitulates the journey of the old man's "heart," *viz*, how it was initially "bound by the purest and most tender regard" for his elder son.

3) That son, as prodigals do, then fell into "unbridled licentiousness." But, she argues, if "Reason" should "light up his virtues" and "give him a new heart," how could the old father bear to deny his son, and be responsible for having

4) "shut up that [son's] heart which was once so open to receive him?" No,

5) the old man's "noble and generous heart," Lise assures him, can't possibly withstand "the repentant tears" of that prodigal, tears which wholly signify his "return to virtue." And to demonstrate the moral certainty of the old man's response to such tears, she announces:

6) "He is here," so that the old man can learn his son's truth not merely from his own lips, but closer to the genuine source of his truth, from "his own heart."

This is the classic sentimental formula: the irresistible persuasion of heart talking directly to heart.

For the fallen one, once Reason touches the Heart, the Heart instills Virtue; that Virtue is signified by Repentant Tears; Tears open and invade even the opposing Resistant Heart; and from that newly warmed Heart flow the Tears of Forgiveness.

For centuries to come, it is the reality, as well as the efficacy, of this psychology, morality, and physiology of the heart that will govern much of the drama's characterological and structural logic.

LISE

O that I may be able to melt the good Euphemon! How my heart flutters and leaps within me! my life or death depends on this important moment. He comes. Hark'ee Martha.

(Old Euphemon enters)

A chair here—pray, sir, be seated. Oh! permit me, sir. My heart esteems and reveres you. Be you my judge, sir, and look into my heart; that judge, I doubt not, will one day be my protector: but hear me, sir, I will speak my own sentiments, perhaps they may be yours also.

(She takes a chair and sits by him.)
Now, sir, tell me; if your heart had for a long time been bound by the purest and most tender regard to an object, whose early years gave the fairest promise of all that is amiable, who every day advanced in beauty, merit, and accomplishments; if, after all, his easy and deluded youth gave way to inclination, and sacrificed duty, friendship, everything, to unbridled licentiousness—If fatal experience should teach him what false happiness he had so long pursued, should teach him that the vain objects of his search sprang but from error, and were followed by remorse; if at length, ashamed of his follies, his reason, instructed by misfortune, should again light up his virtues, and give him a new heart; if, restored to his natural form, he should become faithful, just, and honest, would you, sir, could you then shut up that heart which once was open to receive him?

O sir, when I have told you all, you will be much more astonished; for heaven's sake, hear me then: I know you have a noble and a generous heart, that never was formed for cruelty; let me then ask you, was not your son Euphemon once most dear to you? He was, I own to you, he was, and therefore it is that his ingratitude called for a severer vengeance. But could you punish him forever? could you still be so unhappy, so miserable, as to hate him? could you throw from you a repenting child, an altered son, whose change would bring back to you the image of yourself? could you repulse this son were he now in tears at your feet? I should not, I know, thus open a wound that bleeds too fresh, and inflict new torments on you: but if he returned to virtue, if he came and asked forgiveness of you? Yes, and he will come to ask it; you shall hear him; and hear him with compassion, too, indeed you shall. If death has not already put an end to his shame and grief, you may perhaps see him dying at your feet with excess of sorrow and repentance.

If he yet lives, he lives to love and honor you. Can you know it? from whom can you learn it? From his own heart. It is time now, and you shall be satisfied.

*(She comes forward a little, and speaks
to young Euphemon behind the scene.)*
Euphemon! Come forth.

169.

MADAME DE CROUPILLAC, OLD AND DECAYING, IS DETERMINED TO WIN BACK HER FALSE LOVER AT ANY COST (oc)

(1736) Voltaire, *The Prodigal*, tr. William F. Fleming, Act II, Sc. 3

[Continues Nos. 167 and 168, above] Western comedies in the eighteenth century whose plots end in the bliss of marriage generally put romantic interest ahead of practical interest—love, that is, ahead of money. But lurking in the delicious satisfactions of their denouements was the certainty of a regular income, and even a stupendous one, for the newlyweds. The matter of the one was not known without the other. But rarely do the two confront one another so baldly as in Voltaire's *The Prodigal*.

Madame de Croupillac, an elderly lady "who wants vastly to be married, is apt to be a little quarrelsome, and almost in her dotage." She confirms for us the only reason Fierenfat is eager to marry Lise: the extraordinary wealth that's to be settled on her husband when she marries. It's the reason, we learn from her, that Fierenfat earlier made addresses to herself—her money—and dropped her when he learned of the larger income attached to marriage with Lise. Madame de Croupillac has arrived to stop the marriage, and drag her "villainous" Fierenfat back to her side and the promised alliance.

To Lise's astonishment, Madame de Croupillac confronts her with the news of her earlier claim, a frank confession of her loss of charms with age and consequently a loss of competitive edge, and the threat to forbid Lise's marriage with the weapon she still has: lawsuit. Her narrative lurches, but her purpose is clear: she, a formidable foe, will stop at nothing to win her "abominable" Fierenfat back. Her intended menace, of course, turns into collaboration with a more than willing Lise and Euphemon for their common advantage. (Fierenfat at the end is left with the alternatives of joining Madame de Croupillac in marriage or a life of lawsuits.)

Madame de Croupillac

Madam, I heartily wish I could steal your charms; it makes me weep to see you so handsome. You cannot comfort me; no, madam, that's impossible. I see, my dear, you may have as many husbands as you please. I had only one, at least I thought so; only one, and that's a melancholy consideration; and trouble enough I had to get him, too, and you are going to rob me of him. There is a time, madam—O dear! how soon that time comes about!—when if a lover deserts us, we lose our all, and one is quite left alone: and let me tell you, madam, it is very cruel to take away all from one, who has little or nothing left. My dear child, there are a great many wrinkled old fools, who fancy that, by the help of paint and a few false teeth, they can stop the course of time and pleasure, and fix wandering love; but, to my sorrow, I am a little wiser: I see too plainly that everything is running away, and I can't bear it.

You cannot make me young again—I know it; but I have still some hopes: perhaps to restore my false one to me, might, in some measure, give me fresh youth and beauty. My ungrateful, cruel almost-husband, whom I have run after so long; and little worthy he is of all my care. The President of this little town, madam—yes, madam: when Croupillac was in her bloom, she would not have talked to presidents; their persons, their manners, their everything was my aversion, but as we grow old, we are not quite so difficult. And so, madam, in short, you have reduced me to a state of misery and despair.

I lived, you must know, at Angouleme, and, as a widow, had the free disposal of my person: there, at that very time, was Fierenfat, a student, then a mere president's apprentice, you understand: he ogled me for a long time, and took it into his head to be most villainously in love with me. Villainously, I say, most horrid and abominable; for what did he make love to? My money. I got some people to write to the old gentleman, his father, who interested themselves too far in the affair, and talked to him in my name: he returned in answer, that he would consider it: so you see the thing was settled. For my part, I had no objection: his elder brother was at that time, so I was informed, engaged to you. But he was a foolish

felow, my dear; though he had then the honor to be in your
good graces. The silly fellow, being quite out at elbows, kicked
out of doors by his father, and wandering about the wide
world, dead, perhaps, by this time (you seem concerned), my
college hero, my President, knowing extremely well, that your
fortune was, upon the whole, much better than mine, has
thought fit to laugh at my disappointment, and go in quest of
your superior income. But do you think, madam, to run in
this manner from brother to brother, and engross a whole
family to yourself? I do here most solemnly enter my protest
against it: I forbid the banns: I'll venture my whole estate, my
dowry, and everything; in short, the cause shall be so
managed, that you, his father, my children, all of us shall be
dead, before ever it is put an end to.

170.
ERNESTINE, ABDUCTED BY COUNT OXTIERN, OVERCOMES HER DESPAIR (YT)

(1791) MARQUIS DE SADE, *OXTIERN*, TR. AUSTRYN WAINHOUSE AND
RICHARD SEAVER, ACT I, SC. 5

There's the private de Sade and the public de Sade. The public one is
exhibited in *Oxtiern*, the play he intended for public performance,
and which was done with some success in the Paris theater. The private and far more characteristic one is visible briefly in these volumes
in excerpt No. 172, below.

The portrait of the villainous Count Oxtiern in the play suggests far
more of de Sade's familiar preoccupations than it specifies. His
henchman Derbac, for example, is shocked at the fate the Count is
contemplating for the abducted Ernestine. "What you are contriving," he exclaims, "is frightful." The Count snickers: "In your eyes, it
may well be, because you are a lackey full of Gothic [i.e., supersti-
tious] prejudices upon which the light of philosophy has not yet
managed to direct its rays.... A few more years at my school, Derbac,
and you will no longer pity a woman for such a peccadillo." The "peccadillo" he means is the rape of Ernestine, already accomplished, his

current abduction of her, her imminent imprisonment in his castle, and her further debauchery and murder to come.

The model for the play is Samuel Richardson's novel, *Clarissa Harlowe*, in which the libertine Lovelace—one of the most famous of all of literature's libertines—abducts Clarissa with the promise of marriage, "ruins" her, and then abandons her. Richardson's abduction model in fiction remained intact throughout the eighteenth, nineteenth and early twentieth centuries, surviving in Lessing's *Miss Sara Sampson* [see Nos. 199 and 201, below] and even in Jane Austen, Dickens, Tolstoy, Chekhov, and many other plays and novels.

De Sade, even in this "public" work, touches on the limit to which "villainy" in the Lovelace tradition can conceivably go. Though his description of the Count's appetites is thoroughly circumspect, the sexual outrages of his *120 Days of Sodom*, or of *Justine* hover just off-stage, kept, with propriety, behind the scenes. But we can recognize even in this veiled version what was implicit in the Lovelace–eighteenth century world—not entirely unique to de Sade: that the mass debaucheries of de Sade's fictional world could be, and were to a degree, real, subject only to *pro forma* restraints for an aristocracy of money, power, and already fading privilege.

What is remarkable in *Oxtiern* is de Sade's ability to give nobility of address and posture to one of the female victims he normally despised. Unlike the Justines of his novels, or the Sara Sampsons of Lessing's tragedy, who in de Sade's terms whimper and whine their way throughout their tormented journeys, and who beg on their knees for the favor of either release or marriage from their tormentors, he gives to Ernestine in this play a voice and address and power of intent that, like the enraged, avenging Evadne in the Jacobean *Maid's Tragedy* [see Vol. 3, No. 79], moves her to plot and win revenge against her victimizer. In the first passage, she spells out her complaints to her maidservant Amelie who is with her at the hostel where Oxtiern's party has stopped on the way to his castle. "Lost, irrevocably lost," she cries, in the breast-beating tradition of the victims deprived of their virgin honor. "My only hope is in death." But she does not stay in that supine posture for long. Escape? No. She "won't lift a finger to flee." Seek protection in the "corruption-ridden Court"? Worse than futile. She opts for nothing less than personal revenge. It must be remembered that, by the 1790s, the fictional daughters of Clarissa had become so cowed by the severe proprieties of custom and so paralyzed by their abject surrender to them that an avenging gesture of their own was hardly to be imagined. De Sade's

Ernestine, like a throwback to the Vittorias and Evadnes of two centuries earlier, does what the melodrama and closet drama and novel of the approaching nineteenth century was almost to lose the memory of: She takes her fate and her vengeance into her own hands.

In the second passage below, she confronts Oxtiern openly, directs the interview on her own terms, expresses her contempt for his unlikely promises of matrimony—the standard ploy to which the abused characteristically madly cling—accuses him directly of his multiple sins against her and her lover Herman, and concludes, in the spirit of a revenging Electra, "Here I must be avenged, or here I must die." She does not die; unique among the sisterhood of victims, she avenges. De Sade obviously has no problem circumventing the pious rule for tragic dramatists that, once tampered with sexually, whether willingly or no, heroines must suffer, at the close, death.

Ernestine

Rest?... I rest? Great God, no!... Oh, no!... there can be no further rest upon this earth for poor Ernestine.

For such cruel desecrations there can never be amends, Amelie. Reflect for a moment how the man, resorting to the most arrant roguery, abducted me from my family... from my lover... from everything I hold dear in this world. And were you aware that he had this man, this worthy Herman whom I love, cast into irons? He has founded his case upon false accusations, resorted to the worst kind of calumnies, made use of informers and traitors. 'Tis they who have brought the poor man low; base gold, and Oxtiern's crimes, have led to his undoing. Herman is a prisoner... perhaps he has already been sentenced... and 'tis upon the very chains of the man I love that this cowardly Oxtiern has come to sacrifice his wretched victim.

What hope is there for me?... What have I to look forward to? Great God! What recourse is left to me?

My father had been absent from Stockholm for some time when Oxtiern, resorting to cruel deceit, invited me to his house, pretending that, were I to come, I would be helping my lover's cause and obtain not only his release but perhaps his hand as well; Oxtiern's brother, the Senator, was to be there and could use his influence to help poor Herman, or so he declared. 'Twas a venture which, for me, was as guilty as 'twas foolhardy, I realize now. How could I ever have dreamt of a betrothal without my father's consent? Heaven has punished me dearly for it... Do you know whom I discovered there, instead of the protector I was expecting? Oxtiern, ravenous Oxtiern, a dagger in his hand, offering me the choice of death or dishonor, nor did he even give me the opportunity to make a choice. Had that choice been mine, Amelie, I swear I would not have hesitated for a single moment; the most frightful torments would have been for me sweeter than the loathsome deeds that perverted man had prepared for me; frightful bonds prevented me from defending myself... The scoundrel!... and, as a crowning blow, Heaven has seen fit to let me live... the sun still casts its rays upon me, and I am lost!

And even were Oxtiern to desire the marriage bond, could I ever consent to spend my life in the arms of a man I loathe?... a man who has done me the most grievous wrong? Can you marry a man by whom you have been debased?... Can you ever learn to love what you deem to be beneath contempt? Ah, Amelie, I am lost, irrevocably lost... All that remain for me are sorrow and tears; my only hope is in death: one does not recover from the loss of one's honor. From any other hurt, but never from that!

(Glancing around her)
There is no one here; who stands in our way, or stops us from fleeing? from going to beg the Court for its protection, a protection not only merited but which it is my bounden duty to claim? But no! *(Proudly)* Were Oxtiern a thousand leagues away, I would do everything in my power to shorten the distance between us, nor would I lift a finger to flee. The traitor has dishonored me; I must avenge myself. I shall not fly to any corruption-ridden Court to ask for a protection which would be denied me; you have no inkling, Amelie, to what extent wealth and influence debase the souls of those who dwell in that house of horror! Monsters! I perhaps would be merely one further morsel for their dreadful desires!

171.

ERNESTINE CONFRONTS HER ABDUCTOR AND THREATENS REVENGE (YT)

(1791) MARQUIS DE SADE, *OXTIERN*,
TR. AUSTRYN WAINHOUSE AND RICHARD SEAVER, ACT II, SC. 5

[See No. 170, above]

ERNESTINE

However painful it is for me to appear before you, Monsieur,
whatever humiliation I may feel in your presence, it is none
the less necessary for me to ask you, following the horrible
deed you have perpetrated, what satisfaction your probity can
offer me.

I trust you do not imagine that this gift you proffer of your
heart can assure my happiness... What reason have you for
proposing it to me?... How, after the baseness wherein you
have wallowed, can you think that savage heart worthy of me?
You offer love!... You? O God! if this is what love inspires, let
my heart be forever free from any feeling so capable of defiling
man!... No, Monsieur, this is in no wise love; that is not the
comforting sentiment, the basis for all good works...; would it
counsel crimes?

"There was a rival." Yes. Indeed, there was. Monster, what have
you done to this rival? You alone stole him from me; you alone
must return him to me. My Herman has been sent to prison.
He is in chains. 'Twas you who forged them! But how can I so
deceive myself that now stoop to ask that you break them!...
Begone, I want nothing from you... I, offer you the chance to
do something generous?... the means wherewith to blot your
horrors from my mind?... You see, Oxtiern, I am losing my
mind... All right, what do you intend to do with your victim?...
Where are you taking me?

To enchain myself to my torturer?... Never, never! For me,
there is no other choice; is there? Traitor, what match can you
propose to me now that you have dishonored me? I would
remain caught forever between opprobrium and humiliation,
a constant prey to grief and tears, trying to captivate my

husband in ties he shall have formed solely out of duty. Tell me, Oxtiern, what moments of peace or contentment can I look forward to upon this earth? Hate and despair on the one hand, constraint and remorse on the other. For us, the marriage tapers would be lighted from the torches of the Furies, serpents would form the bonds between us, and death would be our only salvation.

As for your repentance, that I shall believe when you break the irons wherewith, thanks to your villainy, my lover is fettered: go and confess your plots to the judges; go and meet the death your crimes deserve; burden the earth no more with a weight which wearies it; the sun is less pure since for shedding light upon your days.

No, I am going no farther; it was in spite of myself that you decoyed me here; here I must be avenged, or here I shall die.

172.

MME. DE SAINT-ANGE INCULCATES IN HER PROTÉGÉ EUGENIE THE MORAL FREEDOMS DEMANDED BY HER NATURE (OC)

(1795) MARQUIS DE SADE, *PHILOSOPHY IN THE BEDROOM*, TR. RICHARD SEAVER AND AUSTRYN WAINHOUSE, DIALOGUE THE THIRD

"Mothers," de Sade wrote in an epigraph to his *Philosophy in the Bedroom*, "will require their daughters to read this work," but in a second edition he unaccountably changed this to read, "Mothers will forbid their daughters from reading this work." Prescribed or proscribed, it remains a work of explicit instruction in de Sade's principles of libertinism. Three practitioners gather with a neophyte, Eugenie de Mistival, a fifteen-year-old virgin, to initiate her into libertine philosophy and into the mysteries of sensual pleasure. Madame de Saint-Ange, a woman of "extreme lubricity," together with two men provide Eugenie with a remarkably well informed faculty of instruction. The treatise is written in dialogue, but like Plato's *Symposium*, it lends itself conceivably but somewhat awkwardly to actual performance.

Written just at the close of the French Revolution, the work adopts the posture of the Revolution's cry for liberty, and adapts it without qualification to the provinces of moral conduct, philosophic speculation, and sexual practice. De Sade abrogates every constraint, without exception, to any vestigial proprieties lingering in either moral speculation or behavior, and argues against the smallest compromise with their total repudiation.

The passage below is de Sade's characteristic flaying of the conventional assumptions of the general (for our purposes most particularly the dramatic) public literature of the eighteenth century—and had de Sade but known, it was even more grimly applicable to the approaching nineteenth. One of the distinctly more moderate flayings is Madame Saint-Ange's lesson below—an early one—to Eugenie. Her argument, first, is that none of the shibboleths and taboos ever taught her are in fact the objects of universal horror; all moral horror is invented by the prejudices of particular times and places. Sexual license, for example, for virgins and for married women alike, is forbidden only because of parental proscriptions which entrap the young in their early education, and are later used to force women into marital entrapment. None of these bonds of obedience is fixed; they're illusory, and are enforced only by the greed, the cupidity, the pride in power, of moral despots, and so their dissolution is imperative: breaking the shackles of "an imbecile mother," an enslaving father, the strictures of continence, of chastity, is imperative.

The overriding principle of her argument is clear, and amounts to a moral discipline in itself. It's manifested most dramatically but also most assertively in sexual practice: the absolute of personal freedom. And the logical appeal, long familiar in philosophic tradition, is to Nature and the presumption of its abhorrence of humanity's manufactured and overlaying constraints. One limit and only one is countenanced by Madame in the exercise of radical liberty: "So long as laws remain such as they are today," the libertine is wise to be discreet in public, but must compensate fully for her discretion by her practices in private.

In the pursuit of Eugenie's education, the instruction of the philosophers in the bedroom goes far beyond the modest goals set by Madame Saint-Ange in this excerpt; it moves to the farther side of de Sade's libertine's recipe to encompass degrees of cruelty that, in strictest logic, remain justified according to his fundamental principles, but they're possibly refutable on other grounds.

Mme. de Saint-Ange

You ask, Eugenie: are there actions in themselves so dangerous and so evil that they have come to be considered from one end of the earth to the other as generally criminal? Are there such? There are none, my love, none, not even theft, nor incest, neither murder nor parricide itself. There are places where they have been honored, crowned, beheld as exemplary deeds, whereas in other places, humaneness, candor, benevolence, chastity, in brief, all our virtues have been regarded as monstrosities.

Let us begin by exposing my opinion upon libertinage in young girls, then upon the adultery of married women. You will listen to me, Eugenie, and you will see how absurd it is to say that immediately a girl is weaned she must continue the victim of her parents' will in order to remain thus to her dying day. It is not in this age of preoccupation with the rights of man and general concern for liberties that girls ought to continue to believe themselves their families' slaves, when it is clearly established that these families' power over them is totally illusory. What is the basis of these young maiden's duties if not the father's greed or ambition? Well, I ask if it is just that a young girl who is beginning to feel and reason be submitted to such constraints. Is it not prejudice which all unaided forges those chains?

And is there anything more ridiculous than to see a maiden of fifteen or sixteen, consumed by desires she is compelled to suppress, wait, and while waiting, endure worse than hell's torments until it pleases her parents having first rendered her youth miserable, further to sacrifice her riper years by immolating them to their perfidious cupidity when they associate her, despite her wishes, with a husband who either has nothing wherewith to make himself loved, or who possesses everything to make himself hated?

Oh, no. No, Eugenie, such bonds are quickly dissolved; it is necessary that once she reaches the age of reason the girl be detached from her paternal household, and after having received a public education it is necessary that at the age of fifteen she be left her own mistress, to become what she wishes. Begin therefore, with the legitimacy of these principles, Eugenie, and break your shackles at no matter what the cost; be contemptuous of the futile remonstrances of an imbecile mother to whom you legitimately owe only hatred and a curse. If your father, who is a libertine, desires you, why then go merrily to him; let him enjoy you, but enjoy without enchaining you; cast off the yolk if he wishes to enslave you; more than one daughter has treated thus with her father. Fuck, in one word, fuck: 'twas for that you were brought into the world; no limits to your pleasure save those of your strength and will; no exceptions as to place, to time, to partner; all the time, everywhere, every man has got to serve your pleasures; continence is an impossible virtue for which Nature, her rights violated, instantly punishes us with a thousand miseries. So long as the laws remain such as they are today, employ some discretion: loud opinion forces us to do so; but in privacy and silence let us compensate ourselves for that cruel chastity we are obliged to obey in public.

EIGHTEENTH-CENTURY ENGLISH

173.

THE YOUNG WIDOW SHARES HER JOY WITH HER MAID AT HER NEW WIDOWHOOD, AND ANTICIPATES NEW JOYS FOR THE FUTURE (YC)

(1701) RICHARD STEELE, *THE FUNERAL*, ACT I, SC. 2

"Lord Brumpton" [quoting from Men's vols. entry: "Sable the Undertaker Rehearses His Regular Mourners for the Coming Funeral"] "is not dead at all, but recovered from his faint, alive, and set to spend the rest of the play discovering who were the hypocrites and who the honest folk grieving over his loss." Among the truly grieving will not be his young widow, whose delight in her new freedom is bubbling over when she meets her faithful Tattleaid to plan strategy for the coming months and years, for a life of unobstructed wealth and independence. And of abandoned pretense: that men are "the rulers! the governors!... [T]hey imagine themselves mighty things, but... we rule them.... In this nation our power is absolute."

For the widow Brumpton, this is no mere giddy assertion. She's prepared for her reign carefully, over time, soliciting her husband to disinherit his son entirely in her favor, and with that substance, she envisions the untrammeled joys to come. These are the joys:

First, her discreet flirtations will bring gold to her as well as to her cooperating Tattleaid; then, in the theater, looking fetching in widow's weeds, she'll turn heads (the "wigs in the pit") in homage and admiration, and command attention for her studied performance of greeting and acknowledgment before the actors begin theirs. And then the game of governing lovers, as she did her husband, they believing the government was theirs. And fnally the particular pleasure of "keeping an obstinate shyness to all our old acquaintants," granting, in other words, nothing to any, and so losing neither authority nor reputation.

But as a character, the widow is not merely pretension and duplicity; she's more the glee underlying the performance of pretension and duplicity, the sheer verve of throwing off the last vestige of constraint to revel in all the vanities of human wishes her imagination can call up. She's clearly limited in the vanities her imagination is capable of calling up, but whatever they are, for her they mean repletion.

*(Enter Widow and Tattleaid, meeting
and running to each other)*

WIDOW

Oh Tattleaid! His and our hour is come! Nay, thou hast ever
been my comfort, my confident, my friend, and my servant;
and now I'll reward thy pains; for tho' I scorn the whole sex of
fellows, I'll give 'em hopes for thy sake; every smile, every
frown, every gesture, humor, caprice and whimsy of mine,
shall be gold to thee girl; thou shalt feel all the sweet and
wealth of being a fine rich widow's woman: Oh! how my head
runs my first year out, and jumps to all the joys of

widowhood! If thirteen months hence a friend should haul one to a play one has a mind to see: what pleasure 'twill be when my Lady Brumpton's footman's call'd (who kept a place for that very purpose) to make a sudden insurrection of fine wigs in the pit, and side-boxes. Then with a pretty sorrow in one's face, and a willing blush for being star'd at, one ventures to look round and bow, to one of one's own quality, thus: *(Very directly)* To a smug pretending fellow of no fortune, thus: *(As scarce seeing him)* To one that writes lampoons, thus: *(Fearfully)* To one one really loves, thus: *(Looking down)* To one's woman acquaintance, from box to box, thus: *(With looks differently familiar)* And when one has done one's part, observe the actors do theirs, but with my mind fixt not on those I look at, but those that look at me—Then the serenades! The lovers! Oh, it makes my heart bound within me; I'll warrant you, I'll manage 'em all, and indeed the men are very silly creatures, 'tis no such hard matter—They rulers! They governors! Ay Tattleaid, they imagine themselves mighty things, but government founded on force only, is a brutal power—We rule them by their affections, which blinds them into a belief that they rule us, or at least are in the government with us—But in this nation our power is absolute; Thus, thus, we sway—*(Playing her fan)* A fan is both the standard, and the flag of England: I laugh to see the men go our errands, strut in great offices, live in cares, hazards and scandals, to come home and be fools to us in brags of their dispatches, negotiations, and their wisdoms—as my good dear deceas'd us'd to entertain me; which I to relieve myself from—would lisp some silly request, pat him on the face—He shakes his head at my pretty folly, calls me simpleton; gives me a jewel, then goes to bed so wise, so satisfyed and so deceiv'd!

I'm sure I was ty'd to a dead man many a long day before I durst bury him—But the day is now my own—Yet now I think on't Tattleaid, be sure to keep an obstinate shyness to all our old acquaintance: Let 'em talk of favours if they please, if we grant 'em still they'll grow tyrants to us, if we discard 'em the chaste and innocent will not believe we could have confidence to do it, were it so, and the wise if they believe it, will applaud our prudence.

INSURRECTION: here, a flurry of excited activity.

174.

LEODICE, SEDUCED AND ABANDONED BY KING ANTIOCHUS, OBSERVES WITH RAGE THE PROCESSION OF THE KING AND HIS NEW BRIDE (YT)

(1701) JANE WISEMAN, *ANTIOCHUS THE KING*, ACT II

In one long wail of pain and rage, Leodice expresses the "confusion" over her loss of the King's love and her place beside him, now stolen by a "usurping" Queen. Leodice is the quintessential tragic Restoration figure suffering a sudden "fall," the fall attended by her sudden recognition of the very quicksand on which her power, her prestige, her dignity, her command of worshippers, actually rests—the recognition that that place of merit is not only lost, but that it was a chimera, that it was never in fact hers but only existed at the whim of her powerful lover. That a moment's about-face, a day's turn of events, could destroy her value, even her meaning as a woman, causes her wail of rage and disappointment. She shares with Statira [No. 139, above] the signature of the Restoration's "debased" heroine.

> *(Shouts at a distance, "Long live
> Antiochus and Berenice." Enter Leodice,
> followed by Artenor and Cypre)*

LEODICE

Oh! Whither shall I flie,
To 'scape the noise of these accursed clamours?
Now I cou'd stoop to banishment, or death,
And give up all my title to revenge;
Oblige the ungenerous, faithless, cruel king,
And free my rival from her evil genius. *(Shouts again.)*
Hark! they shout again! Now plagues and tortures,
Great as those I feel, seize on them all,
And teach their bellowing, hoarse plebeian tongues
To rave and curse as I do.

Ungrateful perjur'd tyrant!
Thus to reward my everlasting love.

How often have I sat in awful state,
And view'd with scorn the trembling wishing crowd,
Where all that lifted their presumptious eyes,
Bow'd to my charms, and offered up their hearts;
Where sighing princes have confess'd my power,
And gaz'd to adoration!
These, these will point at my prodigious fall;
Laugh at my wrongs, and glory in my fate.
Oh that distraction wou'd relieve my brain,
And free me from the sense of what I am!
Disgrac'd and banish'd! Oh, my swelling heart!
Give me revenge, ye Gods, or I shall burst.
Tell me of poison, daggers, death, confusion,
These be the subjects I wou'd treat on now;
These be our theme, but mention hope no more.

He's marry'd!
And Berenice must live and die a queen.
Had his bewitching charms betray'd her vertue,
His soft, resistless, dear, deluding arts
Deceiv'd her to his arms, as they did me,
I then might hope.
I know my youth and beauty great as hers,
And cou'd not fear, upon the square of fate;
But she, with curst Egyptian subtlety
Has wrought my ruin, sure, and bound him fast.
Gods! Must I see this env'd, hated rival
Shine on a throne which I shou'd have adorn'd?
Must her curst race possess the daz'ling crown?
And will no power prevent her lavish fortune?
Was every blessing cast and stampt for her?
That thus he doats upon the worthless Bauble,
Crowning her pleasures with excessive love.
Confusion, that he basely robs me of:
From me he catch'd the first uniting sparks;
I kindled in his breast the generous flame;
And from my store he has inrich'd the queen.
Oh! Torture, treachery, and wrongs unparallel'd!

I will be calm; but yet 'tis very hard
To enjoy the chiefest blessings Heaven cou'd give,
And lose them all on one unlucky hour!
To fall from love and empire in one day!
Who but my self wou'd have out-liv'd the loss?

175.

LEODICE, KNEELING BEFORE HER BETRAYER ANTIOCHUS, THREATENS SUICIDE (YT)

(1701) JANE WISEMAN, *ANTIOCHUS THE KING*, ACT III

[See No. 174, above]

(Leodice kneels and holds the King's robe.)

LEODICE

Turn your all gracious eyes, most mighty sovereign;
And for one moment listen to my prayers:
Not as partaker of these high diversions
Came I here, but to intreat your mercy.

I am descended from a noble family,
Whose bright prosperity and rigid vertue
Were of equal wonder. Impartial death
Snatch'd my dear parents from my heedless youth.
'Ere half their race was finish'd;
Who dying, left me for a lasting pledge,
A jewel of inestimable value,
And charg'd me to esteem it as my life;
Then told me it included secret power
To make me bless'd, belov'd, admir'd and happy;
That when I lost it, misery wou'd ensue:
My fame be blasted, and my peace destroy'd.
I heard with due regard, and promis'd fair;
Swore to preserve it to my latest hour:
And visiting the silent, sacred urn,
Where afterwards their pious dust was laid,
Again I often did renew my vow.

Yet see
How fruitless my resolves! how vain my care!
In one unguarded hour came a robber,
Who bore the prize triumphantly away.
I wou'd have rais'd my voice to loud complaint,

But long he sooth'd my rage, and flatter'd me to peace,
'Till I believ'd the sad predictions false.
But Oh, too lately I am undeceiv'd:
The victor grown unmindful of my wrongs,
Now treats me with ungenerous disdain,
And drives me like a vagabond away;
The only shame of all my spotless race,
Who from their happy seats above look down,
And own my sufferings greater than my crime.
To you, great monarch, I appeal for justice:
Oh save me, save me from approaching ruin.
I love the foe that has procur'd my fall.
Let him restore me to his dear embrace,
Return my passion, and forget his hate;
What have I done that you shou'd hate me thus?
Besides my guilty love of false Antiochus,
Stay, I conjure you; if you go, I die.

    (Draws a dagger)
See, I'm prepar'd; and well you know, I dare.
Oh, that I cou'd return thy barbarous hate!
But 'tis in vain I wish, in vain I strive.
My rage is feign'd, and I am still Leodice;
That foolish, doating, lost, abandon'd wretch!
Still you are dearer to my soul than peace;
Than life; or pleasing dreams of what I was.
Oh! look upon me, kneeling at your feet:
Think in this posture what I might have gain'd
Once, all that you cou'd grant; then hear me now,
Thus when malicious devils have seduc'd
And plung'd our poor unwary souls in sin,
Themselves with black infernal cruelty
Stand first accusers of those crimes they've urg'd.
If vertue be the only thing you love,
And has alone the power to keep you true,
Why does your treacherous sex take so much pains
To undermine the beautiful foundation?
Oh! Let all fond believing maids by me be warn'd,
And hate as I do, base ungenerous man;
Whom if you trust, you're sure to be betray'd.
Fly from their power, laugh at their complaint;
Disdain their love, and baffle their designs;
So you may scape my sufferings, and my faults.
Fallen to mean desires: I'll ask like what I am.
Revoke my banishment, and let me stay

In some unminded corner of the court;
Confine me if you please, with iron bars,
To see you through the melancholy grates,
At distance as you pass, is all I ask.

176.

CALISTA, SCORNING HER HUSBAND, YEARNS FOR THE FAITHLESS LOTHARIO (YT)

(1703) NICHOLAS ROWE, *THE FAIR PENITENT*, ACT II, SC. 1

"Hide me from the base world, from malice and from shame," Calista pleads. She is addressing her confidante Lucilla, but mercilessly condemning herself. *The Fair Penitent* is not unusual in using the hard and fast rules of sexual conduct in their most uncompromising form, but in the vein of "she-tragedy" [see Men's vols. entry: "Essex, Abject, Begs the Queen for Return to Favor..."], manages at the same time to weep for the woman in default. In this instance, the victim, by standing proudly above the consolation of the tears that readily flow for she-tragedy heroines, becomes genuinely worthy of them.

Calista is the victim of a single "misstep," but it's fatal. Seduced by the indifferent libertine Lothario, she not only assented, but welcomed the act, and ever since becomes obsessed by her longing for her seducer. In her own judgment, her seduction and subsequent obsession leave her beyond the pale of forgiveness or redemption. What is remarkable about this particular victim, though, is that for all her self-condemnation and despair, she refuses to live with either, most particularly with the condemnation of others. She refuses shame. Why?

Calista has the strength of enormous self-regard. Misstep or no, she knows herself as great, as noble, as greatly worthy. For that worth to be subject to the judgment and "malice" of others is for her insupportable; she prefers death. Later, she will bear actively the role of self-executioner, she will demand that privilege. But at first—the equivalent of death—a mournful solitude, out of the reach of "malice," somewhere in a dark wood inhabited if at all only by skeletal remains. "For 'tis the solemn counsel of my soul/ Never to live with public loss of honor." And then, almost in the same breath, she contradicts herself: She must meet one more time with her seducer, to vent her indignation and be done with it—and then be done with life itself. And then she contradicts *that* intent: for all her loathing of his falseness, if he were to beg forgiveness, even falsely, she would at once pardon him.

The bridegroom—Altamont—approaches (it's their wedding day), and Calista at once takes umbrage from his loving good cheer: with respect to her suffering, he's irrelevant and has no place in her confidence. She dissembles and does not dissemble: she will lie about her "warring passions," of course, but not for an instant will she pretend love or regard for him. Lying and not lying, until her "sin" is later discovered, her integrity remains at war with her lack of it.

(Enter Calista and Lucilla)

CALISTA

Be dumb forever, silent as the grave,
Nor let thy fond officious love disturb
My solemn sadness with the sound of joy.
If thou wilt soothe me, tell some dismal tale
Of pining discontent and black despair;
For oh! I've gone around through all my thoughts,
But all are indignation, love, or shame,
And my dear peace of mind is lost forever.
My sad soul
Has formed a dismal, melancholy scene,
Such a retreat as I would wish to find;
An unfrequented vale, o'ergrown with trees
Mossy and old, within whose lonesome shade
Ravens and birds ill-omened, only dwell;
No sound to break the silence but a brook
That, bubbling, winds among the weeds; no mark
Of any human shape that had been there,
Unless the skeleton of some poor wretch
Who had long since, like me by love undone,
Sought that sad place out to despair and die in.
There I fain would hide me
From the base world, from malice, and from shame;
For 'tis the solemn counsel of my soul
Never to live with public loss of honor;
'Tis fixed to die rather than bear the insolence

Of each affected she that tells my story,
And blesses her good stars that she is virtuous.
To be a tale for fools! Scorned by the women,
And pitied by the men! Oh, insupportable!
My genius drives me on;
I must, I will behold him once again:
Perhaps it is the crisis of my fate,
And this one interview shall end my cares.
My lab'ring heart, that swells with indignation,
Heaves to discharge the burden; that once done,
The busy thing shall rest within its cell,
And never beat again.
I have been wronged enough to arm my temper
Against the smooth delusion, but alas!
(Chide not my weakness, gentle maid, but pity me)
A woman's softness hangs about me still.
Then let me blush, and tell thee all my folly.
I swear I could not see the dear betrayer
Kneel at my feet and sigh to be forgiven,
But my relenting heart would pardon all,
And quite forget 'twas him that had undone me.
Ha! Altamont? Calista, now be wary,
And guard thy soul's accesses with dissembling,
Nor let this hostile husband's eyes explore
The warring passions and tumultuous thoughts
That rage within thee and deform thy reason.

177.

CALISTA, FORCED INTO A MARRIAGE SHE ABHORS, DECRIES WOMAN'S BONDAGE (YT)

(1703) NICHOLAS ROWE, THE FAIR PENITENT, ACT III, SC. 1

[See No. 176, above] Sciolto, Calista's father, at first bewildered, then angered at her refusal to smile kindly on and love her future husband, approaches her tentatively: his own love for her and joy in her forthcoming marriage forbids him from putting evil designs on her conduct. But Calista refuses to reassure him. She will grant only that she's obeyed his commands, not that she likes them. In fact, she hates the very code that assumes willing filial obedience not only for one's acts, but for one's emotions. The "sorrow," she assures him, that he's recognized and deplored is, she explains, now "native" to her, and will dissolve only with her death.

Her father gone, Calista unburdens herself of the problem that lies behind her problem: the code of womanly obedience itself. First fathers, then husbands—and rather remarkably, the complaint of Lysistrata against Athenian husbands [see Vol. 3, No. 33], that they imprison wives within the boundaries of domestic idiocy, is, so many centuries later, intact. Why not, demands Calista, speaking for "high-souled" women like herself, shake off "vile obedience... and claim an equal empire o'er the world?" Why not?

Because the new focus in "she-tragedy," understood to be newly compassionate toward women, was in fact anything but compassionate. The burden of honor, the fundamental subject of tragic cogitation, was largely removed from the shoulders of men and laid squarely on the shoulders of women. It is they, center stage, who now wrestle with the terms of the code, and it is their actions that are weighed endlessly for proof of honorable subscription to honor. Was it so before? Yes, but never with such compassionate venom. So that what was remarkable in the Princesse de Cleves [see No. 145, above] is expected to be commonplace in these heroines: the investiture of the terms of the code of filial and marital obedience, sexual purity, and unending self-punishment for transgression. The code must reside so deeply within the soul that there is nothing left of the character of a woman but the unabating expression, in action and word, of those principles. These female soldiers in the war of honor are, and can do, nothing they do not register any single level of interest other than their obedience to whosoever's male property they are, and to the safe-keeping of those men's honors by their woman-soldier's single task of shielding their own virginity. Sexual betrayal is their single mode of treachery, and that treachery is death.

The portrait of Calista is of a woman refusing to be caught in these toils, refusing to succumb to the postures of obedience and self-flagellation except on her own terms: in private, away from the sight of "the world" and its judgment, independent of any judgment but her own—damaging enough, but her own. Until the accusation that she has "sinned" is publicly proven and no longer avoidable, she lies, she averts it, she accuses the bearer of calumny, of himself lying. But with that discovery, and her "sin" out in the open, the Calista who held herself beyond the judgment of others, corrodes; her judgment is instantly at one with theirs. She-tragedy inflicts pious retribution, as did tragedy before it, but it does so with an excruciating, punishing elongation of pain.

Calista is on the rack for the two final acts, but that is hardly a record in she-tragedies—heroines can weep and smite their consciences for as long as five acts, the tragedy beginning with sin behind them, and with nothing left for them to do but expiate it.

But given the "high-souled" Calista, even when she is wallowing in guilt and moral pain in the style of other she-tragedy sinners, her style exceeds theirs. Her self-laceration goes so far beyond the bounds of the expiations of "softer" heroines ("I am all contagion, death, and ruin, And Nature sickens at me") that at the final moment, when she is on the verge of killing herself, she expresses contempt for the too-tender ways of Heaven, offering as it does too easy terms. "[H]eaven... is atoned by penitence and prayer. Cheap recompense! Here [on earth] 'twould not be received: Nothing but blood can make the expiation And cleanse the soul from inbred, deep pollution." She takes the dagger willingly offered from her father's hands, and conforming to both their verdicts, "Thus," she says to the world, as she offers to remove from it this "plague," herself, "thus I set you free."

CALISTA

Is then the task of duty half performed?
Has not your daughter giv'n herself to Altamont,
Yielded the native freedom of her will
To an imperious husband's lordly rule
To gratify a father's stern command?
For pity, do not frown then,
If in despite of all my vowed obedience,
A sigh breaks out, or a tear falls by chance;
For oh! that sorrow which has drawn your anger
Is a sad native to Calista's breast,
And, once possessed, will never quit its dwelling
Till life, the prop [of] all, shall leave the building
To tumble down and molder into ruin.

(Sciolto exits)
How hard is the condition of our sex,
Through ev'ry state of life the slaves of man!
In all the dear, delightful days of youth
A rigid father dictates to our wills,
And deals out pleasure with a scanty hand;

To his, the tyrant husband's reign succeeds;
Proud with opinion of superior reason,
He holds domestic bus'ness and devotion
All we are capable to know, and shuts us
Like cloistered idiots from the world's acquaintance,
And all the joys of freedom; wherefore we are
Born with high souls but to assert ourselves,
Shake off this vile obedience they exact,
And claim an equal empire o'er the world?

178.

CALISTA, WALLOWING IN GUILT, JUSTIFIES VENGEANCE AGAINST HERSELF (YT)

(1703) Nicholas Rowe, *The Fair Penitent*, Act V, Sc. 1

[See No. 177, above]

Calista

Oh! 'tis too much for this offending wretch,
This parricide, that murders with her crimes,
Shortens her father's age and cuts him off
E'er little more than half his years be numbered.
That I must die—it is my only comfort;
Death is the privilege of human nature,
And life without it were not worth our taking;
Thither the poor, the prisoner, and the mourner
Fly for relief and lay their burdens down.
Come then, and take me now to thy cold arms,
Thou meagre shade; here let me breathe my last,
Charmed with my father's pity and forgiveness
More than if angels tuned their golden viols
And sung a requiem to my parting soul.
Now think thou, cursed Calista, now behold
The desolation, horror, blood, and ruin
Thy crimes and fatal folly spread around
That loudly cry for vengeance on thy head;
Yet heaven, who knows our weak, imperfect natures,

How blind with passions and how prone to evil,
Makes not too strict enquiry for offences,
But is atoned by penitence and prayer.
Cheap recompense! here 'twould not be received:
Nothing but blood can make the expiation
And cleanse the soul from inbred, deep pollution.

And dost thou bear me yet, thou patient earth?
Dost thou not labor with my murd'rous weight?
And you, ye glittering, heavenly host of stars,
Hide your fair heads in clouds, or I shall blast you,
For I am all contagion, death, and ruin,
And nature sickens at me; rest, thou world,
This parricide shall be thy plague no more;
Thus, thus, I set thee free.

(Stabs herself)

179.

MRS. CLERIMONT, WHILE STUDYING HER MIRROR, DEPLORES THE ENGLISH FOR NOT BEING DECENTLY FRENCH (oc)

(1705) RICHARD STEELE, *THE TENDER HUSBAND*, ACT III, SC. 1

From the pages of Moliere's *Les Precieuses Ridicules*, Steele borrows the portrait of inept silliness imitating a manner for which it has no fitness. Only for staunchly British Steele, it is the British affection of French manners that he parodies in those weak vessels who are not sharing in the growing parochialsim of the English toward the French, the Italian—in word, toward the continental, which in the face of the continuing popularity of Italian music and French anything, is flying in the face of English fashion for warlike zealous posturing and proud insularity.

Mrs. Clerimont is a female francophile of a tender English husband for whom she has infinite respect, even love. But respect, she's concluded, "has something too solemn for soft moments." And so she turns to "pretty Beau Titmice" and "pert Billy Butterflies" to play with her in her hours of continental dalliance. Her husband, who has concluded, "I find I am to be a cuckold out of her pure esteem of me," eventually wins her back to bully-beef English, and she, penitent, abandons her French dalliance, and swears, "I must correct every idea that rises in my mind, and learn every gesture of my body anew. I detest the thing I was."

But before her thorough transformation, Mrs. Clerimont dallies not only with Frenchified Butterflies, but with her mirror as well. And in a scene reminiscent of Lady Wishfort's in *The Way of the World* [see No. 159, above], she happily studies her mirror, puts corrective touches to her face, enjoys the temporary freedom of being out of her corset stays, instructs her maid Jenny on the significant differences between the English and French underservant, frowns at her too great success in the marks of her beauty being aped by her acquaintance, and holds up the French, and her own, capacity for flowing volubility to the dullness and dumbness of English conversation.

Mrs. Clerimont

The English are so saucy with their liberty—I'll have all my lower servants French—there cannot be a good footman born out of an absolute monarchy—

Indeed, Jenny, I could wish thou wer't really French; for thou art plain English in spite of example—your arms do but hang on, and you move perfectly upon joints. Not with a swim of the whole person—But I am talking to you, and have not adjusted my self to day: what pretty company a glass is, to have another self! To converse in soliloquy! To have company that never contradicts or displeases us! The pretty visible echo of our actions. How easy too it is to be disencumber'd with stays, where a woman has any thing like shape, if no shape, a good air—But I look best when I'm talking.

I'm always talking—that disquiets thy sullen English temper, but I don't really look so well when I am silent—If I do but offer to speak—then I may say that—Oh, bless me, Jenny, I am so pale, I am afraid of my self—I have not laid on half red enough—What a dough-bak'd thing was I before I improv'd my self, and travell'd for beauty—However, my face is very prettily design'd to day. The ladies abroad us'd to call me Mademoiselle Titian, I was so famous for my colouring; but prethee, wench, bring me my black eye-brows out of the next room.

No, hang it, I'll wear these I have on, this mode of visage takes
mightily, I had three ladies last week came over to my
complexion—I think to be a fair woman this fortnight, till I
find I'm ap'd too much—I believe there are an hundred copies
of me already. It is a very pretty piece of ill-nature, for a
woman that has any genius for beauty, to observe the servile
imitation of her manner, her motion, her glances, and her
smiles.

Indeed, the French mien is no more to be learn'd, than the
language without going thither—Then again to see some poor
ladies who have clownish, penurious, English husbands, turn
and torture their old cloaths into so many forms, and dye 'em
into so many colours, to follow me—

What say'st, Jenny? What say'st? not a word? Nay, I believe,
Jenny, thou hast nothing to say any more than the rest of thy
country-women—The splenaticks speak just as the weather
lets 'em—They are mere talking barometers—abroad the
people of quality go on so eternally, and still go on, and are
gay and entertain—In England discourse is made up of
nothing but question and answer—I was t'other day at a visit,
where there was a profound silence, for, I believe, the third
part of a minute. They infected me with their dullness, who
can keep up their good humour at an English visit—They sit
as at a funeral, silent in the midst of many candles—one,
perhaps, alarms the room—'tis very cold weather—then all
the mute play their fans—till some other question happens,
and then the fans go off again—Speak, simpleton!

TITIAN (1477–1576): Italian Renaissance painter. MIEN: bearing, air, aspect. SPLENAT-
ICK: ill humored, bad tempered, spiteful.

180.

LADY EASY DOWNS HER OUTRAGE AT HER HUSBAND'S INFIDELITY, AND DUTIFULLY BLAMES HERSELF (YC)

(1705) COLLEY CIBBER, *THE CARELESS HUSBAND*, ACT V, SC. 5

Lady Easy discovers her husband and her maid "asleep in two easy chairs"—damning evidence of what they'd been up to—and has three violent reactions one after the other. Her first response to the "killing sight" is the urge to "throw this vizor of my patience off"—patience was heretofore her only stratagem for dealing with her husband's infidelities—and confroting him with his shame "until he blushes." But she bethinks herself: she'll be bereft, at once, of everything she's held dear; she will, by accusing him at all, be guilty of violating her marital vow of obedience and worst, his fault may in fact be her fault for being insufficiently appealing to him to "warm the heart of love."

Having taken the fault on herself, she notices that the poor man is sleeping with his wig off, and "who knows?" she frets, heaven, offended by his crime, might be readying to punish him with a cold. To forestall it, Lady Easy drapes her neck kerchief over her husband's head, still speculating that when he wakes, her "too busy" gesture may offend rather than please him.

But her gesture, on the contrary, produces one of the seminal moments in the annals of English drama—the moment when Lord Easy, recognizing his wife's gesture for the kindness and implicit forgiveness it signified, undergoes so radical a change of heart that his sentiments and language at once leap to a level of moral propriety that accords perfectly with his wife's. It is indeed the quintessential moment of moral conversion in the development of Sentimental or, as it was called, "Tearful" comedy. And Lady Easy herself serves permanently as one of the models for the essential characteristic of women of virtue in sentimental drama—fretful, anxious self-negation.

LADY EASY

Ha!
Protect me virtue, patience, reason!
Teach me to bear this killing sight, or let
Me think my dreaming senses are deceived!

For sure a sight like this might raise the arm
Of duty, even to the breast of love. At least
I'll throw this vizor of my patience off,
Now wake him in his guilt,
And barefaced front him with my wrongs.
I'll talk to him till he blushes, nay till he
Frowns on me, perhaps—and then
I'm lost again. The ease of a few tears
Is all that's left to me—
And duty, too, forbids me to insult
Where I have vowed obedience. Perhaps
The fault's in me, and nature has not formed
Me with the thousand little requisites
That warm the heart to love.
Somewhere there is a fault,
But heaven best knows what both of us deserve.
Ha! Bareheaded and in so sound a sleep!
Who knows, while thus exposed to the unwholesome air,
But heaven, offended, may o'ertake his crime,
And, in some languishing distemper, leave him
A severe example of its violated laws.
Forbid it mercy, and forbid it love!
This may prevent it.

(Takes a steinkirk from her neck and
lays it gently over his head)
And if he should wake offended at my too-busy care, let my
heartbreaking patience, duty, and my fond affection plead my
pardon.

STEINKIRK: neckcloth, scarf.

106

181.

MISTRESS SULLEN BEMOANS HER MARRIAGE TO A COUNTRY BLOCKHEAD (YC)

(1707) George Farquhar, *The Beaux' Stratagem*, Act II, Sc. 1

Dorinda, hearing Mrs. Sullen's perpetual complaints against her husband, who is Dorinda's own brother, wonders: "What can you urge against your husband?" He's constant, she argues, "never sleeps from you," allows you a maintenance "suitable to your quality," and most attractive (presumably) of all, "you share in all the pleasures that the country affords." Mrs. Sullen, however, having been nurtured in London, having previously spied out "the country" from the distance of published pastoral poetry, with its nymphs and swains and their amatory pleasures in copses and groves; having tangled with nature only in the drives and walks of London's parks, having been married to this unconscionable boor to whom she has brought a dowry of ten thousand pounds, having been dragged by him to rustic Lichfield, where he is fortified by his sister Dorinda and his mother Lady Bountiful, who concocts and furnishes herbs and simples and restorative liquids for the cure of her neighbors, having been suffering not only boorish taste and temper and behavior by that blockhead husband but physical abuse from his as well, has a case:

Mrs. Sullen

Country pleasures! Racks and torments! Dost think, child, that my limbs were made for leaping of ditches, and clambering over stiles? or that my parents, wisely foreseeing my future happiness in country pleasures, had early instructed me in the rural accomplishments of drinking fat ale, playing at whisk, and smoking tobacco with my husband? or of spreading of plasters, brewing of diet-drinks, and stilling rosemary water, with the good old gentlewoman my mother-in-law?

Not that I disapprove rural pleasures, as the poets have painted them; in their landscape, every Phillis has her Corydon, every murmuring stream, and every flowery mead, gives fresh alarms to love. Besides, you'll find that their couples were never married.

But yonder I see my Corydon, and a sweet swain it is, Heaven knows! Come, Dorinda, don't be angry; he's my husband, and your brother; and between both, is he not a sad brute? O sister, sister! I shall never ha' good of the beast till I get him to town; London, dear London, is the place for managing and breaking a husband.

'Tis a standing maxim in conjugal discipline, that when a man would enslave his wife, he hurries her into the country; and when a lady would be arbitrary with her husband, she wheedles her booby up to town.—A man dare not play the tyrant in London, because there are so many examples to encourage the subject to rebel.

Sister! if ever you marry, beware of a sullen, silent sot, one that's always musing, but never thinks. There's some diversion in a talking block-head; and since a woman must wear chains, I would have the pleasure of hearing 'em rattle a little. Now you shall see—but take this by the way: he came home this morning at his usual hour of four, wakened me out of a sweet dream of something else, by tumbling over the tea-table, which he broke all to pieces; after his man and he had rolled about the room, like sick passengers in a storm, he comes flounce into bed, dead as a salmon into a fishmonger's basket; his feet cold as ice, his breath hot as a furnace, and his hands and his face as greasy as his flannel nightcap. O matrimony! He tosses up the clothes with a barbarous swing over his shoulders, disorders the whole economy of my bed, leaves me half naked, and my whole night's comfort is the tuneable serenade of that wakeful nightingale, his nose! Oh, the pleasure of counting the melancholy clock by a snoring husband!

STILES: a series of steps for climbing over a fence or wall. FAT ALE: ale brewed in a vat (barrel). WHISK: an early name of the card game now known as whist. PLASTERS: bandages spread with a healing preparation. DIET-DRINKS: medicinal drinks, or daily drinks, or both. STILLING ROSEMARY WATER: distilling water with the fragrant evergreen rosemary shrub. PHILLIS... CORYDON: names conventionally used in pastoral poetry.

182.

MISTRESS SULLEN RAILS AGAINST THE LAWS OF DIVORCE (YC)

(1707) GEORGE FARQUHAR, *THE BEAUX' STRATAGEM*, ACT III, SC. 2 AND ACT IV, SC. 1

[Continues No. 181, above] "I dare not keep the thought about me," frets Mrs. Sullen, as she contemplates the marriage which has "cheated [her] into slavery" and imprisoned her in the country home where she lives remote from bearable society in "a wilderness of solitude." Even in the vein of comedy, Farquhar commiserates with the victimized Mrs. Sullen by giving her justifications for divorce that are taken from the grave and powerful pen of the Puritan poet and pamphleteer Milton, whose *Tracts on Divorce* cut such wide swaths through the very narrow permissible exits granted by conventional divorce law. Milton argues—and Mrs. Sullen echoes him—for a principle that flies in the face of the pieties of family values: it isn't adultery but incompatibility that is the true curse of lingering marriages. The echo is precise:

(1) Mrs. Sullen: "Law! What law can search into the remote abyss of nature, what evidence can prove the unaccountable disaffection of wedlock? Can a jury sum up the endless aversions that are rooted in our souls, or can a Bench give judgment upon antipathies?"

Milton: "Christ so left it, preaching only to the conscience, and not authorizing a judicial court to toss about and divulge the unaccountable and secret reasons of disaffection between man and wife, as a thing most improperly answerable to any such kind of trial.... [O]ftimes the causes of seeking divorce reside so deeply in the radical and innocent affections of nature, as is not within the diocese of Law to tamper with."

(2) Mrs. Sullen: "O sister, casual violation [i.e., adultery] is a transient injury, and may possibly be repaired, but can radical hatreds ever be reconciled? No, no, sister, Nature is the first lawgiver, and when she has set tempers opposite, not all the golden links of wedlock, nor iron manacles of law can keep 'um fast."

Milton: "[N]atural hatred whenever it arises is a greater evil in marriage, than the accident of adultery, a greater defrauding, a greater injustice....This being but a transient injury and soon amended... but that other being so unspeakable and unremitting sorrow and offense....To couple hatred therefore though wedlock try all her golden links and borrow to her aid all the iron manacles and fetters of Law, it does but seek to twist a rope of sand."

Nevertheless Mrs. Sullen's sister-in-law Dorinda counsels patience, even in the face of Mrs. Sullen's bald demonstration of her husband's brutal indifference. Mrs. Sullen explodes: "Patience!" But common to the Western imagination the farther it projects its fantasies into the remote recesses of the East, is the view that in the teaching of Islam women had "no souls and no rights in law." In fact, the property rights of married women were stronger in Islamic countries than those governing Mrs. Sullen's England in her time.

Finally, "diverting" Mrs. Sullen from her despondency, a countrywoman arrives to consult with Lady Bountiful, Mrs. Sullen's rustic mother-in-law whose remedies "cure all her neighbors of all distempers." She, like everything else in her bucolic kingdom, is anathema to Mrs. Sullen, and since she is absent, Mrs. Sullen takes it on herself to prescribe a remedy for a husband's sore leg.

Mrs. Sullen

Patience! the cant of custom—Providence sends no evil
without a remedy—should I lie groaning under a yoke I can
shake off, I were accessory to my ruin, and my patience were
no better than self-murder. But how can I shake off the yoke?
My divisions from my husband, you say, don't come within
the reach of the law for a divorce. But what law can search into
the remote abyss of nature? what evidence can prove the
unaccountable disaffections of wedlock? Can a jury sum up
the endless aversions that are rooted in our souls, or can a
bench give judgment upon antipathies! Casual violation is a
transient injury, and may possibly be repaired, but can radical
hatreds be ever reconciled?

No, no, sister, nature is the first lawgiver, and when she has set
tempers opposite, not all the golden links of wedlock nor iron
manacles of law can keep 'um fast.

Were I born an humble Turk, where women have no soul nor
property, there I must sit contented. But in England, a
country, whose women are its glory, must women be abused?
where women rule, must women be enslaved? nay, cheated
into slavery, mocked by a promise of comfortable society into
a wilderness of solitude? I dare not keep the thought about

me.—Oh, here comes something to divert me.

(Enter a Country Woman)
Well, good woman!—what, woman? A cure for your husband's
sore leg? Well, I'll tell you what you must do. You must lay
your husband's leg upon a table, and with a chopping-knife
you must lay it open as broad as you can; then you must take
out the bone, and beat the flesh soundly with a rolling-pin;
then take salt, pepper, cloves, mace, and ginger, some sweet
herbs, and season it very well; then roll it up like brawn, and
put it into the oven for two hours.

CANT: jargon. TURK: here, Mohammedan woman. WHERE WOMEN RULE: England's
queens: the two Marys (1553–1558) and (1688–1702); Elizabeth (1558–1603); Anne
(1702–1714). BRAWN: a boar or pork meat.

183.

ALICIA, MAD WITH JEALOUSY OF JANE SHORE, RISES TO FURY (OT)

(1714) NICHOLAS ROWE, *THE TRAGEDY OF JANE SHORE*, ACT V, SC. 1

Alicia's vow to her friend Jane Shore becomes prediction: "If I not
hold [you] nearer to my soul, Than every other joy the world can
give, Let poverty, deformity and shame, Distraction and despair seize
me on earth."

It was the "fatal love" of King Edward, deceased, which is now the
ruin of Jane Shore. Her goods have already been seized, and she is
abandoned by all her intimate friends but Alicia. What is left to her is
a jewel case which she puts into the hands of Alicia for safe-keeping
against a possible time of "utmost wretchedness." And it is Lord
Hastings whom she trusts to befriend and plead her cause to the
Duke of Gloucester (soon to become Richard III), the same Lord
Hastings whom Alicia loves, unknown to Jane, with jealous passion.
Alicia's jealousy misinterprets and condemns Jane until she is persuaded that Jane has won Hastings' love, and is responsible for his
execution at the command of Gloucester (for his opposition to
Gloucester's ambition for the throne). Distracted by his death, Alicia
is on the verge of madness when Jane, now utterly bereft, comes to her

door begging for help—even for bread. Alicia's greeting goes beyond wrath, and becomes madness.

(*Enter Alicia in disorder, two Servants following*)

ALICIA

What wretch art thou whose misery and baseness
Hangs on my door; whose hateful whine of woe
Breaks in upon my sorrows, and distracts
My jarring senses with thy beggar's cry?
Dost thou come to me, to me for bread?
I know thee not.—Go, hunt for it abroad,
Where wanton hands upon the earth have scattered it,
Or cast it on the waters.—Mark the eagle
And hungry vulture, where they wind the prey;
Watch where the ravens of the valley feed,
And seek thy food with them—I know thee not.
Ha!—let me look upon thee well—
'Tis true—I know thee now—A mischief on thee!—
Thou art that fatal fair, that cursed she,
That set my brain a madding. Thou hast robbed me;
Thou hast undone me.—Murder! Oh, my Hastings!
—See, his pale, bloody head shoots glaring by me!
Give him me back again, thou soft deluder,
Thou beauteous witch—
Avaunt! and come not near me—
Where is thy king, thy Edward,
And all the smiling, cringing train of courtiers
That bent the knee before thee?
Mercy? I know it not—for I am miserable,
I'll give thee misery, for here she dwells.
This is her house, where the sun never dawns;
The bird of night sits screaming o'er the roof,
Grim spectres sweep along the horrid gloom,
And nought is heard but wailings and lamentings.
Hark! something cracks above!—It shakes, it totters!
And see, the nodding ruin falls to crush me!
—'Tis fall'n, 'tis here! I feel it on my brain!
A waving flood of bluish fire swells o'er me;
—And now 'tis out, and I am drowned in blood.
—Ha! what art thou, thou horrid headless trunk?
It is my Hastings!—See, he wafts me on!
Away! I go! I fly! I follow thee.

—But come not thou with mischief-making beauty
To interpose between us; look not on him;
Give thy fond arts and thy delusions o'er,
For thou shalt never, never part us more.

(She runs off, her Servants following.)

184.

INDIANA DEFENDS HER PROTECTOR'S HONOR AGAINST HER AUNT'S CONJECTURES (YC)

(1722) RICHARD STEELE, *THE CONSCIOUS LOVERS*, ACT II, SC. 2

"'Tis artifice," sneers Indiana's guardian Isabella concerning the young Bevil's unaccountable conduct toward Indiana. "'Tis all skill and management.... Mr. Bevil carries his hypocrisy the best of any man living, but still he is a man, and therefore a hypocrite." Isabella knows the way of the world, but not the new interior world inhabited by the principal lovers in Steele's comedy, in which severity of obligation, delicacy of address, and mute perception of inner feeling have taken over from the crass egocentrism of the Restoration's libertines. The behavior, even the thoughts, of Bevil Junior and Indiana, the paragons of this new breed of lovers, are governed by a new and startlingly complex code. To quote from entry in Men's vols.: "Bevil Junior, Constrained but Courteous, Counters His Father's Choice of Wife for Him":

"By 1722, when *The Conscious Lovers* was written, English sentimentality, like middle-class manners, had added to its four-square virtues a continental refinement it very much emulated and very much needed: French sensibility. Sensibility was a drawing-room version of *Generosité*, a code [originally for] those who added refinement of feeling to heroic [battlefield] acts. [I]t meant a dignified forbearance, an indulgent understanding, a generous granting of a rival's or an enemy's claim to considerations of personal honor, or even, in its most generous form, to considerations of the heart....

"In the eighteenth century, the man of *generosité* became the Man of Feeling. He was not only responsive to the feelings of the other, and also and equally deeply responsive to his own, but became feeling's votary, Feeling itself becoming the supreme moral guide to his conduct. Knowing the flutterings, the whims and desires, the shames and mortifications within his own heart, he was honor bound to detect them with equal accuracy, intensity, and forbearance in the other, and to respond first and foremost to the claims of that forbearance. To violate, or even in very small ways to impinge on the feeling of the other, was the equivalent of physical assault.... For dramatic characters to qualify for Feeling's status, they had to be ideally attuned to the operative code of conduct and feeling in the other, to act on the other's silent instructions and exhortations."

It is this extraordinary genius that both Indiana and her lover Bevil have in common. So perfectly attuned are they to one another's never-mentioned, never-suggested desire—guessed from such signs as the turn of the head, the furtive glance, the lowering of the eyes—that they intuit purity of soul and motive in the other with no cavil and no vacillation. It's this remarkable way of *knowing* that makes Indiana proof against her guardian's warnings, and in the face of common sense, against the oddity of Bevil's behavior toward her.

It certainly is odd: Bevil rescued Indiana from an evil stepbrother, installed her in thoroughly comfortable, thoroughly respectable quarters, provides her with money and furnishings with never a hint of their source, and yet makes no protestations to her of anything but his devoted friendship. But Indiana is aware of the reason behind his hesitation. His father has engaged him to an heiress, and Bevil's delicate sensibility forbids his confronting his father with a blunt rejection of so generous a gift. Father and son tread carefully around one another's sensibilities; Bevil and Indiana wait in silence for the plot to turn in their favor, and Indiana heroically withstands the suspicions of her guardian.

INDIANA

Will you persuade me there can be an ill design in supporting me in the condition of a woman of quality, attended, dressed, and lodged like one; in my appearance abroad and my furniture at home, every way in the most sumptuous manner, and he that does it has an artifice, a design in it? And all this without so much as explaining to me that all about me comes from him! If he is an ill man, let us look into his stratagems. Here is another of them.

(Showing a letter)

Here's two hundred and fifty pound in bank notes, with these words, "To pay for the set of dressing plate which will be brought home to-morrow." Why, dear aunt, now here's another piece of skill for you, which I own I cannot comprehend,—and it is with a bleeding heart I hear you say anything to the disadvantage of Mr. Bevil. When he is present, I look upon him as one to whom I owe my life and the support of it. Then again, as the man who loves me with sincerity and honor. When his eyes are cast another way and I dare survey him, my heart is painfully divided between shame and love. This is my state of mind in his presence; and when he is absent, you are ever dinning my ears with notions of the arts of men,—that his hidden bounty, his respectful conduct, his careful provision for me, after his preserving me from the utmost misery are certain signs he means nothing but to make I know not what of me.

I have, when I am with him, ten thousand things besides my sex's natural decency and shame to suppress my heart that yearns to thank him, to praise, to say it loves him. I say thus it is with me while I see him; and in his absence I am entertained with nothing but your endeavors to tear this amiable image from my heart and in its stead to place a base dissembler, an artful invader of my happiness, my innocence, my honor.

I will not doubt the truth of Bevil, I will not doubt it. He has not spoken it by an organ that is given to lying. His eyes are all that have ever told me that he was mine. I know his virtue, I know his filial piety and ought to trust his management with a father to whom he has uncommon obligations. What have I to be concerned for? My lesson is very short. If he takes me forever, my purpose of life is only to please him. If he leaves me (which Heaven avert) I know he'll do it nobly, and I shall have nothing to do but to learn to die, after worse than death has happened to me.

Therefore [I] desire you will not make my life uneasy by these ungrateful jealousies of one to whom I am, and wish to be, obliged, for from his integrity alone, I have resolved to hope for happiness. All the rest of my life is but waiting till he comes. I only live when I'm with him.

(Exit)

185.

INDIANA DEFENDS TO MR. SEALAND HER HONORABLE FRIENDSHIP WITH BEVIL JR. (YC)

(1722) RICHARD STEELE, *THE CONSCIOUS LOVERS*, ACT V, SC. 3

The merchant Sealand, not attuned to the lofty virtues of lovers of "delicacy" [see No. 184, above] has reason for anxiety. His daughter, a wealthy heiress, is engaged to Bevil Junior who, Mr. Sealand surmises from rumor, keeps an abandoned mistress, an Indiana, with whom he wallows, and in all likelihood will continue to wallow in sin after marriage. Before his daughter and her dowry are given up to such a voluptuary, Mr. Sealand is determined to get to the bottom of rumor, and in a famous confrontation scene (which subsequently turns into a recognition scene) meets with Indiana. But she, with the dignity and innocence native to her, disabuses him first of his suspicions concerning her own character, and then of Bevil Junior's. Recognizing her own lack of standing in the commerce of a marriage transaction, she generously supports the propriety of her lover's claim to Mr. Sealand's desirable daughter. But at cost.

While behaving with reason, emotional control, and extraordinary generosity during her interview with Mr. Sealand, Indiana, in fact, inwardly suffers a pulverizing emotional journey that fitfully emerges. But it is as active throughout her interview as is her studied equanimity, and when it bursts into the open, it explodes. The double layering of emotion, hardly novel in dramatic history, is now, in dramas awash in sentimentality and sensibility, to be exploited to the full, and Indiana's alternating performance of tight suppression and violent expression is the harbinger of many heroines' later performances and many scenes to come in which the murky waters of emotion below hold the whole truth, and the rational palaver covering them holds only lies.

But her portion doesn't remain "bitterness and sorrow." Subsequently, in one of the most popular and tearful scenes in eighteenth-century drama, Providence takes a hand. In her raving, a few hints concerning the facts of her past escape Indiana, and they register alarmingly with Mr. Sealand. Is it possible...? Can she be...? She is. Already persuaded of her virtue, and now of his paternity, he has little trouble welcoming his newfound daughter into his wealthy arms, and in an instant transferring her and a portion of that wealth into the arms of Bevil Junior.

INDIANA

Sir, you are going into very great errors; but as you are pleased to say you see something in me that has changed at least the color of your suspicions, so has your appearance altered mine, and made me earnestly attentive to what has any way concerned you to enquire into my affairs and character.

Good sir, be seated, and tell me tenderly—keep all your suspicions concerning me alive, that you may in a proper and prepared way—acquaint me why the care of your daughter obliges a person of your seeming worth and fortune to be thus inquisitive about a wretched, helpless, friendless—*(weeping)*. But I beg your pardon: though I am an orphan, your child is not; and your concern for her, it seems, has brought you hither. I'll be composed.

How could Mr. Bevil injure—? Sir, you wrong him; he has not injured me; my support is from his bounty. But my own fears tell me all. You are the gentleman, I suppose, for whose happy daughter he is designed a husband by his good father, and he has, perhaps, consented to the overture. He was here this morning, dressed beyond his usual plainness—nay, most sumptuously—and he is to be, perhaps, this night a bridegroom. His actions, sir, his eyes, have only made me think he designed to make me the partner of his heart. The goodness and gentleness of his demeanor made me misinterpret all. 'Twas my own hope, my own passion, that deluded me; he never made one amorous advance to me. His large heart and bestowing hand have only helped the miserable; nor know I why, but from his mere delight in virtue, that I have been his care, the object on which to indulge and please himself with pouring favors.

Let not me, miserable though I may be, do injury to my benefactor. No, sir, my treatment ought rather to reconcile you to his virtues. If to bestow without a prospect of return; if to delight in supporting what might, perhaps, be thought an object of desire, with no other view than to be her guard against those who would not be so disinterested—if these actions, sir, can in a careful parent's eye commend him to a daughter, give yours, sir—give her to my honest, generous Bevil! What have I to do but sigh and weep, to rave, run wild, a lunatic in chains, or, hid in darkness, mutter in distracted starts and broken accents my strange, strange story!

All my comfort must be to expostulate in madness, to relieve with frenzy my despair, and shrieking to demand of fate, "Why—why was I born to such variety of sorrows?" No, 'twas heaven's high will I should be such—to be plundered in my cradle! tossed on the seas! and even there an infant captive! to lose my mother, hear but of my father! to be adopted! lose my adopter! then plunged again in worse calamities!

Yet then to find the most charming of mankind, once more to set me free from what I thought the last distress; to load me with his services, his bounties and his favors; to support my very life in a way that stole, at the same time, my very soul itself from me!

Yet then, again, this very man to take another, without leaving me the right, the pretence, of easing my fond heart with tears! For, oh! I can't reproach him, though the same hand that raised me to this height now throws me down the precipice. My portion here is bitterness and sorrow.

186.

MRS. PEACHUM RAILS AT POLLY'S FOLLY IN GETTING MARRIED (OC)

(1728) JOHN GAY, THE BEGGAR'S OPERA, ACT I, SC. 8

[Quoting from Men's vols. entry: "Peachum Considers Which... Henchmen He Will Betray" and "Peachum Warns Against the Evil of Marriage":] "In The Beggar's Opera, John Gay satirizes not only the pretensions of Italianate opera and the vogue for the sentimental and the romantic, but politics in particular.... The parody of the Whig politician runs deep. Peachum is portrayed as a Whitehall clone in the back alleys of London. Note how he deals with a fanciful premise when it clashes with the real world. The premise is Mrs. Peachum's, who argues a bit tearfully that if their daughter Polly is in love, she will naturally want to marry her lover, how could she possibly not? Peachum's response, in both manner and logic, is impeccably true to the sober, politely set forth calculation of a skilled cabinet man.... He sets out his points on a platter of objective fact and reason. And the facts and reason, then, speak for themselves."

To Mrs. Peachum's notion that the girl will marry whom she loves, Peachum explains: "Gamesters and highwaymen [Peachum's laborers] are generally very good to their whores, but they are the very devils to their wives.... A handsome wench in our way of business is as profitable as at the bar of a Temple coffee-house, who looks upon it as her livelihood to grant every liberty, but one.... I would indulge the girl... in anything but marriage! After that, my dear, how shall we be safe? Are we not then in her husband's power? For a husband hath the absolute power over all a wife's secrets but her own."

Polly's possible marriage to Macheath, then, is iniquity without profit. Mrs. Peachum learns her husband's lesson sufficiently thoroughly to greet the news, when it tragically comes, that Polly is in fact already married to Macheath, the highwayman in Peachum's employ, responding as her husband responded to the very suggestion, but without his careful politician's sobriety.

MRS. PEACHUM

You baggage, you hussy! you inconsiderate jade! had you been hanged, it would not have vexed me, for that might have been your misfortune; but to do such a mad thing by choice!—The wench is married, husband.

I knew she was always a proud slut; and now the wench hath played the fool and married, because forsooth she would do like the gentry. Can you support the expense of a husband, hussy, in gaming, drinking and whoring? have you money enough to carry on the daily quarrels of man and wife about who shall squander most? There are not many husbands and wives who can bear the charges of plaguing one another in a handsome way. If you must be married, could you introduce nobody into our family but a highwayman? Why, thou foolish jade, thou wilt be as ill used, and as much neglected, as if thou hadst married a lord!

With Polly's fortune, she might very well have gone off to a person of distinction. Yes, that you might, you pouting slut!

How the mother is to be pitied who hath handsome
daughters! Locks, bolts, bars, and lectures of morality are
nothing to them; they break through them all. They have as
much pleasure in cheating a father and mother as in cheating
at cards. Then all the hopes of our family are gone for ever
and ever!

"But I love him," she says. Love him! worse and worse! I
thought the girl had been better bred.

187.

MILLWOOD ATTACKS THE PREDATIONS OF MEN (OT)

(1731) GEORGE LILLO, *THE LONDON MERCHANT*, ACT I, SC. 2

Millwood's speeches of justification are the eighteenth century's classic statements of women's victimization, but backhanded, since
they're intended, in the moral framework of the play, to demonstrate
the false, overwrought reasoning of the fallen woman. Inadvertently,
though, Lillo put into her mouth arguments—and the passion of
those arguments—that resonate still, certainly more now than then,
with incredible, and persuasive, conviction.

Millwood is explaining to her maidservant Lucy the genesis of
her hatred of men, of the world as man's world, of the policy she pursues for their undoing, in consideration of revenge, and for their
exploitation, in consideration of her livelihood. She traffics in the
innocent, the young, who have as yet no guilt and therefore no suspicion (basic principle for choosing victims), and having fixed on
young Barnwell—having detected on him, money, and in him, desire
(basic prognosis for success), she calls up a final maxim for a first
meeting—to seem and speak the opposite of what one is and means;
and that, with the cooperation of "Nature," will suffice. For more on
The London Merchant, see Men's vols. entries on Barnwell and
Thorowgood.

There's little question that Millwood is the paragon of the female
villain who entices and traps vulnerable innocents, but there is also little question of the universality of the male villainy with which she's
competing. When, at her capture, her wrath explodes [No. 188, below],

the power of her argument comes into its own. Not merely focussed on her immediate motive and her immediate act, her diatribe goes wide, and embraces more than the hypocrisy of men in their relations to women, but the hypocrisy of men in all their essential relations: the corruption, the greed, the cruelty of "the reverend priesthood," the inherent evil of religion itself, the law as first the protective screen and then the punishing arm of the villains in power, and finally, once again, all this visited on womankind, "your universal prey." Of the many condemnations in dramatic literature, not only of men but of maleness itself as a bludgeon in social intercourse, few have reached as large and as violent a bill of particulars as Millwood's, at her end, in the arms of the law and a step from the gallows.

Millwood

Wit and beauty first made me a wretch, and still continue me so. Men, however generous or sincere to one another, are all selfish hypocrites in their affairs with us. We are no otherwise esteemed or regarded by them but as we contribute to their satisfaction. We are but slaves to men. Slaves have no property, no; not even in themselves. All is the victor's. I would have my conquests complete, like those of the Spaniards in the New World, who first plundered the natives of all the wealth they had, and then condemned the wretches to the mines for life to work for more. It's a general maxim among the knowing part of mankind; that a woman without virtue, like a man without honor or honesty, is capable of any action, though never so vile; and yet what pains will they not take, what arts not use, to seduce us from our innocence, and make us contemptible and wicked, even in their own opinions! Then is it not just, the villains, to their cost, should find us so? But guilt makes them suspicious, and keeps them on their guard; therefore we can take advantage only of the young and innocent part of the sex, who, having never injured women, apprehend no injury from them.

Such a one, I think, I have found. As I've passed through the City, I have often observed him, receiving and paying considerable sums of money; from thence I conclude he is employed in affairs of consequence. Having long had a design on him, and meeting him yesterday, I made a full stop, and, gazing wishfully on his face, asked him his name. He blushed, and bowing very low, answered: "George Barnwell." I begged his pardon for the freedom I had taken, and told him that he was the person I had long wished to see, and to whom I had an affair of importance to communicate at a proper time and place. He named a tavern; I talked of honor and reputation, and invited him to my house. He swallowed the bait, promised to come, and this is the time. I expect him.

(Knocking at the door)
Somebody knocks;—d'ye hear, I am at home for nobody today but him.

(Exit Lucy)
Less affairs must give way to those of more consequence, and I am strangely mistaken if this does not prove of great importance to me and him too, before I have done with him. Now, after what manner shall I receive him? Let me consider—what manner of person am I to receive? He is young, innocent and bashful; therefore I must take care not to put him out of countenance at first. But then, if I have any skill in physiognomy, he is amorous, and, with a little assistance will soon get the better of his modesty.—I'll e'en trust to Nature, who does wonders in these matters. If to seem what one is not, in order to be the better liked for what one really is; if to speak one thing, and mean the direct contrary, be art in a woman—I know nothing of nature.

188.

MILLWOOD, APPREHENDED, VOWS "TO PLAGUE MANKIND" (OT)

(1731) GEORGE LILLO, *THE LONDON MERCHANT*, ACT IV, SC. 2

[See No. 187, above]

MILLWOOD

Fool, hypocrite, villain—devil! That imaginary being is an emblem of thy cursed sex collected—a mirror, wherein, each particular man may see his own likeness and that of all mankind.

Well may I curse your barbarous sex, who robbed me of mind and body. 'Ere I knew their worth; then left me, too late, to count their value by their loss. Another and another spoiler came, and all my gain was poverty and reproach. My soul disdained, and yet disdains, dependence and contempt. Riches, no matter by what means obtained, I saw, secured the worst of men from both. I found it therefore necessary to be rich, and to that end I summoned all my arts. You call 'em wicked; be it so! They were such as my conversation with your sex had furnished me withal.

Men of all degrees and all professions I have known; yet found no difference but in their several capacities; all were alike wicked to the utmost of their power. In pride, contention, avarice, cruelty and revenge, the reverend priesthood were my unerring guides. From suburb-magistrates, who live by ruined reputations, as the unhospitable natives of Cornwall do by shipwrecks, I learned that to charge my innocent neighbors with my crimes, was to merit their protection; for to screen the guilty is the less scandalous when many are suspected, and detraction like darkness and death, blackens all objects and levels all distinction. Such are your venal magistrates, who favor none but such as, by their office, they are sworn to punish. With them, not to be guilty is the worst of crimes, and large fees privately paid are every needful virtue.

O, I know you and I hate you all. I expect no mercy and I ask for none; I followed my inclinations, and the best of you every day. All actions seem alike natural and indifferent to man and beast, who devour, or are devoured, as they meet with others weaker or stronger than themselves.

I am not fool enough to be an atheist, though I have known enough of men's hypocrisy to make a thousand simple women so. Whatever religion is in itself, as practised by mankind it has caused the evils you say it was designed to cure. War, plague, and famine, has not destroyed so many of the human race as this pretended piety has done, and with such barbarous cruelty, as if the only way to honor heaven were to turn the present world into hell. What are your laws of which you make your boast, but the fool's wisdom and the coward's valor—the instrument and screen of all your villainies, by which you punish in others what you act yourselves, or would have acted had you been in their circumstances? The judge who condemns the poor man for being a thief had been a thief himself had he been poor. Thus you go on deceiving and being deceived, harassing, plaguing, and destroying one another: but women are your universal prey.

Women, by whom you are, the source of joy,
With cruel arts you labor to destroy;
A thousand ways our ruin you pursue,
Yet blame in us those arts first taught by you.
O may, from hence, each violated maid,
By flatt'ring, faithless, barb'rous man betrayed,
When robbed of innocence and virgin fame,
From your destruction raise a nobler name;
To right their sex's wrongs devote their mind,
And future Millwoods prove, to plague mankind!

SUBURB-MAGISTRATES...REPUTATIONS: magistrates in the environs of London; i.e., outside the "City," had no regular salary, but subsisted upon their fees; many of them therefore encouraged vice in order to increase their profits. THE UNHOSPITABLE... SHIPWRECKS: during the eighteenth century the practice of plundering shipwrecked vessels became increasingly common, especially in Cornwall, in the Highlands of Scotland, and on the western coast of Ireland.

189.

AGNES, DAZZLED BY THE SIGHT OF THE TRAVELER'S CONCEALED TREASURE, IS TEMPTED TO MURDER (OT)

(1737) GEORGE LILLO, *FATAL CURIOSITY*, ACT III, SC. 1

Agnes' son is the wealthy traveler returning to his impoverished family after years abroad. Intending to reveal his identity the next morning, when he would bless his family with the treasure he carries with him, he retires for the night, but his mother's fatal curiosity discovers the treasure concealed in his case, which discovery leads to her son's murder. The play itself inspired the rash of "fate-tragedies" written in the early nineteenth century, and in the twentieth it was the basis of Camus' *Le Malentendu* (translated as *Cross-Purposes*). But for the puritanical Lillo, it signified neither the irony of fate nor radical absurdity, but simply the moral lesson of the evils of temptation. In Agnes' hovering over the traveler's case, Lillo is spelling out the step by step grip of temptation as it seizes, releases, and seizes again, until her mind is entirely captured by the "thought." It is another version of the devil's several ways of winning victims to sin. Lillo's didactic warning becomes implanted later in the edifying lessons of formal psychology, and Agnes' struggle through no—yes—no—yes becomes a familiar one in crime melodrama.

It is the dead of night; Agnes, alone, her hands on the case, talks to herself in whispers:

AGNES

Who should this stranger be? And then this casket—
He says it is of value, and yet trusts it,
As if a trifle, to a stranger's hand.
His confidence amazes me. Perhaps
It is not what he says. I'm strongly tempted
To open it and see. No, let it rest.
Why should my curiosity excite me
To search and pry into th'affairs of others,
Who have t'employ my thoughts so many cares
And sorrows of my own? With how much ease
The spring gives way! Surprising! Most prodigious!
My eyes are dazzled and my ravished heart
Leaps at the glorious sight. How bright's the lustre,
How immense the worth of these fair jewels!
Aye, such a treasure would expel forever
Base poverty and all its abject train:
The mean devices we're reduced to use
To keep famine and preserve our lives
From day to day, the cold neglect of friends,
The galling scorn or more provoking pity
Of an insulting world. Possessed of these,
Plenty, content, and power might take their turn,
And lofty pride bare its aspiring head
At our approach and once more bend before us.
A pleasing dream!—'Tis past, and now I wake
More wretched by the happiness I've lost.
For sure it was a happiness to think
Though but a moment, such a treasure mine.
Nay it was more than thought. I saw and touched
The bright temptation, and I see it yet.
'Tis here—'tis mine—I have it in possession!
Must I resign it? Must I give it back?
Am I in love with misery and want,
To rob myself and court so vast a loss?
Retain it, then! But how? There is a way—

Why sinks my heart? Why does my blood run cold?
Why am I thrilled with horror? 'Tis not choice,
But dire necessity, suggests the thought!

190.

MRS. OAKLY ASSAILS HER HUSBAND FOR NON-EXISTENT DUPLICITIES (oc)

(1761) GEORGE COLMAN THE ELDER, *THE JEALOUS WIFE*, ACT I, SC. 1

Mrs. Oakly is the jealous wife of the play's title, and seen out of the context of that comic cliche, she veers toward the tragic as much as toward the comic. Like the Morose of Ben Jonson's *Epicoene* (see, in Men's vols.: "Morose, Who Can Bear No Noise, Instructs His Servant Mute"), Mrs. Oakly exceeds the easy classification of the "humours" character in the earlier Jonsonian tradition, and shares with Morose that "tendency toward excess" which becomes excess to the point of mania. She is, like him, the victim of uncontrollable urgencies that have nothing to do with a fixed, rational belief (as with Molière's monomaniacs), but with self-governing urgencies that result for her to perpetually seek reasonable justification for the suspicions that she is helpless to forgo. Automatically, she pounces on every sign, gesture, word, and object, and with keen intelligence, sees their significance in the pattern she's woven in advance of certain knowing. What she assumes as given is her husband's philandering. What she accumulates moment by moment—in her private fantasy—is proof.

If it were possible to put aside for a moment the meanness of spirit with which Mrs. Oakly inflicts pain on her husband, and recognize the degree to which she sees his falsehood as real, one might understand the degree to which she feels her victimization, and the degree of watchful zeal she feels demanded of her to avoid becoming an imposter's laughing stock.

She's intercepted a letter to her husband about his nephew Charles and the disappearance of his beloved Harriot, and assumes a scheme on the part of her husband, using the ruse of Charles' role as abductor, to conceal his own abduction of the young lady.

Mrs. Oakly

(Within) Don't tell me! I know it is so. It's monstrous, and I will not bear it! Nay, nay...

(Enter Mrs. Oakly, with a letter, Oakly
following)

Say what you will, Mr. Oakly, you shall never persuade me but this is some filthy intrigue of yours. Don't I know your—Tell me, I say, this instant, every circumstance relating to this letter. Look you, Mr. Oakly, this usage is not to be borne. You take a pleasure in abusing my tenderness and soft disposition. To be perpetually running over the whole town, nay, the whole kingdom too, in pursuit of your amours! Did not I discover that you were great with Mademoiselle, my own woman? Did not you contract a shameful familiarity with Mrs. Freeman? Did not I detect your intrigue with Lady Wealthy? Have not I found you out a thousand times? And have I not this moment a letter in my hand, which convinces me of your baseness?

Heaven be praised! I stopped it. I suspected some of these doings for some time past. But the letter informs me who she is, and I'll be revenged on her sufficiently. O, you base man, you! But I am not to be made such a fool. I am convinced of your perfidy, and very sure that—No, you are a base man, and I will not hear you.

(Going)

Go to your mistresses, and leave your poor wife to her miseries. How unfortunate a woman am I! I could die with vexation.

(Throwing herself into a chair)

O! I know you hate me; and that your unkindness and barbarity will be the death of me. *(Whining)* O, I am an unhappy woman! *(Weeping)* You see I have detected you. Tell me this instant where she is concealed. What! are you confounded with your guilt? Have I caught you at last?

O, is it Charles?! O that wicked Charles! To decoy a young lady from her parents in the country! The profligacy of the young fellows of this age is abominable. Charles, is it!—Charles!— There's a sudden turn now! You have a ready wit for intrigue, I find. Mighty fine, Mr. Oakly!—Go on, sir, go on! I see what you mean. Your assurance provokes me beyond your very falsehood itself. So you imagine, sir, that this affected concern, this flimsy pretense about Charles, is to bring you off. Matchless confidence! But I am armed against everything. I am prepared for all your dark schemes. I am aware of all your low stratagems. O, you do it well! Prodigiously well, sir! You do it very well. Nay, keep it up, carry it on, there's nothing like going through with it. O you artful creature! But, sir, I am not to be so easily satisfied. Give me the letter. *(Snatching the letter)* You shall sorely repent this vile business, for I am resolved that I will know the bottom of it.

191.

MRS. OAKLY, EATEN UP WITH SUSPICION, PLOTS TO UNCOVER THE DEPTH OF HER HUSBAND'S INIQUITIES (oc)

(1761) GEORGE COLMAN THE ELDER, *THE JEALOUS WIFE*, ACT II, SC. 2

[Continues No. 190, above] Mrs. Oakly, much relieved, learns the good news from her husband, his brother, and the much relieved Charles that Harriot has disappeared on her own to escape an unwanted marriage. But when Mr. Oakly suggests that they give safe harbor to Harriot in their own home and under Mrs. Oakly's own protection, she smells treachery: her husband intends to make her, his own wife, his "convenience woman" in his affair with Harriot.

MRS. OAKLY

After all, that letter was certainly intended for my husband. I see plain enough they are all in a plot against me: my husband intriguing, the Major working him up to affront me, Charles owning his letters, and so playing into each other's hands. They think me a fool, I find; but I'll be too much for them yet. I have desired to speak with Mr. Oakly, and expect him here immediately. His temper is naturally open, and if he thinks my anger abated, and my suspicions laid to sleep, he will certainly betray himself by his behavior. I'll assume an air of good humor, pretend to believe the fine story they have trumped up, throw him off his guard, and so draw the secret out of him. Here he comes. How hard it is to dissemble one's anger!

O, I could rate him soundly! But I'll keep down my indignation at present, though it chokes me.

(Enter Oakly)

O, my dear! I am very glad to see you. Pray sit down. *(They sit)* I longed to see you. It seemed an age till I had an opportunity of talking over the silly affair that happened this morning. Nay, don't look so grave now. Come, it's all over. Charles and you have cleared up matters. I am satisfied.

And really sometimes it is very ridiculous. My uneasiness this morning, for instance! ha, ha, ha! to be so much alarmed about that idle letter, which turned out quite another thing at last. Was not I very angry with you? ha, ha, ha! *(Affecting a laugh)*

I am apt to be too violent: I love you too well to be quite too easy about you. *(Fondly)* Well; no matter. What is become of Charles? Poor fellow! he is on the wing, rambling all over the town in pursuit of this young lady. Where is he gone, pray? An aunt of hers in the neighborhood? Lady Freelove! O, ho! gone to Lady Freelove, is he? You are well acquainted with her? Indeed! But, pray—a—a—a—I say,—a—a—*(Confused)* I say—a—a—*(Stammering)* Is she handsome? Prodigiously handsome! And is she reckoned a sensible girl? Charles will be mighty happy. I am convinced of it. Poor Charles! I am much concerned for him. He must be very uneasy about her. I was thinking whether we could be of any service to him in this affair. I would do anything to serve Charles, and oblige you. But what's your proposal? Bring her home here!! Amazing! this is even beyond my expectation. Was there ever such assurance! Take her under my protection! What! Would you keep her under my nose? You thought I would have approved! What! make me your convenient woman? no place but my own house to serve your purposes? Why, surely you imagine me an idiot, a driveller. Charles, indeed! Yes, Charles is a fine excuse for you. You have made it very clear to me. Now I am convinced. I have no doubt of your perfidy. But I thank you for some hints you have given me, and you may be sure I shall make use of them. Nor will I rest until I have full conviction, and overwhelm you with the strongest proofs of your baseness towards me. Go, go! I have no doubt of your falsehood. Away!

192.

LYDIA COMPLAINS THAT HER IMITATING THE PLOT OF A SENTIMENTAL NOVEL HAS CAUSED HER TO LOSE HER LOVER (YC)

(1775) RICHARD BRINSLEY SHERIDAN, *THE RIVALS*, ACT I, SC. 2

"Madam," pronounces Sir Anthony Absolute for the benefit of Lydia's aunt and guardian, Mrs. Malaprop, "a circulating library in a town is an ever-green tree of diabolical knowledge!—It blossoms through the year!—And depend on it, Mrs. Malaprop, that they who are fond of handling the leaves, will long for the fruit at last."

Lydia Languish so longs. Mocked though she is in Sheridan's play for a sentimental simpleton (as her name tells us), still in her way she is also a rebel, flouting her elders who deplore the newly popular circulating libraries (from which the Lydias with small budgets can rent books for tiny sums), the elders not wanting the young to learn discontent from books, and very much wanting their wives and daughters to stay low—at least lower than themselves—in education. Sheridan's sneer at the circulating libraries shares with the Sir Anthonys their scorn of the libraries for "pandering fiction" to women and servants and the previously illiterate, and laughs at Lydia for not only devouring sentimental/romantic fiction, but for emulating the life within it. Lydia's a believer, a devotee, and is programming her reality to conform to romantic fantasy. For instance:

The course of Lydia's secret love with Beverley has been running smooth, and so its plot is ripe for a lover's quarrel. Well and good, she's managed the quarrel, but her aunt Mrs. Malaprop has ruined her premeditated timetable for ending it, and Lydia is in danger of losing her lover altogether because of this irrelevant intrusion from real life. She complains to her bosom friend, Julia. But in the midst of her complaining, the very intruders who are most unwelcome, Mrs. Malaprop and Sir Anthony Absolute, arrive, and Lydia scrambles with her maid Lucy to hide the offense of harboring literature.

LYDIA

Ah, Julia, I have a thousand things to tell you!—Then before we are interrupted, let me impart to you some of my distress!—I know your gentle nature will sympathize with me, though your prudence may condemn me!—My letters have informed you of my whole connexion with Beverley;—but I have lost him, Julia!—my aunt has discovered our intercourse by a note she intercepted, and has confined me ever since! Unfortunately I had quarreled with my poor Beverley, just before my aunt made the discovery, and I have not seen him since, to make it up. I don't know how it was, as often as we had been together, we had never had a quarrel, and, somehow, I was afraid he would never give me an opportunity. So, last Thursday, I wrote a letter to myself, to inform myself that Beverley was at that time paying his addresses to another woman. I signed it *your friend unknown,* showed it to Beverley, charged him with his falsehood, put myself in a violent passion, and vowed I'd never see him more. 'Twas the next day my aunt found the matter out. I intended only to have teased him three days and a half, and now I've lost him for ever.

What's here? Oh, here is Sir Anthony Absolute just come with aunt. They are both coming upstairs.—Adieu, my dear Julia. There, through my room you'll find another staircase.

(Exit Julia)

Here, my dear Lucy, hide these books. Quick, quick! Fling *Peregrine Pickle* under the toilet—throw *Roderick Random* into the closet—put *The Innocent Adultery* into *The Whole Duty of Man*—Thrust *Lord Aimworth* under the sofa—cram *Ovid* behind the bolster—there—put *The Man of Feeling* into your pocket—so, so,—now lay *Mrs. Chapone* in sight, and leave *Fordyce's Sermons* open on the table. O burn it, the hairdresser has torn away as far as *Proper Pride.* Never mind—open at *Sobriety,*—fling me *Lord Chesterfield's Letters,*—Now for 'em.

ROUT: a large evening party.

193.

MRS. MALAPROP RAGES AT HER NIECE TO GIVE UP HER LOVER, AND OUTLINES FOR SIR ANTHONY DECENT LIMITS FOR A YOUNG GIRL'S EDUCATION (OC)

(1775) RICHARD BRINSLEY SHERIDAN, *THE RIVALS*, ACT I, SC. 2

[Continues No. 192, above] The Mrs. Malaprop who so intrudes is the legendary character whose name has entered the language for her foible of using the wrong words in the right places. Having discovered her niece's infatuation for the mysterious pauper Beverley, she rages at her, sends her off, and then shares with Sir Anthony her aversion for Lydia's choice of "a fellow not worth a shilling." Sir Anthony concurs, and also concurs in Mrs. Malaprop's condemnation of the cause of her niece's infatuation with romance: reading. Both are at once on the constraints necessary for a young lady's education. Given the bushelful of malapropisms Mrs. Malaprop lavishes in her dissertation on those constraints, she effectively undermines her own thesis.

(Enter Mrs. Malaprop, and Sir Anthony Absolute)

MRS. MALAPROP

There, Sir Anthony, there sits the deliberate simpleton, who wants to disgrace her family, and lavish herself on a fellow not worth a shilling! You will promise to forget this fellow—to illiterate him, I say, quite from your memory. It is not so easy to forget!? But I say it is, miss; there is nothing on earth so easy as to forget, if a person chooses to set about it.—I'm sure I have as much forgot your poor dear uncle as if he had never existed—and I thought it my duty so to do; and let me tell you, Lydia, these violent memories don't become a young woman. Don't attempt to extirpate your-self from the matter; you know I have proof controvertible of it.—But tell me, will you promise to do as you're bid?—Will you take a husband of your friend's choosing?

No preference! Your aversion! What business have you, miss, with preference and aversion? They don't become a young woman; and you ought to know, that as both always wear off, 'tis safest in matrimony to begin with a little aversion. I am sure I hated your poor dear uncle before marriage as if he'd been a black-a-moor—and yet, miss, you are sensible what a wife I made!—and when it pleased heav'n to release me from him, 'tis unknown what tears I shed!—But take yourself to your room.—You are fit company for nothing but your own ill-humors.

(Exit Lydia)

There's a little intricate hussy for you! It is not to be wondered at, Sir Anthony. All this is the natural consequence of teaching girls to read.—by heaven! I'd as soon have them taught the black art as their alphabet!

Observe me, Sir Anthony.—I would by no means wish a daughter of mine to be a progeny of learning; I don't think so much learning becomes a young woman; for instance—I would never let her meddle with Greek, or Hebrew, or Algebra, or Simony, or Fluxions, or Paradoxes, or such inflammatory branches of learning—neither would it be necessary for her to handle any of your mathematical, astronomical, diabolical instruments;—but, Sir Anthony, I would send her, at nine years old, to a boarding-school, in order to learn a little ingenuity and artifice.—Then, sir, she should have a supercilious knowledge in accounts;—and as she grew up, I would have her instructed in geometry, that she might know something of the contagious countries;—but above all, Sir Anthony, she should be mistress of orthodoxy, that she might not mis-spell, and mis-pronounce words so shamefully as girls usually do; and likewise that she might reprehend the true meaning of what she is saying.—This, Sir Anthony, is what I would have a woman know;—and I don't think there is a superstitious article in it.

ILLITERATE: (instead of) obliterate. EXTIRPATE: to remove utterly, do away with; (instead of) exonerate. CONTROVERTIBLE: (instead of) incontrovertible. INTRICATE: (instead of) ingrate (?). PROGENY: (instead of) prodigy. SIMONY: (instead of) ciphering (?). FLUXIONS: calculus, in Newtonian geometry. PARADOXES: in astronomy: Parallaxes (?). SUPERCILIOUS: (instead of) superficial. GEOMETRY: (instead of) geography. CONTAGIOUS: (instead of) contiguous. ORTHODOXY: (instead of) orthography. REPREHEND: (instead of) comprehend. SUPERSTITIOUS: (instead of) superfluous.

194.

JULIA, HAVING SUFFERED FAULKLAND'S CRUELEST TEST OF HER FIDELITY, BIDS HIM A FINAL FAREWELL (yc)

(1775) RICHARD BRINSLEY SHERIDAN, *THE RIVALS*, ACT V, SC. 1

The much-maligned character of Julia in *The Rivals* deserves redemption. That her role is "serious," and adds nothing to the humor or wit of the comedy, is blatantly true. But if it doesn't add humor, it certainly adds sense as well as a new subtlety and dignity to the portrait of female "delicacy." Julia suffers the torments of the patient Griselda—that medieval sufferer who is maliciously tortured in order to prove—which she does—her unabating loyalty to the lord and future husband who is testing her worth. In the Eighteenth Century's novel commitments to "delicacy," much the same tests—psychological rather than physical—are, as in the case of Indiana, ideally endured [see No. 185, above].

Faulkland, Julia's lover, in his quest for certainty regarding Julia's fidelity—not only her fidelity but her deep, perfect, abiding, and unabating love—drives her to the limits of forbearance. But just as Griselda, in a final test that goes beyond the limit of endurance (she's left to float in a tiny boat on the ocean waves for endless days without food or water), so Julia is told the tale of Faulkland's having to go into exile with no money at all, so that she, like Griselda, will prove her perfect loyalty and perfect love, and join him willingly in a life of unredeemable beggary. She passes the test; she willingly vows to join him. But the tale is false. Faulkland, in a state of rapture, confesses it, and rewards Julia at last with his perfect trust.

But what had been in the Middle Ages a lord's prerogative, has become in the eighteenth century merely a lover's psychological aberration, since his demand is measured not only against the protocol of a woman's "delicacy," but for Julia, also against her "pride." The barrier is still low, to be sure but the limit of the woman's self-abasement in the exchanges of love is fixed by the level of her assertion of self-worth. Julia, after the painful pride she took in her fidelity to her aberrant lover, and in the very delicacy which to her *was* the badge of her dignity, accosted by the profound insult to that dignity by Faulkland's demeaning test, leaves him for good.

Or would have. The exigencies of Act V bring about the reconciliation of the lovers in casual but perfect contradiction of the logic of their tale.

Julia

Has no such disaster happened as you related? It was all pretended? Hold, Faulkland!—that you are free from a crime, which I before feared to name, Heaven knows how sincerely I rejoice! These are tears of thankfulness for that! But that your cruel doubts should have urged you to an imposition that has wrung my heart, gives me now a pang more keen than I can express!

Yet hear me. My father loved you, Faulkland! and you preserved the life that tender parent gave me; in his presence I pledged my hand—joyfully pledged it—where before I had given my heart. When, soon after, I lost that parent, it seemed to me that Providence had, in Faulkland, shown me whither to transfer, without a pause, my grateful duty, as well as my affection: hence I have been content to bear from you what pride and delicacy would have forbid me from another. I will not upbraid you by repeating how you have trifled with my sincerity.

After such a year of trial, I might have flattered myself that I should not have been insulted with a new probation of my sincerity, as cruel as unnecessary! I now see it is not in your nature to be content, or confident in love. With this conviction—I never will be yours. While I had hopes that my persevering attention, and unreproaching kindness, might in time reform your temper, I should have been happy to have gained a dearer influence over you; but I will not furnish you with a licensed power to keep alive an incorrigible fault, at the expense of one who never would contend with you.

But one word more. As my faith has once been given to you, I never will barter it with another. I shall pray for your happiness with the truest sincerity; and the dearest blessing I can ask of Heaven to send you, will be to charm you from that unhappy temper, which alone has prevented the performance of our solemn engagement. All I request of *you* is, that you will yourself reflect upon this infirmity, and when you number up the many true delights it has deprived you of, let it not be your *least* regret, that it lost you the love of one who would have followed you in beggary through the world!

(Exit)

PROBATION: test, trial.

195.

LYDIA, MORTIFIED, REFUSES THE LOSS OF HER ANTICIPATED ELOPEMENT FOR THE INDELICACY OF A SANCTIONED MARRIAGE (YC)

(1775) RICHARD BRINSLEY SHERIDAN, *THE RIVALS*, ACT V, SC. 1

[Continues No. 192, above.] It turns out badly for Lydia. She had manufactured a sentimental romance for herself and her lover Beverley, with the bliss of their secret meetings in the snow and frost beneath her window, and the rapture of her elopement down a rope ladder from her bedroom window, and the anticipated escape in the dead of night to the door of a Sottish parson for an outrageous wedding in darkness and solitude, and a delicious public scandal to follow. Her fiction thrived until it was betrayed by Beverley himself—who behind his romantic disguise was none other than the proper bridegroom being foisted on her by her elders—that Captain Absolute whose very name she detested for its propriety. But Lydia at play's end is reconciled to her fate—a mundane happiness with a well-heeled, well-descended Captain Absolute, never to be the equal of her adored, impoverished Beverley.

LYDIA

Oh Julia, I am come to you with such an appetite for consolation. Lud! child, what's the matter with you? You have been crying! Ah! whatever vexations you may have, I can assure you mine surpass them. You know who Beverley proves to be? Young Absolute! I'll never have him.

Why, is it not provoking? when I thought we were coming to the prettiest distress imaginable, to find myself made a mere Smithfield bargain of at last. There had I projected one of the most sentimental elopements!—so becoming a disguise!—so amiable a ladder of ropes! Conscious moon—four horses—Scotch parson—with such surprise to Mrs. Malaprop—and such paragraphs in the newspapers! Oh, I shall die with disappointment!

Now—sad reverse!—what have I to expect, but, after a deal of flimsy preparation, with a bishop's license, and my aunt's blessing, to go simpering up to the altar; or perhaps be cried three times in a country church, and have an unmannerly fat clerk ask the consent of every butcher in the parish to join John Absolute and Lydia Languish, spinster! Oh, that I should live to hear myself called spinster!

How mortifying, to remember the dear delicious shifts I used to be put to, to gain half a minute's conversation with this fellow! How often have I stole forth, in the coldest night in January, and found him in the garden, stuck like a dripping statue! There would he kneel to me in the snow, and sneeze and cough so pathetically! he shivering with cold and I with apprehension! and while the freezing blast numbed our joints, how warmly would he press me to pity his flame, and glow with mutual ardour! Ah, Julia, that was something like being in love.

SMITHFIELD: the London cattle market.

196.

MRS. CANDOUR RECAPITULATES ALL THE SCANDAL SHE DEPLORES (OC)

(1777) RICHARD BRINSLEY SHERIDAN, *THE SCHOOL FOR SCANDAL*, ACT I, SC. 1

The malice of the members of the cabal in *The School for Scandal* is made evident, with no concession to subtlety, by their names: Lady Sneerwell, Snake, Sir Benjamin Backbite, Crabtree, and Mrs.

Candour, though none is so precisely the standard bearer of their name as is Mrs. Candour. She is and is nothing but the efflorescence of candor, unable to withhold from instant publication the slander she revels in and gleefully deprecates. If dramatic characters are artificial constructs—and they are—Mrs. Candour and the rest of this band are made of single bricks, each splashed with a single color, and the motive and policy each pursues is confined entirely to the nature belonging to their limiting name. In *The School for Scandal*, they form a backdrop of mild grotesquerie to the principal characters—Lord and Lady Teazle, Joseph and Charles Surface, Maria—who beyond their "leading characteristic" take on more persuasive dimensions. But these others are, in other words, throwbacks to the "character" writing that began with Theophrastus and remained a live and revived tradition since the Renaissance, in which a "type" is reductively defined by duplicative instances of behavior, dress, speech, etc. Sheridan's reductive characters of the "scandal" cabal are, theatrically, extraordinarily viable, puppets in lively motion, but they have no other reality but as instances of a noun (their type) and an adjective (their behavioral bent.) Paradoxically, though, comedy, particularly satiric comedy, and even great comedy—as is *The School for Scandal*—thrives on narrowly defined, unidimensional characters, embodiments of quickly graspable and approximately just representations of one moral bent or another. Actors contributing their private personalities, rather than heavily underscoring the single trait of these paperweights, make them seem alive.

Mrs. Candour

My dear Lady Sneerwell, how have you been this century? Mr. Surface, what news do you hear?—though indeed it is no matter, for I think one hears nothing else but scandal.

Ah, Maria! child,—what, is the whole affair off between you and Charles? His extravagance, I presume—the town talks of nothing else. But there is no stopping people's tongues. I own I was hurt to hear it; as indeed I was to learn, from the same quarter, that your guardian, Sir Peter, and Lady Teazle have not agreed lately so well as could be wished. But what's to be done? People will talk—there's no preventing it.—Why, it was but yesterday I was told that Miss Gadabout had eloped with Sir Filigree Flirt.—But, Lord! there's no minding what one hears—though, to be sure, I had this from very good authority. But the world is so censorious, no character escapes.—Lord, now who would have suspected your friend,

Miss Prim, of an indiscretion? Yet such is the ill-nature of people, that they say her uncle stopped her last week, just as she was stepping into the York Diligence with her dancing-master. No foundation in the world, I dare swear; no more, probably, than for the story circulated last month; of Mrs. Festino's affair with Colonel Casino;—though that matter was never rightly cleared up.

To be sure tale-bearers are as bad as the tale-makers—'tis an old observation, and a very true one—but what's to be done, as I said before? how will you prevent people from talking? To-day, Mrs. Clackit assured me Mr. and Mrs. Honeymoon were at last become mere man and wife, like the rest of their acquaintances. She likewise hinted that a certain widow; in the next street, had got rid of her dropsy and recovered her shape in a most surprising manner. And at the same time Miss Tattle, who was by, affirmed that Lord Buffalo had discovered his lady at a house of no extraordinary fame—and that Sir Harry Bouquet and Tom Saunter were to measure swords on a similar provocation. But, Lord, do you think I would report these things! I confess, Mr. Surface, I cannot bear to hear people attacked behind their backs, and when ugly circumstances come out against one's acquaintance I own I always love to think the best.—By the bye, I hope it is not true that your brother is absolutely ruined?—I heard so—but you must tell him to keep up his spirits—everybody almost is in the same way! Lord Spindle, Sir Thomas Splint, Captain Quinze, and Mr. Nickit—all up, I hear, within this week; so, if Charles is undone, he'll find half his acquaintances ruined too—and that, you know, is a consolation.

YORK DILIGENCE: the stage-coach scheduled for York. DROPSY: an illness involving swelling.

197.

MRS. HALLER, IN TORMENTS OF CONSCIENCE, CONFESSES HER SIN (OT)

(1798) BENJAMIN THOMPSON, *THE STRANGER*, ACT III, SC. 2

A translation of Kotzebue's German drama of the most pure and gentle sentimentality, *The Stranger* represents the complete departure of sentimental drama from its earlier alliance with moral punishment. Punishment, the controlling term of earlier bourgeois sentimental plots [as in *The London Merchant*: see, in Men's vols.: "Barnwell Executes a Murder Against His Will" and "Barnwell Suffers Agonies of Remorse...."] is displaced by Forgiveness, in deference to the "heart" psychology so fervently espoused by the eighteenth-century Enlightenment's benevolent morality. The story here, and in plays like it, is of clouds of self-denigration and longings for punishment dispersing, and universal forgiveness covering all. We have, once again, the case of the fallen woman wracked with guilt, and suffering the delusion that the world hates her sin as much as she hates herself. She, the Countess Adelaide Waldbourg, "ran away with a villain," as she confesses, having done so for slight and delusional causes, leaving a husband and children. She is now in the service of the Countess Wintersen, hiding her shame under the assumed name of Mrs. Haller, but stricken with woe and constantly in tears. The Countess, more than curious, eventually drags her story out of her. The Countess's first response to Mrs. Haller's confession is an instant, "Begone!" but taking counsel with herself, she reconsiders, and instructs herself: "Be still awhile, remorseless prejudice, and let the genuine feelings of my soul avow: 'They do not truly honor virtue who can insult the erring heart that would return to sanctuary.'" And here is the salve of forgiveness that will be extended to Mrs. Haller universally—by her rediscovered husband (the play's Stranger), by her children, by the entire cast, by the spectators. The degree to which she deserves forgiveness is determined by the degree to which she refuses to countenance it. Repentance itself earns forgiveness; the punitive side of Christianity in the earlier sentimental plays is wholly replaced by its softer, benevolent face.

MRS. HALLER

(Checking her tears) Spare me! I am a wretch. The sufferings of

three years can give me no claim to your friendship—No, not even to your compassion. Oh! spare me!

(Going) Alas! But a frank reliance on a generous mind is the greatest sacrifice to be offered by true repentance. This sacrifice I will offer. *(Hesitating)* Did you never hear—Pardon me—Did you never hear—Oh! how shocking it is to unmask a deception, which alone has recommended me to your regard! But it must be so.—Madam—Fie, Adelaide! does pride become you?—Did you never hear of the Countess Waldbourg? She plunged an honourable husband into misery. She ran away with a villain.

(Clasping her hands) Do not cast me from you. My conscience never martyrs me so horribly, as when I catch my base thoughts in search of an excuse! No, nothing can palliate my guilt; and the only just consolation left me, is to acquit the man I wronged, and own I erred without a cause of fair complaint.

To attempt to account for my strange infatuation—I cannot bear it. I thought my husband's manner grew colder to me. 'Tis true, I knew, that his expenses, and his confidence in deceitful friends, had embarrassed his means, and clouded his spirits; yet I thought he denied me pleasures and amusements still within our reach. My vanity was mortified! My confidence not courted. The serpent tongue of my seducer promised everything. But never could such arguments avail, till, assisted by forged letters, and the treachery of a servant, whom I most confided in, he fixed my belief that my lord was false, and that all the coldness I complained of was disgust to me, and love for another; all his home retrenchments but the means of satisfying a rival's luxury. Maddened with this conviction (conviction it was, for artifice was most ingenious in its proof), I left my children—father—husband—to follow—a villain.

I did not remain long in my delusion, but long enough to make sufficient penitence impossible. 'Tis true, that in a few weeks the delirium was at an end. Oh, what were my sensations when the mist dispersed before my eyes! I called for my husband, but in vain!—I listened for the prattle of my children, but in vain!

Allow me a moment to compose myself!—*(Exit Countess)* I pause!—Oh! yes—to compose myself! *(Ironically)* She thinks little it is but to gain one solitary moment to vent my soul's remorse. Once the purpose of my unsettled mind was self-destruction; Heaven knows how I have sued for hope and resignation. I did trust my prayers were heard—Oh! spare me further trial! I feel, I feel, my heart and brain can bear no more.

198.

ELVIRA, CONDEMNED TO DEATH, VOWS TO DIE NOBLY, CALLING FOR VENGEANCE AGAINST HER OWN "CORRUPTION" (OT)

(1799) RICHARD BRINSLEY SHERIDAN, *PIZARRO*, ACT IV, SC. 2

The enlightened European literature of the eighteenth century deplored the way that wealth of the eighteenth century was being hoarded. It was uneasy about the slave trade, it decried the "insatiate avarice" that visited barbarities on the "wretched, unoffending" races in America. But it confined its hand-wringing to the style, not the substance, of these undertakings. For instance, in Sheridan's historical melodrama translated from Kotzebue's German *The Spaniards in Peru*, the "barbarian" is Pizarro, who fights against the native Peruvians with a cruelty born of avarice. His "abhorrent lust for gold forsook the duties of humanity." His greed is so abhorrent that the virtuous in his army forsake him: Alonzo, his chief officer, goes over to the enemy, the kindly, family-oriented Peruvians.

Elvira is caught in this tussle between the inhumanity of her lover Pizarro and the virtue of the Peruvians—as well as the virtue of Pizarro's own followers who have deserted him. She, a woman of noble breeding, infatuated with the image of the "brave" Pizarro, has followed him aboard ship to the new world, and trekked over land from one battle to another, only to discover in the course of his dealings with the Peruvians, the range of his crimes and the depth of his cruelty. Her being his wellborn camp follower is reason enough for her uneasiness, but when he captures Alonzo and is on the verge of executing him—a prisoner of war!—Elvira has had enough. He shall "never more receive the pledge of love," and he shall meet, if he can, "an injured woman's fury."

Her fury goes so far as to help Alonzo escape from his imprisonment, and to join in the attempt to assassinate Pizarro. Her betrayal moves him to sentence her to death. But for Elvira, there was no treachery in her act. "Such was the greatness of the cause that urged me, I shall perish glorying in the attempt." The "cause" was upholding universal values of humanity over the barbarous "greed" of the Pizarros. But invasion done with propriety, with honor, with kindly bearing—like the Alonzos do—would be unobjectionable to her, both Christian and noble.

Whatever the logic of her principles, Elvira means them with passion and declares them with high sentence. When the guards attempt to take hold of her, she shrugs them off with an aristocratic gesture—the great Mrs. Siddons played Elvira—and turning toward Pizarro, her former lover and now her abhorrence, she declares her guilt in loving him, the wracking punishments due her for that crime (the obligatory revenge on the self with which every innately noble "fallen woman" redeems her nobility), and the nobility of her final act.

ELVIRA

Touch me not, at the peril of your souls;—I am your prisoner, and will follow you. Didst thou but know the spell-like arts by which this hypocrite first undermined the virtue of a guileless heart! how, even in the pious sanctuary wherein I dwelt, by corruption and by fraud, he practiced upon those in whom I most confided—'till my distemperate fancy led me, step by step, into the abyss of—guilt—

Soldiers—but a moment more—'Tis to applaud your General—It is to tell the astonished world, that, for once, Pizarro's sentence is an act of justice: Yes, rack me with the sharpest tortures that ever agonized the human frame; it will be justice. Yes—bid the minions of thy fury—wrench forth the sinews of those arms that have caressed, and—even have defended thee! Bid them pour burning metal into the bleeding cases of these eyes, that so oft—oh, God!—have hung with love and homage on thy looks—then approach me bound on the abhorred wheel—there glut thy savage eyes with the convulsive spasms of that dishonoured bosom, which was once thy pillow!—Yet, will I bear it all; for it will be justice, all! And when thou shalt bid them tear me to my death, hoping that thy unshrinking ears may at last be feasted with the music of my cries, I will not utter one shriek or groan—but to the last gasp, my body's patience shall deride thy vengeance as my soul defies thy power.

And now, farewell, world!—Farewell, thou condemned of Heaven. *(To Pizarro)* For repentance and remorse, I know will never touch thy heart.—We shall meet again.—Ha! be it thy horror here, to know that we shall meet hereafter! And when thy parting hour approaches—hark! to the knell, whose dreadful beat will strike to thy despairing soul. Then, will vibrate on thy ear the curses of the cloistered saint from whom you stole me. Then, the last shrieks which burst from my mother's breaking heart, as she died, appealing to her God against the seducer of her child! Then the blood-stifled groan of my murdered brother—murdered by thee, fell monster!—seeking atonement for his sister's ruined honour.—I hear them now! To me, the recollection's madness!—At such an hour,—what will it be to thee?

I have spoken—and the last mortal frailty of my heart is past.—And now, with an undaunted spirit, and unshaken firmness, I go to meet my destiny. That I could not *live* nobly, has been Pizarro's act. That I will *die* nobly, shall be my own.

(Exit, guarded)

EIGHTEENTH-CENTURY GERMAN

199.

SARA PLEADS WITH HER ABDUCTOR
FOR THE SAVING RITE OF MARRIAGE (YT)

(1755) Gottfried Ephraim Lessing, *Miss Sara Sampson*,
tr. Ernest Bell, Act I, Sc. 7

Probably the most effective continental example of the influence of
cold, puritanical English morality on the one hand and warm, tearful
English sentimentality on the other is Lessing's *Miss Sara Sampson*.
These influences, with the overlay of a home-grown, Germanic,
strenuously applied, duty-oriented, heaven-watching, instantly punishing, instantly rewarding religiosity, produce the most characteristic mode of fictionalizing of young, virtuous heroines throughout the
eighteenth and nineteenth centuries. In Lessing's play, and in many to
follow, these tendencies combine to produce heroines of an entirely
passive, entirely self-demeaning, entirely self-accusing, and entirely
other-forgiving character. Sara is the ultimate instance of these mar-
tyr-heroines, the absolute of self-denigration, the absolute of willed
helplessness, the absolute of godly virtue and of punishing self-judg-
ment. Astonishingly, her character is almost identical to that of de
Sade's contemptuously drawn portrait of the many-times-abused but
still prayerful Justine, although Sara's total passivity exceeds even
Justine's by degrees.

   Lessing follows the tradition of the abduction-plot in Richardson's
Clarissa Harlowe, in which a virtuous girl is seduced and abducted
with a promise of marriage. Like Clarissa, Sara is genuinely in love
with her Mellefont, is aware of none of his "weaknesses of character,"
and certainly none of his vices. There, similarity ends. No matter
what evidence is staring her in the face, Sara is determined to see no
ill in her lover, and to a degree that might seem to pass all reason,

maintains with stolid faith that a happy outcome awaits her temporarily compromising position.

The happy outcome is of course marriage, promised and promised again by Mellefont, but its fixed date is subject always to unaccountable delays. In a sentimental/puritanical world given to perpetual conscience-smiting, Mellefont himself is not immune, and he, unlike the libertines from whom he derives, is torn by conscience. He cannot give a straight answer to Sara's anxieties because he is still enticed by a diabolical but desirable woman who has borne him a small daughter, Arabell. She, Marwood, stands ready to blackmail Mellefont or to reclaim him, whichever she can manage. Through a series of increasingly suspenseful crises, Mellefont remains of two minds: to return to Marwood and his illegitimate but beloved daughter, or to wed the newly compromised Sara.

In her campaign to win a wedding date from her abductor, Sara is morbidly conscience-smitten that she must urge him at all: such an undertaking suggests she doubts him—a feeling she will not tolerate, since it slanders love. And yet, not knowing, not being certain, puts her in jeopardy not only with the Almighty, but with her father, both of whom, on the face of how matters stand, have reason to abandon her as fallen—a turn of events that causes her unbearable anguish and guilt. Lest he suppose that she wants marriage to bask in the name of wife suggests a selfishness of intent that she shrinks from: let him never acknowledge her openly as wife if he so pleases, but not to have the sacred ceremony betrays her patriarchal gods. And yet to press for it too vigorously betrays her faith in her lover. Between this Scylla and Charybdis, Sara must negotiate.

Sara

Ah, Mellefont! Why is it that we think so differently about this ceremony! Yield a little to the woman's way of thinking! I imagine in it a more direct consent from Heaven. In vain did I try again, only yesterday, in the long tedious evening, to adopt your ideas, and to banish from my breast the doubt which just now—not for the first time, you have deemed the result of my distrust. I struggled with myself; I was clever enough to deafen my understanding; but my heart and my feeling quickly overthrew this toilsome structure of reason. Reproachful voices roused me from my sleep, and my imagination united with them to torment me. What pictures, what dreadful pictures hovered about me! I would willingly believe them to be dreams—

A single act, Mellefont, a single blessing bestowed upon us by a messenger of peace, in the name of the Eternal One, can restore my shattered imagination again. Do you still hesitate to do a few days sooner for love of me, what in any case you mean to do at some future time? Have pity on me, and consider that, although by this you may be freeing me only from torments of the imagination, yet these imagined torments are real torments for her who feels them. Ah! could I but tell you the terrors of the last night half as vividly as I have felt them. Wearied with crying and grieving—my only occupations—I sank down on my bed with half-closed eyes. My nature wished to recover itself a moment, to collect new tears. But hardly asleep yet, I suddenly saw myself on the steepest peak of a terrible rock. You went on before, and I followed with tottering, anxious steps, strengthened now and then by a glance which you threw back upon me. Suddenly I heard behind me a gentle call, which bade me stop. It was my father's voice—I unhappy one, can I forget nothing which is his? Alas if this memory renders him equally cruel service; if he too cannot forget me!—But he has forgotten me. Comfort! cruel comfort for his Sara!—But, listen, Mellefont! In turning round to this well-known voice, my foot slipped; I reeled, and was on the point of falling down the precipice, when just in time, I felt myself held back by one who resembled myself. I was just returning her my passionate thanks, when she drew a dagger from her bosom. "I saved you," she cried, "to ruin you!" She lifted her armed hand—and—! I awoke with the blow. Awake, I still felt all the pain which a mortal stab must give, without the pleasure which it brings—the hope for the end of grief in the end of life.

But do not misinterpret my urgent request. Another woman, after having forfeited her honour by an error like mine, might perhaps only seek to regain a part of it by a legal union. I do not think of that, Mellefont, because I do not wish to know of any other honour in this world than that of loving you. I do not wish to be united to you for the world's sake but for my own. And I will willingly bear the shame of not appearing to be so, when I am united to you. You need not then, if you do not wish, acknowledge me to be your wife, you may call me what you will! I will not bear your name; you shall keep our union as secret as you think good, and may I always be unworthy of it, if I ever harbour the thought of drawing any other advantage from it than the appeasing of my conscience.

200.

MARWOOD URGES MELLEFONT TO REMAIN WITH HIS "SAINT" SARA, THEN RETURN TO HERSELF (OT)

(1755) GOTTFRIED EPHRAIM LESSING, *MISS SARA SAMPSON,*
TR. ERNEST BELL, ACT II, SC. 3

[Continues No. 199, above] Unlike Sara, Marwood understands Mellefont entirely, the motives of conscience and desire that govern such not-altogether-committed lovers of virtue on the one hand, and not-altogether-committed lovers of randy libertinism on the other. Rejected, she no longer fumes and bridles at the outrage of neglect (as did the spurned villainesses in Restoration drama), but, studying the balance of desire and restraint in her prize, calculates within a hair the perfect enticements for both sides of his nature. She reverses precisely the significance of his alternatives: duty is owing not to Sara but to her, Marwood, and her abandoned child (to which his conscience will inevitably respond); his desire is temporarily aroused not by jaded experience but by fresh innocence (of which he will inevitably, and quickly, tire). This, the first engagement in her campaign to win him back, is performed gently, reasonably, not threateningly; but it's only the first of several. She's settled in the hotel where Mellefont has fled with Sara, and engineers interviews with both of them. Subsequently, her threat of blackmail, and her move to criminality, supplant gentle enticement.

MARWOOD

Just listen, my dear Mellefont! I see your position now. Your desires and your taste for this country girl are at present your tyrants. Never mind, one must let them wear themselves out. It is folly to resist them. They are most safely lulled to sleep, and at last even conquered, by giving them free scope. They wear themselves away. Can you accuse me, my fickle friend, of ever having been jealous, when more powerful charms than mine estranged you from me for a time? I never grudged you the change, by which I always won more than I lost. You returned with new ardour, with new passion to my arms, in which with light bonds, and never with heavy fetters I encompassed you. Have I not often even been your confidante though you had nothing to confide but the favours which you stole from me, in order to lavish them on the other. Why should you believe then, that I would now begin to display a capriciousness just when I am ceasing, or, perhaps have already ceased, to be justified in it. If your ardour for the pretty country girl has not yet cooled down, if you are still in the first fever of your love for her; if you cannot yet do without the enjoyment she gives you; who hinders you from devoting yourself to her, as long as you think good? But must you on that account make such rash projects, and purpose to fly from the country with her?

Your new mistress is a girl of fine moral sentiments, I suppose. You men surely cannot know yourselves what you want. At one time you are pleased with the most wanton talk and the most unchaste jests from us, at another time we charm you, when we talk nothing but virtue, and seem to have all the seven sages on our lips. But the worst is, that you get tired of one as much as the other. We may be foolish or reasonable, worldly or spiritual; our efforts to make you constant are lost either way. The turn will come to your beautiful saint soon enough. Shall I give you a little sketch? Just at present you are in the most passionate paroxysm over her. I allow this two or at the most three days more. To this will succeed a tolerably calm love; for this I allow a week. The next week you will only think occasionally of this love. In the third week, you will have to be reminded of it; and when you have got tired of being thus reminded, you will so quickly see yourself reduced to the most utter indifference, that I can hardly allow the whole of a fourth week for this final change. This would be about a month altogether. And this month, Mellefont, I will overlook with the greatest pleasure; but you will allow that I must not lose sight of you. I will not detain you any longer. Go to her again; she might grow suspicious. But I trust that I shall see you again today.

201.

SARA, LONGING TO RECEIVE HER FATHER'S LETTER, REFUSES TO READ IT IF IT CONTAINS HIS FORGIVENESS FOR HER SHAME (YT)

(1755) GOTTFRIED EPHRAIM LESSING, *MISS SARA SAMPSON*,
TR. ERNEST BELL, ACT III, SC. 3

[See No. 199, above] Sara's father, Sir William, and his daughter play the game of Sensibility [see, in Men's vols.: "Bevil Junior, Constrained but Courteous, Counters His Father's Choice..."]—the game of intuiting the feeling of the other, and calculating a response that simultaneously keeps the secret of one's own feeling, spares the other the discomfort of its being found out, and still answers delicately to the need of the other's equally undivulged feeling. His grief over her downfall is immense, but his care lest she feel the weight of that grief and the judgment it implied, is equally vast. His letter to her is calculated to reveal neither grief nor judgment, but—in response to her assumed need—only benign forgiveness. Sara, equally attuned to these strategies, at the sight of the unopened letter, guesses at once what he has done, and adamantly refuses his offer. Why? It would signify that she intuited his pretended feeling, and grossly pretending she believed that to be his real feeling, responded to that rather than the feeling he was, she also intuited, masking. It's a delicate not to say devious operation in which the two indulge, but the failure to outmaneuver the skill of the other could lead—as Sara clearly concludes here—to a moral lapse in sensibility of even greater consequence than the one she has already inflicted on her father's feeling by her current and still unreconstructed sin. As she explains with lawyerly precision to her father's loyal servant, Waitwell, were she to pretend to believe the forgiveness lying in the unopened letter before her, she would have stolen the happiness of her father's forgiveness from him at the expense of his ongoing masked unhappiness—a crime that only the morally gross could conceivably contemplate.

SARA

From whom? From my father? To me? Give it me, Waitwell.

But no! I will not take it before you tell me what it contains. Does he write with love? Forgiveness? If that is so, then keep your cruel letter. It is just this which I fear. To grieve a father such as he, this I have had the courage to do. But to see him forced by this very grief—by his love which I have forfeited, to look with leniency on all the wrong into which an unfortunate passion has led me; this, Waitwell, I could not bear. If his letter contained all the hard and angry words which an exasperated father can utter in such a case, I should read it—with a shudder it is true—but still I should be able to read it. I should be able to produce a shadow of defence against his wrath, to make him by this defence if possible more angry still. My consolation then would be this—that melancholy grief could have no place with violent wrath and that the latter would transform itself finally into bitter contempt. And we grieve no more for one whom we despise.

His yearning for me misleads him, perhaps, to give his consent to everything. But no sooner would this desire be appeased a little, than he would feel ashamed before himself of his weakness. Sullen anger would take possession of him, and he would never be able to look at me without silently accusing me of all that I had dared to exact from him. Yes, if it were in my power to spare him his bitterest grief, when on my account he is laying the greatest restraint upon himself; if at a moment when he would grant me everything I could sacrifice all to him; then it would be quite a different matter. I would take the letter from your hands with pleasure, would admire in it the strength of the fatherly love, and, not to abuse this love, I would throw myself at his feet a repentant and obedient daughter. But can I do that? I shall be obliged to make use of his permission, regardless of the price this permission has cost him. And then, when I feel most happy, it will suddenly occur to me that he only outwardly appears to share my happiness and that inwardly he is sighing—in short, that he has made me happy by the renunciation of his own happiness. And to wish to be happy in this way,—do you expect that of me, Waitwell?

So take your letter back! If my father must be unhappy through me, I will myself remain unhappy also. To be quite alone in unhappiness is that for which I now pray Heaven every hour, but to be quite alone in my happiness—of that I will not hear.

202.

EMILIA, APPROACHED BY THE PRINCE, IS OVERCOME WITH SHAME (YT)

(1772) GOTTFRIED EPHRAIM LESSING, *EMILIA GALOTTI*,
TR. LEON KATZ, ACT II, SC. 6

Emilia, on the day of her wedding to the honorable Count Appiani, is permitted—through the carelessness of her mother—to attend church alone to give thanks for the much desired blessing to come. The Prince of this small principality, however, a monarch obligated to observe no restraint within that domain, has seen her and seen her picture, and having recently divested himself of a former mistress, is inflamed with the possibility of investing Emilia. He follows her to church, and—as Emilia reports in this passage—attempts in whispers to move her feeling. She is overcome with shame, and dares not respond one way or the other (to encourage him by a word or look would be in itself a downfall; to make the slightest sign of rejection would subject her to instant scandal in the eyes of passersby). She moves, in a daze, away from the church and arrives home—in a state of such terror as to imagine the Prince is still following her inside her own home.

What is chiefly notable in Emilia's terrified response to the incident at church is the conditions of constraint under which she lives. In the seventeenth century, it was not unusual in both comedy and tragedy for young girls to be imprisoned in their own homes or in convents to maintain their virtue until marriage; but it was not characteristic for them to enjoy it. Emilia, in the puritanical bourgeois world of the eighteenth-century Germany of petty principalities, is represented as happy in cage and terrified in open air.

The determinants of virtue and the limitations surrounding its safekeeping have, by the mid-century, ratcheted down so far that the range of either physical or imaginative motion has reached a stage of near-immobility. The places to tread: home and church; the imaginative terrain to explore: bible and prayer; the range of volition: unqualified submission, are what are left of her parameters. The play itself is a cautionary tale warning of the widening of those limits by a hair: her foray into church alone and without chaperone leads to the Prince's abduction, the assassination of her fiance, and eventually her father's and her own hand in her suicide to prevent her violation.

EMILIA

> *(Rushing in, much alarmed)*
> God be praised! I'm safe now.—Has he followed me here?

> *(Throwing back her veil and espying
> her mother)*
> Has he, mother?—No, thank Heaven. What have I had to listen to?—And where have I been forced to hear it? But what are churches and altars to vicious men like him?—Oh, mother!

> *(Throws herself into Claudia's arms)*
> Never should my devotion have been more fervent and sincere than on this day. But never was it less than it ought to have been. I had just fallen to my knees, further from the altar than usual—for I arrived too late. I had just begun to raise my thoughts towards Heaven—when someone placed himself behind me—so close behind me! I could neither move forwards nor aside, however much I desired to, afraid that the devotion of my neighbour might interrupt my prayers. Devotion was the worst thing I suspected. But it was not long before I heard a deep sigh close to my ear, and then heard—not the name of a saint—no—the name—do not be angry, mother—the name of your daughter.—My own name! Oh, if only a peal of thunder had at that moment made me deaf to the rest. The voice spoke of beauty and love—and complained that this day, the day of my wedding, which was to crown my happiness, sealed his misery for ever. He begged me—all this I was obliged to hear, but I did not look round. I tried to seem as if I was not listening. What more could I do? Nothing but pray that my guardian angel would strike me with deafness— even with eternal deafness. This was my prayer—the only prayer which I could utter. At length it was time to rise; the service came to an end. I trembled at the idea of being obliged to turn round—trembled at the idea of beholding the man whose impiety had so much shocked me—and when I turned—when I beheld him I thought I should have sunk into the earth—it was—Himself! The Prince.

After the glance by which I recognized him, I had not courage to cast a second. I fled. The Prince followed. I did not know it until I had reached the porch, where I felt my hand seized—by him. Shame compelled me to stop; as an effort to free myself would have attracted the attention of every one who was passing. This was the only reflection of which I was capable, or which I at present remember. He spoke, and I replied—but what he said, or what I replied, I don't know. At present I remember nothing more. My senses had left me.—I cannot remember how I got away from him, and escaped from the porch. I found myself in the street—I heard his steps behind me—I heard him follow me into the house, and pursue me up the stairs—No. He dared not follow me so far. That was only my fancy.—In my terror, I imagined—What a silly, timid thing I am! I must be calm now. I must be calm, mother.— Oh, my terror cannot but appear ridiculous.

203.

THE COUNTESS ORSINA, NO LONGER IN THE PRINCE'S GRACES, DEMANDS TO SEE HIM (OT)

(1772) GOTTFRIED EPHRAIM LESSING, *EMILIA GALOTTI*, TR. ERNEST BELL, ACT IV, SC. 3

[See Nos. 200 and 202, above] The Countess Orsina, desperate for an audience with the Prince Gonzaga who has abandoned her, hears but disregards the sounds of distress coming from the inner rooms of the palace. While Marinelli, the Prince's chamberlain and henchman, is resisting the Countess's determination to confront the Prince, the sounds of distress issuing from the inner rooms are Emilia's, whom the Prince has abducted. To the Countess, neither the fact nor the meaning of those sounds matters much; she's inured to the underside of court and civic life, and takes for granted the prerogatives of power in the little principalities that dot the German (disguised by Lessing as Italian) landscape, each a world within itself of despotic rule.

The Countess is altogether too familiar with the sexual politics at court not to know that railing and fuming are hopeless strategies for recovering a lover's interest. The alternative is to outface the facts, and to pretend that a temporary lapse of courtesy is responsible for the servants' momentary neglect. But the "facts" soon speak with jarring contempt: the Prince has not even bothered to read her letter. For an instant, she's enraged. But quickly, she recovers sufficient poise to deal openly with the plain fact: she's no longer loved. And in the interest of successfully recovering her poise, she quickly reverses in her fantasy her psychological posture vis-a-vis Marinelli: he to whom she was in effect pleading becomes the "lackey" with whom she deigns to share her "philosophic" speculation on the notions of "nothing" and "contempt" and "indifference." And in a single arc of feeling, she rises to a higher posture of confident superiority which in the very act of formulation turns into its opposite: a demand which is indistinguishable from a plea.

ORSINA

> *(Without perceiving Marinelli)*
> What does this mean? No one comes to greet me, but a shameless servant, who endeavours to obstruct my entrance. Surely I am at Dosalo, where, on former occasions, an army of attendants rushed to receive me—where love and ecstasy awaited me. Yes. The place is the same, but—Ha! you here, Marinelli? I am glad the Prince has brought you with him. Yet, no. My business with his Highness must be transacted only with himself. Where is he?
>
> How you stand staring, Marquis! What surprises you? Where is he? He is certainly in the chamber from where I heard sighs and sobs as I was passing. I wished to enter, but the impertinent servant would not let me pass. I heard a woman screaming. What does that mean, Marinelli? Tell me—if I am indeed your "dearest Countess"—tell me.
>
> But—no, it isn't proper that I should waste my time in idle conversation with you in the ante-chamber, when the Prince is waiting for me in the salon. But the Prince cannot speak, you say? Does not wish to speak? And nevertheless is here? He is here in answer to my letter. Which he did receive, you say— but did not read. *(Violently)* Not read! *(Less violently)* Not read it! *(Sorrowfully, and wiping away a tear)* Not even read it!
>
> Contempt! Contempt! To me! *(In a milder tone)* It is true that

he no longer loves me. That is certain. And in the place of love something else has filled his soul. That is natural. But why should it be contempt? Indifference would have been enough. Indifference, yes, in the place of love!—That means, nothing in the place of something. For learn, you mimicking court-parrot, learn from a woman, that indifference is only an empty word, a mere sound which means nothing. The mind can only be indifferent to objects about which it does not think, to things which have no existence for it. Can only be indifferent for a thing that is, for it, nothing—in other words: not indifferent. Is that logic beyond you, man?

True, yes, I am a philosopher. And that, you lackey, is such a shame! If I've shown it often, it's no wonder the Prince despises me. How can a man love a creature who, in spite of him, can *think*? A woman who thinks is as silly as a man who paints his face. She ought to laugh—do nothing but laugh, so that the mighty lords of creation may be kept in good humour—And do you know what makes me laugh now, Marinelli? Why, the accidental circumstance that I should have written to the Prince that I would come here—that he should not have read my letter, and that nevertheless I've come. Ha! ha! ha! It's an odd accident, very pleasant, very amusing. Could it be an accident that the Prince, who little thought that he would see me here, *must* see me?—Accident! Believe me, Marinelli, the word accident is blasphemy. Nothing under the sun is accidental, and least of all this, of which the purpose is so evident.—Almighty and all-bounteous Providence, pardon me that I joined this poor weak sinner in giving the name of accident to what so plainly is Thy work—yes, Thy immediate work.

Oh, my head, my head!—*(Puts her hand to her forehead)*—See to it that I speak to the Prince immediately, or I shall soon have no strength to speak to him. You see, Marinelli, that I must speak to him—that I am resolved to speak to him.

(The Prince advances)

Ha! there he is.

204.

LADY MILFORD DEPLORES HER YIELDING TO HER SOVEREIGN, BUT AS SHE INSISTS, WITHOUT LOVE (OT)

(1783) FRIEDRICH SCHILLER, *INTRIGUE AND LOVE*, TR. CHARLES E. PASSAGE, ACT II, SC. 1

The tyrannical Duke of a small European principality is on the verge of marriage to a new Duchess, and is obliged to remove his mistress, the Lady Milford, "for form's sake." To make the illusion that she is gone more complete, she will marry; he has already selected the groom. What the Duke and his court intriguers—his President, his Chamberlain—are not aware of is that the Lady Milford has outfoxed them all, and engineered the entire ruse out of love for the man whose choice they presumed was theirs.

Lady Milford, in this passage, reveals to her maidservant Sophie the painful life she has been enduring of luxury and deceit as the Duke's mistress. It is true and it is not true. Her motives and her acts are sifted carefully through the rest of the drama: an English lady reduced to near-starvation, she succumbed quickly to the Duke's arrangements for a mistress at the cost of her public reputation—she is spoken of familiarly out of hearing as the Duke's whore. But her innate allegiance to the values of an English gentlewoman—Schiller's reading casts its glow—prompts her secretly to aid the victims of the Duke's rule, and though spared the poverty she had fallen into, and basking in the power of her position, she is in fact disturbed by both the anomaly and incidentally the boredom of her court life. The longing she expresses at the end of this passage for a love that transcends the life she is living is in fact so powerful a longing that it serves, after trials of jealousy, disappointment, and attendant agonies, to motivate her surrender of the evils of that life altogether. She is, in effect, a rethinking of the role of the "fallen woman" in the play from which *Intrigue and Love* is derived: the English bourgeois tragedy *The London Merchant* [see Nos. 187 and 188]. In that play, her counterpart, Millwood, under the virulent Puritanism that attends that tragedy's sentimentality, demonstrates to the bitter end the unreconstructed soul of evil. In the spirit of the later eighteenth-century Enlightenment, the fallen are more and more into the habit of winning dramatic redemption by rediscovering their "real" selves, a habit in drama that persists.

Lady Milford is nervously awaiting a visit from the courtier, President von Walter, and to calm her, her maid Sophie suggests she gather in a set of courtiers to her home for talk, for cards, for anything to distract her. But Lady Milford is more horrified at the thought of spending an evening with the robotic courtiers than at the thought of an evening of nervous anxiety or even solitary boredom.

LADY MILFORD

(Throwing herself down on the sofa) Oh please, spare me! I'll give you a diamond for every hour that I can get them off my neck. Am I to paper my rooms with these people? ... They are wretched, sorry persons who are horrified if a warm and heartfelt word escapes me, who stand with mouths and noses wide open as if they saw a ghost ... slaves of a single marionette-string, which I control more easily than my crochet-work. ... What am I to do with people whose souls work just like their watches? Can I find pleasure in asking them anything when I know in advance what they will answer? Or in exchanging words with them when they do not have the heart to be of a different opinion from me? ... Away with them! It is vexing to ride a steed that won't even take the bit into his teeth.

You say people envy me. Poor thing! They should pity me, rather. Of all those who drink at the breasts of Majesty, the favorite comes off worst, because she alone sees the great and wealthy man in beggar's posture... It is true, he can, with the talisman of his greatness, summon up every desire of my heart, like a fairy palace, out of the ground. ... He can set the essence of two Indias upon a table ... evoke paradises out of wildernesses ... make the springs of his country leap in proud arches toward the sky, or let his subjects' marrow go up in the puff of a piece of fireworks ... But can he also command his *heart* to beat *greatly and ardently* against a *great and ardent heart*? Can he wring his starving brain to a single beautiful emotion? . . . My heart is famished amid all this fullness of the senses, and what good to me are a thousand better feelings when all I can do is check upsurges of passion?

It is true, dear Sophie . . . I sold my honor to the sovereign; but my heart I have kept free . . . a heart, good friend, which is still perhaps worthy of a man . . . over which the poisoned wind of the court has passed only like a breath upon a mirror. . . Believe me, my dear, I would long since have asserted it against this sorry sovereign if I could but prevail upon my ambition to yield my rank to a lady of the court.

Sophie *(significantly, as she lets her hand fall upon Sophie's shoulder)* we women can choose only between *ruling* and *serving*, but the highest bliss of *power* is still but a wretched makeshift if we are denied the *greater* bliss of being slaves to a man we love.

Isn't it obvious by this childish wielding of the *scepter* that we are fit only for *leading-strings*? Have you not seen by my moody fickleness... by these wild pleasures of mine, that they were meant only to drown out still wilder desires in my bosom? Satisfy these! Give me the man I am now thinking of... whom I worship... whom I must *possess*, Sophie, or die. *(Melting)* Let me hear it from his mouth, that tears of love gleam more beautifully in our eyes than jewels in our hair, *(Ardently)* and I'll throw this sovereign's heart and his princedom at his feet, I'll flee with this man, flee to the remotest wilderness in the world.

You turn pale?... Have I perhaps said too much?... Hear still more... hear everything... The union with the Major... you and the world are under the illusion that it is a *court intrigue*... Sophie... do not blush... do not be ashamed of me... it is the work... *of my love.* They let themselves be talked into things, Sophie... the weak sovereign... the cunning courtier Walter... the preposterous Chamberlain... Each one of them will swear that this marriage is the most infallible means of rescuing me for the Duke and knitting the bond between us all the more securely.... Yes! Of undoing it forever! Of breaking that shameful chain forever!... Liars belied! Outwitted by a weak woman!... You yourselves are now bringing me my beloved. That was precisely what I wanted... Once I have him... I have him... Oh then *forever* Good Night, hateful grandeur.

205.

ELIZABETH, IN CONFRONTATION WITH MARY STUART, MOVES FROM ANGER TO SNEERING CONTEMPT (OT)

(1800) FRIEDRICH SCHILLER, *MARY STUART*,
TR. CHARLES E. PASSAGE, ACT III, SC. 4

"I'm asking for an important favor," Mary of Scotland petitions Paulet, her keeper in Fotheringhay Castle, where she is being held as Elizabeth's prisoner. "An audience with her whom I have never seen.... Elizabeth is my blood, my rank, My sex. To her, a woman and a queen, To her, my sister, I can bare my heart." The meeting between the two women, when it is at last and with much maneuvering accomplished, is generally regarded as one of the greatest confrontation scenes in Western drama. Its power derives from the extraordinary stature of the two women, both inflexible, both harboring old hatreds and suspicions against the other, both sullenly meeting presumably to negotiate a peace, and quickly running headlong into the iron obstacle of the other's revulsion. Their reach for harmony corrodes finally into a battle of deadly insult, in which, oddly, the stature of both women enlarges rather than diminishes, as in each there emerges more and more powerfully the enormity of her pride.

Historically, the imprisonment of Mary lasted for nineteen years. Her claim to the English throne, in her Catholic view and that of her supporters, superseded Elizabeth's, but Elizabeth, as the monarch of a newly Protestant England, could not countenance such a threat. A long history of conspiracies to free Mary from her captivity as well as to assassinate Elizabeth forced the issue, and Elizabeth, long wavering, at last signed a death warrant.

In Schiller's drama, the meeting between the two women occurs after Mary has been—illegally—condemned to death for treason by an English court; but their verdict has no effect until Elizabeth concurs. While their judgment waits for her signature, considerable maneuvering by followers of both queens accomplish their meeting. Mary labors to control her revulsion toward Elizabeth in order to negotiate successfully for her freedom. It is a labor lost almost from the start, since Elizabeth from the beginning is prepared to catalogue the sins Mary and her followers have committed against Elizabeth's "profoundly outraged Queenship," and is moved finally to counter Mary's accusation of her own illegitimacy with recollections not only of the Catholic conspiracies in which Mary colluded, but her immorality and collusion in murder.

(Mary collects herself and starts to walk towards Elizabeth, then stops half way with a shudder; her gestures express the most vehement struggle.)

ELIZABETH

What's this, my Lords?
Who was it then that told me of a woman
In deep humility? I find a proud one
No wise subdued by adverse fortune.

(Stepping back)
Lady Mary, you are in your place!
And thankfully I praise the favor of
My God, who did not will that I should lie
At your feet as you now lie here at mine.

(Coldly and severely)
What do you have to tell me, Lady Stuart?
You wished to speak to me. I disregard
My Queenship, my profoundly outraged Queenship,
So I may do my duty as a sister.
I grant the solace of beholding me.
My generous impulse leads me on, and I
Expose myself to righteous censure by
Such low descending—for, as you
Well know, you did attempt to have me murdered.
My lucky star protected me from putting
The adder in my bosom.—You should not
Accuse the fates, but rather your black heart,
The wild ambition of your family.
Between us nothing hostile had occurred.
And then your uncle, that ambition-crazed
Proud priest that stretches out his impious hand
To seize all crowns, threw down his challenge to me,
Befooled you till you took my coat-of-arms,
Till you assumed my royal title, till
You entered with me into battle to
The death—Whom did he not enlist against me?

The tongues of priests, the swords of nations, and
The frightful weapons of religious frenzy;
Here in the peaceful seat of my own kingdom
He blew the flames of revolution up—
But God is with me, and that haughty priest
Has not maintained the field—The blow was aimed
At my head, but it is your head that falls!
Your uncle set
The model for all monarchs of this world
Of *how* to make peace with one's enemies.
The Saint Bartholomew shall be my school!
What is blood-kinship, or the law of nations,
To me? The Church absolves all bonds of duty
And blesses breach of faith and regicide;
I practice only what your own priests teach.
What pledge would guarantee you for me if
I were so generously to set you free?
What lock would I put on your loyalty
Without Saint Peter's key unlocking it?
The only safety lies with force, for with
The breed of serpents can be no alliance.
Out yonder, Lady Stuart is your circle
Of friends, your home is with the Papacy,
Your brother is the monk—Proclaim you as
My heir! A treacherous, deceiving snare!
So that you might seduce my people in
My lifetime, so that like a sly Armida
You might entice the young men of my kingdom
By cunning to your nets for paramours—
So everyone could turn to the newly rising sun.
Do you admit at last that you are beaten?
Are your plots done? No other murderer
Is on his way? Will no adventurer
Attempt his sorry chivalry for you?
—Yes, Lady Mary, all is over. You
Will tempt no more. The world has other cares.
No one is anxious to be your fourth husband,
Because you kill your suitors as you kill
Your husbands!

> (Looks at her with a long look of proud
> contempt)

So these, my Lord of Lester, are the charms
Which no man with impunity has seen,
With which no other woman dares to vie!

Indeed! *This* fame was cheap to come by: it
Costs nothing to become the world-wide beauty
But to have all the world hold one in common!

saint bartholomew: the St. Bartholomew's Day Catholic massacre in 1572 of
Protestants in France. st. peter's key: the Papacy.

206.

MARY STUART, CONFRONTING ELIZABETH'S CONTEMPT, IS MOVED TO RAGE (OT)

(1800) Friedrich Schiller, *Mary Stuart*, tr. Charles E. Passage,
Act III, Sc. 4

[See No. 205, above]

Mary

Be it so! I shall submit even to this.
Hence, impotent pride of the noble soul!
I shall forget now who I am and what
I have endured; I shall bow down before her
Who thrust me down to this ignominy.

> *(She turns toward the Queen.)*
Heaven has decided for you, Sister!
Crowned with triumph is your happy brow,
And I adore the deity that raised
You up.

> *(She kneels before her.)*
Be generous in turn, my Sister!
Let me not lie here in ignominy.
Stretch forth your hand, your royal right hand give
Me now, to raise me up from my deep fall!
Think of the change that comes to all things human!
Gods do exist who punish arrogance!
Revere them, dread them, they are terrible,
And they have cast me down before your feet

For the sake of these stranger witnesses,
Respect yourself in me! Do not dishonor
Or put to shame the Tudor blood that flows
In my veins as in yours—O God in Heaven!
Do not stand there so inaccessible
And rugged, like a cliff that shipwrecked men
Vainly strive and struggle to attain.
My life, my destiny, my all, now hangs
Upon the power of my words and tears.
Release my heart so that I may touch yours!
When you look at me with that icy glance,
My heart shrinks shuddering and closes shut,
The stream of tears is stopped, and frigid horror
Chokes my words of entreaty in my bosom.

Where shall I start, how shall I prudently
Contrive my words so that they may have their
Effect upon your heart, yet not offend it!
O God, lend power to my speech and take
From it all thorns that could cause any wounds!
I cannot any way plead for myself without
Accusing you, and that I do not want.
—You have dealt with me in a way that is
Not proper, for I am, like you, a Queen,
And you have held me as a prisoner.
I came to you a suppliant, and you,
Scorning in me the sacred rights of nations
And sacred laws of hospitality,
Had me shut up in prison walls; my friends
And servants were most cruelly removed;
I was myself left in unseemly hardship;
I was called up to an outrageous court—
No more of that! Oblivion shall forever
Enshroud the cruel things I have endured.
—See! I shall term those things of fate's contriving,
You are not guilty, nor am *I* to blame.
An evil spirit rose from the abyss
To kindle hot the hatred in our hearts
That had already split our tender childhood.
It grew with us, and wicked people fanned
The wretched flame and blew their breath upon it;
Insane fanatics armed with sword and dagger
Officious hands that had no right to meddle—
For this is the accursed fate of rulers,
That once they are at odds, they rend the world

And set at large the Furies of all discord.
You always looked upon me only as
An enemy and stranger. If you had
Proclaimed me as your heir, as was my due,
Then gratitude and love would have retained
A loyal friend and relative in me.
But—Rule in peace!
All claims upon this kingdom I renounce.
Alas, my spirit's pinions have been lamed,
I am no longer lured by greatness.—You
Have gained your end. I now am but the shadow
Of Mary. Prison's shame has broken my
Proud spirit.—You have done your uttermost
To me, you have destroyed me in my bloom!
—Now, Sister, make an end! Pronounce those words
Which you have come here to pronounce. For never
Will I believe that you have come here to
Make cruel mockery of me as victim.
Pronounce those words! Say to me: "Mary, you
Are free! My power you have felt, but now
You shall revere my generosity."
Say that, and from your hand I shall accept
My life, my freedom, as a gift.—One word,
And all will be as if it never happened.
I wait. O let me not await too long!
And woe to you if you do not close with
Those words! For if you do not leave me now
With blessing, grandly, like a goddess,—Sister!
Not for this whole rich island, not for all
The countries that the sea surrounds, would I
Stand here before you as you stand with me!
O God! God! Give me self-control!
I erred, but in a human, youthful way.
I was seduced by power. I did not
Conceal or make a secret of it. With
A royal candor I disdained false seeming.
The world has known the worst of me, and I
Can say that I am better than my name.
But woe to you if from your deeds they once
Rip off the cloak of honor which you use
To hide the wild heat of your secret lusts.
It was not chastity your mother left you;
We all know what the virtue was for which
Anne Boleyn climbed the scaffold to the block.
Self-control! I have

Endured all that a mortal can endure.
Hence and be gone, lamb-hearted resignation!
Fly up to Heaven, patient tolerance!
Burst from your bonds at last, and from your cavern
Come forth, you long-suppressed resentment now!
And you who gave the angered basilisk
His murderous glance, lay now upon my tongue
The poisoned dart—
A bastard has profaned the throne of England,
The noble-hearted British people has
Been cheated by a crafty, cheap imposter.
—If right prevailed, you would be lying in
The dust before me for *I* am your King.

(Elizabeth swiftly leaves.)

TUDOR BLOOD: Elizabeth's mother, Anne Boleyn, the second wife of Henry VIII, was Protestant. Mary of Scotland was the granddaughter of Henry's sister Margaret, and daughter of the French Catholic Mary of Guise. **PINIONS**: feathers, wings. **ANNE BOLEYN**: Since Elizabeth's mother, Anne Boleyn, was never bound in Catholic marriage to Henry VIII, she is therefore called "whore" by Mary; Anne Boleyn was beheaded by Henry when she failed to bear him a male child. **THE FABULOUS REPTILE BASILISK**: (serpent, lizard or dragon) was said by ancients to kill by its breath or look.

NINETEENTH-CENTURY FRENCH TRAGEDY

207.

MARGARET OF BURGUNDY VISITS HER ENTRAPPED, CHAINED ENEMY, AND GLOATS (OT)

(1832) ALEXANDRE DUMAS PÈRE, *THE TOWER OF NESLE,*
TR. ADAM L. GOWANS, TABLEAU VI, SC. 4–5

The skill, the manipulation of motive against motive, secret weapon against secret weapon, character against character, truth against lie, so controls the changes of fortune from moment to moment in the Romantic/melodramatic/well-made-play plots of Dumas *pere* that they sustain the breathless, suspenseful attention of the spectator with nothing sacrificed in their art but credibility. Nothing, to be sure, is believable, but everything is surprising, or at least engaging, or at most positively thrilling.

Margaret of Burgundy, Queen of France, is confronted by an enemy with an assumed name, Buridan, who has given a tablet for safe-keeping into the hands of the Queen's lover, Gaultier, which spells her ruin. Sad mistake. She easily manages to wrest the incriminating document from Gaultier, and its absence spells the ruin of Buridan. So much so that he is at the moment in the bottommost dungeon of the Grand Chatelet, bound hand and foot, to be tried the next morning. But the fate the vengeful, pleased Queen has in store for him is not so happy: Lest he have the opportunity in the course of the trial to speak out, he will be reported to have strangled himself in his cell this very night, and so have no such opportunity.

Not to worry. Another secret in his repertoire recited to the Queen during their interview, and she will be once again cowed and in his power. The cycle is to be repeated one more time before the denouement, in which both Queen and Buridan, each equally guilty of a terrible crime in which both collaborated in the past (their ultimate secret), are subjected to a hideously ironic justice.

But on the night before the trial, Buridan, knowing the Queen from the past as an angel in beauty, a demon in act, is certain she will want to see him again this night "if only to taunt me with my death." She comes indeed, cautiously, with her secret henchman Orsini for protection, to witness with angry pleasure her enemy lying altogether helpless, and altogether without hope. And to taunt him as well with the serious lapse in judgment that is to cost him his life: that he trusted a lover's pledged word as a man of honor to count for more than his devotion to his love. And so it will be possible for her to pass on to Buridan the murder of the young nobleman that she herself committed. So thoroughly is he doomed that with special relief she takes particular pleasure in sealing his fate: "No, no, you cannot escape me, and I go."

She's of course mistaken. He calls her back, utters another secret from the past that makes her blanch, and untie his bonds, promise to give him half the power of her rule, and herself lead him out of the dungeon.

MARGUERITE

(*Entering by a secret door, holding a lamp in her hand; to Orsini*)
Is he bound so that I can approach him without fear? Then wait for me there, Orsini; and at the slightest cry come to my assistance.

(*Exit Orsini*)
(*Approaching*) Did you not expect to see some one again before you died? No, you counted on my coming. But without hope, did you not? You know me well enough to know that, after having reduced me to fear, brought me to entreaties, neither fear nor entreaties can soften my heart. Oh! your measures were well taken, Buridan; only, you had forgotten that when love, ungovernable love enters a man's heart, it eats away all other feelings there, it lives there at the expense of his honour, of his good faith, of his pledged word; and you confided to the word, the good faith, the honour of a man in love, in love with me, the proof, the only proof you had against me! See, there it is, the precious leaf from your tablets, there it is! *I die assassinated by the hand of Marguerite of Burgundy. Philippe d'Aulnay.* Last adieu of brother to brother,

given by that brother to me. Why, look, look!

(Taking the lamp)
Perish, with this last flame, your last hope!... Am I free now, Buridan? Can I do with you what I choose? Are you not arrested as the murderer of Philippe d'Aulnay? What is done with murderers?

A tribunal? Why, you are mad! Are men tried who carry such secrets within them? There are poisons so strong that they break the glass that holds them. Your secret is one of those poisons. Buridan, when a man like you is arrested, he is bound as you are bound, he is placed in a dungeon like this one. If it is not desired to destroy his soul as well as his body, at midnight a priest and a hangman are brought into his prison: the priest begins. There is, in that prison, an iron ring like this one, walls as silent and as thick as these, walls that deaden cries, that stifle sobs, that absorb the death-agony. The priest goes out first, the hangman next; then, next morning, when the warden enters the prison, he mounts again in alarm, and tells that the criminal, whose hands had imprudently been left free, has strangled himself, a proof that he was guilty.

And now your pride revolts at my victory; you would like to make me believe that you have some means of escaping me to torment my sleep or my pleasures; but no, no, your smile does not deceive me; the damned laugh also, that it may be thought they have no pain. No, you cannot escape me, can you? It is impossible, you are securely tied, these walls are very thick, these doors very solid; no, no, you cannot escape me, and I go... Adieu, Buridan.

208.

MARY TUDOR PRETENDS TO BELIEVE THE LIES OF HER LOVER FABIANI (ot)

(1833) Victor Hugo, *Mary Tudor*, tr. Anon., Act II, Sc. 1

Even in translation, there is a sheer music sounding in Hugo's Queen Mary Tudor's tirades. There's an almost incantatory flow of cuttingly ironic, nasty innuendo in this passage, and in the later scene's violently forthright invective [in No. 209, below], out of the mouth of a powerful, imperious queen who brooks neither contradiction nor evasion nor gratuitous flattery. Her Italian lover Fabiani is guilty of the deadliest of miscalculations: He's been supposing that he can enjoy the bed of his royal mistress and at the same time indulge in other affairs. Mary, with the aid of spies, easily uncovers his lies and covert betrayals, and most of all his villainous treatment of an Englishwoman, Lady Jane. She first confronts him with barely concealed scorn that sounds to the insensitive ear of Fabiani like flattery, and then stages a large scene of revelation with Lady Jane, who is a present and incontrovertible contradiction of all Fabiani's feeble excuses [in No. 209, below]. Mary's wrath rises to the height of verbal violence, and the venting of her rage not satisfied, she transcends the merely verbal and indulges in physical violence before condemning the hapless culprit to the final ignominy of arrest and certain execution.

So much for the exploitation, in fanciful historical romantic melodrama, of the "Bloody Mary" of popular misconception, portrayed on the narrow canvas of love affairs and personal intrigues rather than on the larger canvas of Schiller's *Mary Stuart*, in which politics joins with psychology to enlarge the scale of dramatic conflict.

Queen

Fabiani, you have a young and beautiful head! You love me, do you not? You love only me? Say it to me again, just like that, with the same eyes! Alas we poor women, we never know just what is passing in a man's heart. We have to trust your eyes; and the handsomest eyes, Fabiani, are often the most false. But yours, my lord, are so full of loyalty, so full of candour, so full of good faith, they could not deceive, those eyes, could they? Yes, my beautiful page, your glances are artless and sincere. Oh, it would be shameful to use such heavenly eyes to betray with! Your eyes are the eyes either of a devil or an angel!

Listen to me, Fabiani. I love you, too. But you are young; there are many beautiful women who smile tenderly on you,—I know it. People get tired of queens as well as of other women.—Don't interrupt me!—If you ever fall in love with another woman, I want you to tell me about it.—Don't interrupt me, dear!—I may forgive you, if you tell me about it. You don't know how much I love you. I don't know myself. It is true, there are moments when I would rather see you dead than happy with another; but there are also moments when I would rather have you happy. Indeed, I don't know why they try to make me out such a wicked woman! Oh, I am jealous sometimes! I imagine,—where is the woman who does not think of these things?—sometimes I imagine that you are false to me. I would like to be invisible, so that I might follow you, and always know what you are doing, what you are saying, where you are! In fairy stories they tell about a ring which makes one invisible; I would give my crown to have such a ring as that. I keep thinking that you go to see the beautiful women in the city. Oh, you must not deceive me, indeed, you must not!

Ah, my lord, how young you are! What beautiful black hair, what a graceful head you have! Come back to me in an hour. Good bye!

> (As soon as he is gone, the Queen rises
> hastily, goes to a concealed door, opens
> it, and ushers in Simon Renard.)

Come in, Sir Bailiff! Well, did you stay there? Did you hear him? Oh, of all men on earth he is the most false, the most deceitful!

You are sure that he goes to this woman at night? You have seen him? It is infamous! Isn't this, sir, a sufficient crime for his execution?

209.

MARY TUDOR EXPOSES FABIANI, REVILES HIM, AND SENDS HIM TO THE TOWER (OT)

(1833) Victor Hugo, *Mary Tudor*, tr. Anon., Act II, Sc. 7

[See No. 208, above]

QUEEN

Yes, my lord! Truly, I have thought of no one but you. So
much so, that I have tried to plan a pleasant surprise for your
return. A meeting which will give you pleasure! Guess! Can't
you guess? Turn around!

(He turns and sees Jane on the threshold
of the little door, which is half open.)
(With the same smile) My lord, do you know this young
woman? You do not?

(Rising and striking him in the face
with her glove)
Ah, you are a coward! You betray one and disown the other!
You don't even know who she is! Do you want me to tell you?
This woman is Jane Talbot, daughter of John Talbot, the good
Catholic lord who perished on the scaffold for my mother.
This woman is Jane Talbot, my cousin: Jane Talbot, Countess
of Shrewsbury, Countess of Wexford, Countess of Waterford,
peeress of England. That is who she is, this woman! Lord
Paget, you are commissioner of the private seal; you will
remember our words. The Queen of England solemnly
recognizes this woman here present, as Jane, daughter and sole
heiress of the last Earl of Waterford. *(Showing the papers)* Here
are the titles and the proofs, which you will have sealed with
the great seal. It is our will.

(To Fabiani.) Yes, Countess of Waterford, and it is proved! And
you will give back her estates, you wretched man! Ah, you
don't know this woman? You don't know who she is? Well, I
am telling you! It is Jane Talbot. Shall I tell you more yet?

(Looking him in the face, in a low voice, between her teeth)
Coward, she is your mistress! That is what she is! Now, this is
what you are! You are a man without soul, a man without
heart, a man without brains. You are a liar and a villain! You
are—By my faith, gentlemen, you need not draw away. I am
quite willing you should hear what I have to say to this man. I
am not lowering my voice, it seems to me! Fabiano, you are a
wretch; a traitor to me, a coward to her; a lying lackey, the
most vile, the lowest of all men. Yet it is true, I made you Earl
of Clanbrotsil, Baron of Dinasmondy and what more? Baron
of Darmouth in Devonshire. Ah, well! I was an idiot! My
lords, I ask your pardon for having forced you to be elbowed

by that man there. You, a knight! you, a noble! you, a lord! Compare yourself a little with those who are such. Look! look around you! There stand noblemen. There is Bridges, Baron Chandos; there is Seymour, Duke of Somerset. There are the Stanleys, who have been Earls of Derby since 1485. There are the Clintons, who have been barons since 1298. Do you imagine you are like these people,—you? You say that you are allied to the Spanish family of Penalver, but it is not true; you are only a bad Italian. Nothing,—worse than nothing! Son of a shoe-maker in the village of Larino! Yes, gentlemen, the son of a shoe-maker! I knew it, and I did not tell it; I concealed it, and I made believe I credited this man when he talked about his nobility. That is the way we are, we women. Oh, Heaven! I wish there were women here; it would be a lesson to them all. This scoundrel! this scoundrel! he betrays one woman and disowns the other. Infamous creature! Oh, yes, indeed you are infamous. What! I have been speaking all this time and he is not yet on his knees? On your knees, Fabiani! My lords, force this man to kneel!

This creature whom I have loaded with benefits! this Neapolitan lackey whom I have made a noble knight and a proud earl of England. Ah, I ought to have expected this! But I am always like that; I am obstinate, and afterwards I see that I am wrong. It is my fault. Italian stands for liar: Neapolitan for coward. Every time that my father made use of an Italian, he repented of it. This Fabiani! You see Lady Jane, unfortunate child, to what a man you have surrendered yourself! But I will avenge you. Oh, I ought to have known it from the first. You will find nothing in an Italian's pocket but a stiletto, nothing in his soul but treachery. Ah!—

Good! Now he will perjure himself; he will descend to the depths of infamy; he will make us blush to our finger-tips before these men,—we women who have loved him. He will not even lift up his head! Then what, Lady Jane, what is our vengeance? An Italian vengeance? Coward? Liar?

> (*Taking hold of both his hands and
> dragging him violently to the front of
> the stage*)

Poison? Dagger? A treacherous, a disgraceful vengeance,—a vengeance from the back, a vengeance such as you take in your country? No, Signor Fabiani, neither dagger nor poison. Do I have to conceal myself? Do I have to hide in the corners of the street at night and make myself small when I want revenge? No, by my faith, I want the daylight! Do you hear, my lord?— the full noonday, the bright sun, the public square, the axe and the stake, the crowds in the street, the crowds at the windows, the crowds on the roofs! A hundred thousand witnesses! I want people to be afraid, do you hear, my lord? I want them to think it splendid, frightful, magnificent. I want them to say, "It is a woman who has been wronged, but it is a Queen who takes revenge!" This much envied favourite, this handsome, insolent young man, whom I have dressed in velvets and satins, I want to see him bent double, terrified and trembling, on his knees before a black cloth, with naked feet, with manacled wrists, hissed by the people, fingered by the executioner. On this white neck, where I have put a golden collar, I want to put a rope. I have seen how Fabiani looks upon a throne, I want to see how he looks upon a scaffold.

Not a word! Not a word! You will mount the scaffold as did Suffolk and Northumberland. This will be a festival such as I have given before to my good city of London. You know how she hates you, this good city of mine! Faith, when one wants vengeance, it's a good thing to be Mary, Queen of England, daughter of Henry VIII, and mistress of four seas. When you are on the scaffold, you can make a long speech to the people, if you like, as Northumberland did, or a long prayer to God, as Suffolk did, in order to give pardon the time to arrive; but God is my witness that you are a traitor, and the pardon will not come. This wretched liar who talked of love to me and this morning even said "thou" to me—Eh, gentlemen, it seems to amaze you that I talk thus openly before you; but I repeat it, what do I care?

(To Lord Somerset) My lord duke, you are constable of the Tower; demand this man's sword!

210.

MARIANNE, REJECTING A PROPOSAL, RECOGNIZES THAT WHETHER A WOMAN ACCEPTS OR REFUSES, SHE IS CONDEMNED (YT)

(1833) ALFRED DE MUSSET, *THE FOLLIES OF MARIANNE*, TR. R. PELLISSIER AND E.B. THOMPSON, ACT II, SC. 1

Coelio, sick with love for the virtuous Marianne (who is married to drama's perennial jealous old man), and too tongue-tied to speak to her, requisitions his friend Octave to woo her for him. Octave, knowing neither shame for himself nor respect for the possible decency of women, urges Marianne farther than even the old bawd Ciuta ventured to go. Marianne, who possesses both virtue and common sense, recognizes the reason for men's license to woo even virtuous, even married women, with no regard for their refusals. Two reasons: one, her refusals are merely a hedge against the too-sudden abandonment of reputation, and two, her desirability leaves her no justification for lasting refusal.

Octave, then, in the first act of *The Follies of Marianne*, posits in its most blatant form the doctrine of woman as object. And Marianne, feeling the force of the credo, explains, with muffled anger, the logical consequence for the woman of Octave's supposition: She is, after consent, discarded and condemned as a whore, or alternatively, she is, after refusal, abandoned and condemned as no woman, "a Bengal rose, without thorns and without perfume." Her anger is hidden in the courtesy and good humor of her reply, but—given Musset's subtle and multiple ironies—we discover much later that what is also hidden in Marianne is her vulnerability.

But to what? Confronted by the unreasonable jealousy of her husband, Marianne makes a wild decision: to have the affair with the love-saturated Coelio after all. But in the course of the drama's paraphernalia of crossed letters and misunderstandings, Coelio meets his death. Marianne is not entirely wracked by his tragedy. Her longing, once laid bare, has fastened not on Coelio but on Octave. Ultimate irony: The "caprice" of Marianne, though not for Coelio, is nevertheless for the intensity and meaning of his love. And though her "caprice" fastens on Octave, he wisely recognizes that she wants in him that very intensity and meaning which Coelio's love alone harbored. Octave, knowing well his capacity's limit is for lust, not love, refuses her. Better than Marianne herself, he knows the unlimited nature of her longing, which is not his to satisfy.

Negotiations in the politics of love are, in the sophisticated novel and drama of the nineteenth century (Musset, Stendhal), rife with newly dark ironies and subtleties, as feelings, "sensibilities," function increasingly independently of conventional patterns of moral belief and behavior, even when such patterns are internalized, and even when independent sensibilities and internalized beliefs are in a character possessed simultaneously of both. Ungovernable libidos and the strictures of propriety strike fewer and fewer bargains, and so produce the characteristic (particularly women's) tragedies of the century: the Emma Bovaries, the Anna Kareninas, the Hedda Gablers still to come. Musset anticipates and in Marianne, delicately pencil-sketches, such a tragedy.

Marianne

My dear cousin, do you not pity a woman's lot? Just look at what happens. Chance wills it that Coelio loves me, or that thinks he loves me, of which Coelio informs his friends, and those friends in their turn decree that, under pain of death, I must be his mistress. The Neapolitan youth deigns to send me, in you, a worthy representative, charged with informing me that I must love the said Signor within the next eight days. Weigh all this carefully, I beg of you. If I give myself up, what will be said of me? Is not a woman vile who at a given place and at a given hour agrees to such a proposition? Will not her reputation be lost; will she not be pointed at and will not her name form the chorus of a drinking song? If, on the contrary, she refuses, is there any monster too vile to be compared with her? Is a statue as cold as she? And the man who speaks to her, and who dares to stop her with her mass book in her hand, in a public place, has he not the right to say to her: "You are a Bengal rose, without thorns and without perfume"?

Are not honesty and one's sworn oath most ridiculous things? And a girl's education, the pride of a heart which has thought itself of some worth? Before throwing to the winds the ashes of its beloved flower, the calyx must be bathed in tears, withered by a few rays of the sun, half opened by a delicate hand? Is not all this a dream, a bubble, which, at the first sigh of a fashionable cavalier, must evaporate in air? After all, what is a woman? The occupation of a moment, a delicate cup that holds a drop of rose water, that one carries to one's lips and then throws aside. A woman! She is a game of pleasure! Might one not say, in meeting one: "There is a beautiful night passing." And would he not be a great scholar in such matters who would lower his eyes before her and say to himself, "Here is perhaps the happiness of an entire life," and allow her to pass?

211.

THE QUEEN OPENLY CONFESSES HER LOVE FOR "DON CESAR" (YT)

(1838) Victor Hugo, *Ruy Blas*, tr. Leon Katz, Act III

Hugo's balance between the grandiloquence of his poetry and the absurdity of his plots was both reverenced and condemned for about thirteen years from 1830 to 1843, and with the disastrous failure of his *Les Burgraves,* French drama left the poetic afflatus of his dramas, and caught up with the realities of contemporary French life—a time of retrenchment from Napoleonic dreams—settling for the thrills of political corruption, commercial buccaneering, and the speculator's paradise: the stock market. As a wise contemporary put it, "[French] Romantic drama was born too late in a world too old."

While it thrived—preeminently in Hugo—it teetered between that poetic grandiloquence and that absurdity. It absorbed every device of contemporary melodrama except its compassionate happy endings; it cluttered the stage with crowds of soldiers and monks, courtiers and citizens, beggars and bandits, for large theatrical and pictorial effect; it ended every act with a line, a gesture, or a twist of plot that thrilled; it startled appetite with wild visual and sonorous contrasts of light and shade, sound and silence, vivid color and total gloom, and high moments of lyric poetry that served as its truest climactic moments, far more than its shriekings, stabbings, and startling appearances and disappearances through windows, doors, panels, and wall hangings, and traps in the stage floor; it thrived on characters in masks and cloaks that covered half their faces, shedding beggar's dress for gorgeous costumes, disguising and concealing their true identities while they uttered vastly long speeches reviewing details of plot, irrelevant history, and fixed emotional states expressed in an abandoned lyricism that then and later found its truest home in operatic aria.

Ruy Blas, a nobody, a commoner, by Act III has risen to be chief power, chief governor of Spain at the end of the sixteenth century, a Spain in serious decline. How risen? Commandeered by the play's villain, Don Salluste, who is determined to revenge himself against the Queen for causing his banishment, Ruy Blas is disguised as a Don Cesar de Bazan (a nobleman turned criminal and presumably disappeared) with orders to become the Queen's lover—the culpability Don Salluste plans to use to destroy her. The plan of their falling in love succeeds so well that within six months the Queen, functioning in place of an absent, indifferent monarch, has elevated "Don Cesar" to virtual ruler of Spain.

Each loves genuinely, rapturously, and secretly, but neither has professed their hidden love. The moment comes when the Queen, concealed behind the council chamber's arras, overhears "Don Cesar's" harangue against the corrupt ministers of state for their bleeding of the country's wealth and power. So moved is she by his passion, honesty, and authority that she reveals herself to "Don Cesar" when the ministers are gone, and their moment of mutual confession is capped by the Queen's transported recital of her long-burning love. It is a passage that genuinely illustrates Hugo's lyricism encroaching on operatic aria.

QUEEN

No, speak, Don Cesar. The tremor of your voice, its very sound, bewitches me. I've never heard such words addressed to me in all my life. Your very soul is in your words, and in that soul, I find my deepest joy. Oh, how much I longed to hear your voice! And longed to find that welcome in your eyes that says, "Rejoice!" I've longed for many months, and suffered when you turned from me, and dropped your eyes, and would not look at me, your Queen!—No, no, I've said too much, I will be silent.

(After a struggle)
I cannot. If it meant my death, I must tell you, Don Cesar, what is in this torn and bitter heart. If it is a crime, so be it. No matter. I will reveal the truth to you, the truth I've struggled many months to hide. For all those months, I saw

you flee from me, and I pursued. And every day I stood inside that secret cabinet, and listened carefully to catch the calm, rich flow of your tongue's eloquence. And then my heart glowed with pride at such wise words in which I recognized the mettle of a man who'd mastered men, the mettle of a king.

It was I, your Queen, who placed you where you are, who summoned you to climb this high, higher than heaven would have ventured but for the secret woman's hand that led you to that place where majesty alone may sit—a majesty, in you, well earned.

But I'm requited. First, a flower, sent every day in secret by your mysterious hand; now an empire, once again restored. I am requited. I saw you first as good; now, now I find you great. Am I doing wrong? My fate is bitter, to be imprisoned in this tomb, without a husband's love, without a shred of hope. One day, the time may come when we're together privately, at leisure, when I will tell you what I suffer, tell you how I'm left forgotten, and humiliated too. Yesterday I asked to change my chamber, it was dark, depressing, and I wished to change, and I was told—I, their Queen!—was insolently told it was forbidden. These are the bars and bolts of courtly etiquette. But heaven and all that's good has sent you here to save a ruined state, and spare its wretched people from that ruin. You will not shrink, I know, from that great work. And you will love this miserable, suffering—

(He falls to his knees.)
Don Cesar, I give my soul to you. I am a Queen, but with a woman's heart. My faith in you is great, it's strong, and I know my honor will not suffer at your hands. Call, and I will come. There's greatness in your heart, my love, and greatness and nobility of soul.

(She kisses his forehead.)
Adieu.

(She leaves.)

212.

ALIX EXPLAINS HER LOVE FOR THE MASKED PRISONER (YT)

(N.D.) VICTOR HUGO, *THE TWIN BROTHERS*,
TR. ANONYMOUS, ACT I, SC. 9

[See No. 211, above] *The Twin Brothers* is Hugo's unfinished dramatic version of the story of the Man in the Iron Mask; it breaks off at the point of his rescue from the dungeon of his imprisonment. The young Alix becomes his rescuer, an "orphan," but—in Hugo's characteristically obfuscating vein—not really an orphan but, unknown to herself, the daughter of Count Jean de Creci, who is himself in disguise as a mountebank and fortune teller. By blind coincidence, he is the man to whom she turns for help in rescuing the masked man.

The Count as mountebank/fortune teller owns a booth in the city square. When Alix comes to him for assistance, she explains the incredible circumstances under which she conceived her love for this Incognito. And to explain, she tells him how her way of life accidentally led to the moment when she followed a mysterious path to the "vaulted dungeon" where she first spied this mysterious figure with the invisible face. Love's exceptional power overcame her, and so she determined to save him.

Noticeable here, as in all of Hugo's prominent characters, is that what gives crystal clarity and great expressive force to their emotions is their single dimension. There is little more before or behind Alix's love for the masked prisoner than the fact; but what the emotion loses in accountability, it gains in assertive force. Neither logic nor psychology justifies either her passions or those of other Hugo characters; nothing does but simply the vigor and thrust of their assertion, which gives them not only what credibility they have, but their—so to speak—"scale." That scale can be overwhelming; sometimes its passion rings [see Nos. 208 and 209, above]

ALIX

Yes, I love him!
And feel Heaven sent me to his aid. You see
To guardians left while yet a little child,
Bereft of parents, friendless and uncared for,

None heeded me, and so my tutors were
The fields and skies alone; and in the depths
Of solitudes I passed my life in dreams.
'Twas thus that God prepared, far from the light,
My soul to hail a love unlike the common.
Do you, who love me also, and whom God
Has sent to aid me, listen to my words?
The road that leads from Montdidier to Roye
Lies near a manor where I was last year.
One evening, as I looked across the plain,
I saw a prisoner and his guards approach.
The guards required possession of my prison.
As chatelaine all my keys are due my King,
My Suzerain, and I obeyed. At night
I dared to creep along a path of which
None knows, but me, the outlet, and I reached,
Curious and unobserved, that vaulted dungeon.
What I saw there I never shall forget.
The grated loop-hole was lit up outside.
The prisoner kept pacing up and down
Beneath the vault. Although you never saw him,
You doubtless know the horrible sight that met
My gaze. I marked four haggard faces in
The shadow; but none spoke. It was a tomb;
And I, with brow more pale than that of one
On whom the axe is falling, chilled with fear,
Gazed on this spectre, moving to and fro,
Guarded by executioners. How long
Did I continue there? I cannot say.
The morrow, at the dawn, captain and guards
All vanished like the phantom of a dream.
What need to tell you more? Since that same hour
My soul is as the soul of one possessed.
Be it for weal or woe, illusion, madness,
One thought absorbs it. Everywhere I go,
That captive follows, passing like a shadow
With outstretched arms, then fades into the night.
I will deliver him. Who is this victim?
'Tis clear he's young and can have done no wrong.
By what right do those executioners
Change life for him into a hideous dream?
What mystery is this? Ah, well! to be
Entirely frank, by dint of pitying him
I learned to love him. I found out he was
Removed to Pierrefonds. I desire to save him,

And save him surely shall! What you're about
To say to me, I to myself have said
A hundred times. 'Tis madness, ruin, frenzy.
I know nought of him, and I might select
Some fair young lord. Well, then, suppose all true—
I love him; and my fixed resolve to free him
Is in me more than purpose, 'tis a flame,
A fury, a volition that devours
My soul! O God! I see him always there!
I know not what name you may give to this;
For me, I feel 'tis love!

CHATELAINE: lady of the manor; landowner's wife. SUZERAIN: supreme ruler.

213.

GERTRUDE ACCUSES HER LOVER OF BETRAYAL, THEN APPEALS, THEN THREATENS (OT)

(1848) HONORE DE BALZAC, *THE STEPMOTHER*,
TR. ELLEN MARRIAGE, ACT III, SC. 1–2

Mme. Gertrude de Grandchamps' is not, as in much Romantic drama, merely the rhetoric of jealousy, but real jealousy, the pain of which drives her to desperation. The wife of a Napoleonic general, she married him only to inherit his money and then to marry her lover Ferdinand, employed in the household as her husband's servant. But Ferdinand's abandoned her, having fallen in love with her stepdaughter Pauline. The battle between the two women for his possession, waged secretly behind the back of the general, is vicious and unrelenting.

Gertrude, knowing that Ferdinand has spent the night before in Pauline's room, is frantic, not only with jealousy but with the sinking feeling of her impending defeat. Next morning, alone, she prepares to confront Ferdinand. When he appears, she is ready to accuse, but then slips into confessing her helplessness and desperation, and then begs him shamelessly. Finally, his scrupulous and unbending coldness affronting her as the worst of insults, she abandons every posture of regard for him or for herself, and threatens the destruction of them all.

GERTRUDE

As the reward for a sacrifice which has lasted for twelve years, and whose agonies can only be understood by women,—for what man can guess at such tortures!—what have I asked? Very little! Merely to know that he is here, near to me, without any satisfaction saving, from time to time, a furtive glance at him. I wished only to feel sure that he would wait for me. To feel sure of this is enough for us, us for whom a pure, a heavenly love is something never to be realized. Men never believe that they are loved by us, until they have brought us down into the mire! And this is how he has rewarded me! He makes nocturnal assignations with this stupid girl! Ah! He may as well pronounce my sentence of death; and if he has the courage to do so, I shall have the courage at once to bring about their eternal separation; I can do it!

But here he comes! I feel faint! My God! Why hast Thou made me love with such desperate devotion him who no longer loves me!

(Ferdinand enters)
Yesterday you deceived me. You came here last night, through this room, entering by means of a false key, to see Pauline, at the risk of being killed by M. de Grandchamp! Oh! you needn't lie about it. I saw you, and I came upon Pauline as you had concluded your nocturnal promenade. You have made a choice upon which I cannot offer you my congratulations. If only you had heard us discussing the matter, on this very spot! If you had seen the boldness of this girl, the effrontery with which she denied everything to me, you would have trembled for your future, that future which belongs to me, and for which I have sold myself, body and soul.

You must admit then that I have the right to detest and make war upon your love for Pauline; for this love has rendered you a traitor and criminal towards me. Yes, you have deceived me. In standing as you did between us two, you made me assume a character which is not mine. I am violent as you know. Violence is frankness, and I am living a life of outrageous duplicity. Tell me, do you know what it is to have to invent new lies, on the spur of the moment, every day,—to live with a dagger at your heart!

Oh! This lying! But for us, it is the Nemesis of happiness. It is disgraceful, when it succeeds; it is death, when it fails. And you, other men envy you because you make women love you. You will be applauded, while I shall be despised. And you do not wish me to defend myself! You have nothing but bitter words for a woman who has hidden from you everything— her remorse—her tears! I have suffered alone and without you the wrath of heaven; alone and without you I have descended into my soul's abyss, an abyss which has been opened by the earthquake of sorrow; and, while repentance was gnawing at my heart, I had for you nothing but looks of tenderness, and smiles of gaiety! Come, Ferdinand, do not despise a slave who lies in such utter subjection to your will!

Do not you men die for your outraged honor, for a word, for a gesture? Well, there are women who die for their love, that is, when their love is a treasure which has become their all, which is their very life! And I am one of these women. Since you have been under this roof, Ferdinand, I have feared a catastrophe every moment. Yes. And I always carry about me something which will enable me to quit this life, the very moment that misfortune falls on us. See! *(She shows him a phial.)* Now you know the life that I have lived!

I swore that I would keep back these tears, but they are strangling me! For you—While you speak to me with that cold politeness which is your last insult,—your last insult to a love which you repudiate!—you show not the least sympathy towards me! You would like to see me dead, for then you would be unhampered by me. But, Ferdinand, you do not know me! I am willing to confess everything to the General, whom I would not deceive. This lying fills me with disgust! I shall take my child, I shall come to your house, we will flee together. But no more of Pauline!

Yes, I know! If I came to you so—you've already warned me— you would kill yourself. Good. Then I, too, would kill myself! Then we should be united in death, and you would never be hers!

214.

GERTRUDE BEGS HER RIVAL TO SURRENDER HER LOVER: TO "RELENT, AND SAVE ME!" (OT)

(1848) HONORE DE BALZAC, *THE STEPMOTHER,*
TR. ELLEN MARRIAGE, ACT III, SC. 7

[Continues No. 213, above] Her final attempt to possess Ferdinand reduces Gertrude to denigrating her own being. Abjectly, she appeals to her rival, Pauline. But laboring to maintain a posture of reasonable persuasion, she fails utterly at sustaining such an absurd contradiction of herself, and falling to her knees, abandons all pretense of reason and conciliation, and begs without shame, crying aloud in utter and final desperation.

Balzac has little interest in the moral equation signified by the actions of his embattled women, but only in the driving, elemental force that moves them without regard for, and beyond the province of, civilized limitation. What is seen by many critics as "melodrama" in Gertrude's action is in fact that dynamic propulsion which is finally unstoppable and uncontrollable—a propulsion that governs many of the most compelling characters in the literature of realism and naturalism that were to follow the path led by Balzac.

GERTRUDE

Pauline, life is just beginning for you. *(A knock is heard.)*
Ferdinand is the first man, young, well educated and
distinguished, for he is distinguished, by whom you have been
attracted; but there are many others in the world such as he is.
Ferdinand has been in a certain sense under the same roof
with you, and you have seen him every day; the first impulses
of your heart have therefore directed you to him. I understand
this, and it is quite natural. Had I been in your place I should
doubtless have experienced the same feelings. But, my dear,
you know not the ways either of the world or of society. And
if, like so many other women, you have been deceiving
yourself—for we women, ah, how often are we thus
deceived!—you still can make another choice. But for me the
deed has been done, I have no other choice to make.
Ferdinand is all I have, for I have passed my thirtieth year, and

I have sacrificed to him what I should have kept unsullied—
the honor of an aged man. The field is clear for you, you may
yet love some other man more ardently than you can love
today—this is my experience. Pauline, child, give him up, and
you will learn what a devoted slave you will have in me! You
will have more than a mother, more than a friend, you will
have the unstinted help of a soul that is lost! Oh! listen to me!

*(She kneels, and raises her hands to
Pauline's corsage.)*

Behold me at your feet, acknowledging you my rival! Is this
sufficient humiliation for me? Oh, if you only knew what this
costs a woman to undergo! Relent! Relent, and save me. Give
my life back to me!

215.

CAMILLE ON HER DEATHBED IS RECONCILED TO HER LOVER ARMAND (YT)

(1852) ALEXANDRE DUMAS FILS, *CAMILLE*,
TR. EDITH REYNOLDS AND NIGEL PLAYFAIR, ACT V

The coarseness of the kept woman's world in Dumas fils' original
novel, *La Dame aux Camellias*, is a little closer to Balzacian realism
than is the sentimentalism of the play derived from it. Somewhat
shaded from the realities of nineteenth-century Parisian gentlemen's
traffic in expensive whores, the lady of the camellias on stage became
and perhaps remains the most popular tear-stained story of love's triumph and tragedy after *Romeo and Juliet*.

Camille, or Marguerite, is young and barely out of her teens when
she finds herself the most desirable courtesan in Paris. In the first act,
hard-headed, feet on the ground, with no illusions about her social
position, her source of income, her staying power, or her imminent
surrender to tuberculosis, she quickly metamorphoses—by the
power of that brand of love that never stopped speaking its name in
nineteenth-century fiction—into the ideal of negative womanhood

that willingly surrenders its wealth and income, its position, its world, even its lover for the sake of sparing that very lover's wealth and income, social position, and world.

In the most famous scene in the play, the scene of her death, Marguerite surrenders the very last claims she has on life—even tokens of her memory should her lover marry later—and interestingly, instead of winning the traditional final sanction of "Heaven" for the purified fallen woman, it is the blessing of "Love" that gives departing sanction to Marguerite—Love, the value that effectively displaced Heaven in the most morbidly deferential of nineteenth-century fictions which lived vicariously inside Love's raptures.

It is Armand's father who persuades Marguerite to give up her idyllic liaison with her lover for the sake of his family's position, and it is that same father whose change of heart brings Armand back to Marguerite's bedside in time to see her expire. At once, Marguerite has fleeting glimpses of a happy future for the reunited lovers, and as quickly, the debilities of dying put an end to her momentary hope. But she persists in making the most of her happiness at Armand's return, and at the happiness of her friends who have just married. It is with her blessing on their future happiness, her own avowal of reconciliation with death on her lips, and a final instant of unreconstructed optimism about her continuing to live, that eases her into a contented death.

(Marguerite rushes to the door. Armand appears, looking ill. She clings to him.)

MARGUERITE

At last! Armand? It is not possible that you have come back, that God has been so good to me! I said this morning that only one thing could save me. I had given up hope for it—and then you came. We must lose no time, beloved. Life was slipping away from me, but you came and it stayed. You haven't heard, have you? Nichette is to be married this morning to Gustave. Let us go to see her married. It would be so good to go to church, to pray to God, and to look on a little at the happiness of others. Bring my outdoor things, Nanine. I want to go out.

We used to speak of you every day. No one else dared to mention your name. It was she who used to comfort me and tell me that I should see you again. And she was right. You have traveled a long way and seen many beautiful countries. You must tell me about them and perhaps take me there one day. *(She sways.)* No, it is nothing. Happiness hurts a little at first and my heart has been desolate for so long.

> *(She sits down and throws back her*
> *head. Then, coming to herself)*

Don't be afraid, dear. I always used to have these moments of faintness, don't you remember? It is nothing. Come, Nanine, give me my shawl and bonnet. *(Having tried to walk, throws down her bonnet and shawl in anger)* I can't. *(Falls onto the sofa)* Sit down here beside me, as close as you can, Armand. Just for a moment. I was angry with death, but I know, now, that it has to come... I am not angry any more, because it has waited long enough for me to see you again. Even if I did not wish it, dear, it would have to be, because it is God's will. Perhaps if things had been different, if I had really been the good girl you should have loved, I might have grieved more at leaving a world where you are, and a future that was so full of promise. But, as it is, the best and purest of me will be yours forever. Believe me, God sees more clearly than we do.

Must I be the one to give you courage? Come, do as I tell you. Open that drawer. You will find a miniature of me, painted for you, in the days when I was still pretty. Keep it, it will help your memory later. If ever you should love and marry some young and beautiful girl, as I hope you may one day, and if she should find the portrait and ask whose it is, tell her that it is a friend who, if God permits, will never cease to pray for you and her. And if she should be jealous of the past, because we women sometimes are, and asks you to give up the picture, do so, dearest. I forgive you, now, already. A woman suffers too deeply when she feels she is not loved.... Are you listening, Armand my darling? Do you hear me? *(Enter Nichette and Gustave)* Nichette, Gustave. I am dying, but I am happy too, and it is only my happiness that you can see.... And so you are married!... What a strange life this first one is, what will the second be?... You will be even happier than you were before. Speak of me sometimes, won't you? Armand, give me your hand. Believe me, it is not hard to die. It is strange. I am not suffering any more. I feel better, so much better than I have ever felt before... I am going to live.

> *(She appears to fall asleep.)*

216.

PAULINE CONFESSES HER IDENTITY AND REVEALS HER PLANS (YT)

(1858) EMILE AUGIER, *OLYMPE'S MARRIAGE*, TR. BARRETT H. CLARK, ACT I

Note the difference. The Millwoods (*The London Merchant*) [see Nos. 187 and 188] and the Marwoods *(Miss Sara Sampson)* [see No. 200, above] in the eighteenth century professed pride in their "villainy" as revenge against the seductions and ravages of men. Nineteenth-century Pauline needs no such radical justification: female "villainy" in the mid-century manages with slighter motive: boredom, for example, or the urge to upgrade income or respectability, or simply to gain independence.

Pauline Morin fancies title. Thoroughly declassé, notorious in Paris, she takes the precaution of having a fictional death in California published under her active pseudonym of Olympe Taverny, then fools the titled Henri into marrying her under her real name; but she is suffering the unexpected dullness and utter boredom of married life. Still, she has plans: Henri's father, her new father-in-law the Marquis de Puygiron, will endorse her respectability, and provide entreé for her, she intends, into titled society.

The duel of wits that follows, the lies, the unearthed secrets, the maneuverings, only gradually reveal the limits of Pauline's "villainy." At play's end, she's smilingly threatening blackmail against the noble family to win marital separation, a sizable maintenance, and retention of her title of "Madame la Comtesse," in itself a convertible commodity. Conservative Augier, fearing for the establishment, gives this lower-class interloper "Olympe" the morals and cunning of Machiavelli, and the terminal fate of evil itself: She is shot to death by the Marquis, who at curtain is loading the gun again to despatch himself. The lesson is cautionary: society must guard scrupulously against invasion from below; its touch not only sullies, it defiles.

But notably in this speech, Pauline is openly confessing her past connivings and future plans to a former lover, whom she suddenly and accidentally meets. Why her openness, her frankness, her ease in confessing? In the genre of the well-made play, there grew up a freemasonry among a genteely mannered but morally low class of characters who easily and at once recognize one another: They share low motive, they share the grasp for gain, they share greed. Quickly, they understand how they may have potential use for one another, and that very possibility guarantees mutually assured protection for each other's secrets. It is the most recognizable distinction between the two moral classes: The virtuous as a matter of honor tell one another nothing; the vicious as a matter of expediency tell one another everything.

Pauline, accosted by an old Parisian lover, the Baron de Montrichard, at first insists he is mistaken in recognizing in her the "dead" Olympe Taverny, but reflecting that they may still have use for one another, gives up the pretense.

PAULINE

How did you recognize me? My face, of course. Ah, then the little pink mark on my neck. The mark you used to adore. You still remembered it!
Dear Edouard, you were my only real love. No, no—Alfred—I'm mixing names. My "only real love" has had so many names! What the devil put it into my head to marry? Well, reason enough, I suppose.

Did you ever notice, when you stepped out into the boulevard, that you had left your cane in the restaurant? And you went back for it? There in the private dining room you saw the wreckage of the orgy: candelabra in which the lights were burned out; tablecloth removed; a candle end on the table which was all covered with grease and stained with wine. Instead of lights and laughter and heavy perfumes, that made the place gay not long since, were solitude, silence, and a stale odor. The gilded furniture seemed like strangers to you, to everyone, even to themselves. Not a single article among all this that seemed familiar, not one was reminiscent of the absent master of the house or awaited his return. Complete abandonment!

Well, my life is rather like that of the private dining room. I must be gay or utterly lonely—there is no possible compromise. Are you surprised then that the restaurant aspires to the dignity of the home?

The career of an honest woman is a fearful undertaking! But it can't compare with ours! If you only knew how much energy it required to ruin a man!

Luckily, Henri took me seriously from the very first. He was most discreet. You must know that I've played my cards well. I talked of going into a convent; then he asked me to marry him, and I accepted. I pretended I was going to California. Henri met me in Brittany; I married him there a year ago, under my real name, Pauline Morin. Is he so big a fool? No, no! He's a very intelligent and charming young man. He never had a mistress—his father was very severe with him. When he became of age, he was as innocent as—a child.

He's not to be pitied, not at all; he's very happy with me. Do I love him? Well, that is not the question. I strew his path with flowers—artificial, perhaps, but they are prettier and more lasting than real ones.

Is the game worth the candle? So far, no. We've been spending ten months alone in Brittany—all by ourselves. For the past two months we've been travelling, alone again. I can't say that we've been hilarious. I live the life of a recluse, going from hotel to hotel; with the maids, servants, and postilions, I am "Madame la Comtesse." All that would be dull enough if I hadn't other dreams for the future—but I have. Now that Olympe Taverny (God rest her soul) has had time to go to California and die and be mourned for in Paris, I can boldly enter society by the front door, which the Marquis de Puygiron is to open for me. If he introduces me as an honest woman, he will not be lying: for a year I have been the personification of virtue. I have a new skin.

Ah—Henri! Here is my husband! My friend, M. le Baron de Montrichard.

217.

PAULINE, BY STRATEGICALLY DEMEANING HERSELF, WINS THE RESPECT OF THE MARQUIS (YT)

(1858) EMILE AUGIER, *OLYMPE'S MARRIAGE*,
TR. BARRETT H. CLARK, ACT I

[Continues No. 216] It is the moment of Pauline's first great test: over-coming the barrier of her father-in-law the Marquis' anticipated disdain. Her preparations are elaborate for winning acceptance into the noble family of the Puygirons as the wife of the family's scion. After the ruse of obliterating her Paris pseudonym and reputation by pretending her own death, and the further ruse of pretending to refuse the young Puygiron strenuously enough and long enough for him to believe her motives were pure for marrying him, she subjected herself to a year of wedded respectability with him in preparation for a meeting with his father, the Marquis himself. Her object: to overcome the Marquis' expected disdain for her class and kind, and then, and most importantly, to be granted entrance into society through him. She carefully arranges the accident of their meeting during travel—in Germany, near Dresden, on neutral ground. Meeting the Marquis, she allows herself at first to be mistaken by him as his son's mistress, then for him to perceive her marriage as a misalliance maneuvered by her. The Marquis' disdain is perfect; he is ready to leave. But then, her brilliant maneuver: in the Marquis' presence, she "confesses" to her naive husband that she knew—though she allowed him to persuade her otherwise—that their marriage would end in disaster. She then reviews the arguments she had presumably concealed from the impetuous Henri, the very arguments the Marquis himself holds silently but determinedly: that her young husband's misalliance would eventuate in his isolation from his own class, a suspicion that is already, she surmises, taking root. Having succumbed to weakness, and surrendered to him, she "confesses" further that she suffers now to see her husband's soon-to-be-realized inevitable remorse. But her suffering, and his, will give birth to her noblest gesture: when remorse overwhelms him, she will give him up, return him to his own class and kind, and as for herself, in her solitary retirement, the memory of "your love for me will be my whole life."

Subsequently, with the Marquis effectively softened, Pauline delivers the coup de grâce. Her own father, she tells the old aristocrat, was a mere farmer, but in the wars, he fought on the side of the Marquis against the Revolutionaries. For the Marquis, that is lineage enough: he is eager to take her into titled society on his own arm.

From the moment Pauline turns to her simple husband, and "confesses" that their courtship was "a cruel comedy," her performance is skilled, smooth, impeccable. So much so that it is indistinguishable from honesty.

PAULINE

It was a comedy, a cruel comedy! Whom could you hope to persuade of my sincerity? Who would admit that a girl of low birth, when she found in you all the intelligence and goodness of heart she had always dreamed, would give up her secret soul to you? You were very simple to believe it—ask your uncle. If I had really loved you, would I not have refused to become your wife? Would I not, M. le Marquis? But I did refuse. I made every possible objection that you yourself would have made. I was defending not only your happiness, but my own.

Do you think I had a beautiful dream, M. le Marquis? If you only knew what I am suffering! But I have no right to complain; I anticipated what was going to happen. *(To Henri)* I asked God for one year of your love in exchange for the happiness of a lifetime. He has kept His bargain, and given me even a little extra for full measure: for you still love me.

Poor dear! You don't realise what is going on within you! Perhaps I'm wrong to tell you—but it's only what you will learn soon enough. Your affection is already waning and you are being worn out by the struggle you are making against the conventions of society. Your family traditions, which you have shattered, and which you call prejudices, are now rising up one after the other. You are resisting, I know, and you are already angry that your happiness is not rewarded enough for the sacrifices you are forced to make, but every day these sacrifices grow greater, and the reward less. When you leave here, you will feel the weight of loneliness bearing down on you; you will see with other eyes the woman who ought always to stand you in stead of family, friends, society—and before long the regret of what you have given up for me will change to remorse.

But never fear, dearest, the day that happens I shall give you back all you have lost for my sake, and your love for me will be my whole life. Good-bye, M. le Marquis, and forgive me for having the honor to bear your name—I am paying dearly for it!

218.

FRANCOISE CONFIDES IN A STRANGER THE MISERY LURKING BEHIND HER HAPPINESS (YT)

(1888) GEORGES DE PORTO-RICHE, *FRANCOISE'S LUCK*,
TR. BARRETT H. CLARK, ONE ACT

At the very moment when Marcel is out trying again to seduce the woman he had an affair with three years ago, her husband, M. Guerin, who had just discovered the three-year-old affair, is at Marcel's home for the purpose of challenging his old friend to a duel to the death. But there Guerin meets Francoise, Marcel's young wife, who knows nothing of the old affair, and nothing of Guerin's intention to challenge her husband to a duel of honor. Instinctively, she trusts him, and what begins as merely friendly conversation becomes a desperate confessional on her part of her love for a husband who has never reconciled himself to marriage. But while listening to the confession of her love for Marcel, Guerin, recognizing the value of Marcel not in himself but in his wife's extraordinary and painful love for him, decides to give up all thought of a duel.

Carving a monologue out of the delicate discourse of *Francoise's Luck* makes its statement seem far more direct, far more easily available, than in fact it is. It betrays too the subtlety of the serious games of concealment and revelation being played continuously by each of its characters. Even in Francoise's lengthy confessional, which moves from her proud assertion of her happiness to the bitter revelation of the constant pain and uncertainty that lies behind her still-genuine happiness, there are the stops and starts of feeling, the inadvertent shifts in the direction of thought, the sudden self-interruption, the sometimes skillful, sometimes clumsy ability to suppress the hidden truths of feeling. Porto-Riche is a master dramatist of the psychology that became increasingly prominent at the turn of the century—the "layered" structuring of personality, in which multiple levels of being reinforce or contradict or rebel against the inherent truth of one another, and in which the fixity of character definition is endlessly and ironically undercut.

FRANCOISE

Then we're friends, are we not? Word of honor?

(Sitting)
Sit down, and let's talk! *(Guerin is uncertain.)* We have so much to say to each other! Let's talk about you first. Yes, about you! Ah, about my happiness! About my great happiness!

But really, happy people never have anything to say. You see, my happiness is complete. I had never imagined that the goodness of a man could make a woman so happy! The goodness—of course. The love? Well—Marcel's love for me—!

Seriously, Monsieur, you know him very well,—how could he possibly be in love with me? Is it even possible? He lets me love him and I ask nothing more. Only to be allowed to continue to do so. I am not at all like other women. I don't ask for rights; but I do demand tenderness and consideration. He is free, I am not—I'll admit that. But I don't mind, I only hope that we may continue as we are!

But I am afraid, Monsieur. My happiness is not of the proud, demonstrative variety, it is a kind of happiness that is continually trembling for its safety. If I told you—

Well, perhaps later! How I pity one who loves and has to suffer for it! I am on the side of the jealous, of the betrayed.

Am I sure of him? He is Marcel! Admit for a moment that he loves me today—I want so to believe it!—Tomorrow will he love me? Does he himself know whether he will love me then? Isn't he at the mercy of whims, a passing fantasy—of the weather, or the appearance of the first woman he happens to meet? I am only twenty, and I am not always as careful as I might be. Happiness is so difficult!

Perhaps, yes, I am too—conscientious, too sincere. I feel that;

yes, I think I am, but every time I try to hide my affection from him, he becomes indifferent, almost mean—as if he were glad to be rid of some duty—of being good! You see, Marcel can't get used to the idea that his other life is over, dead and buried, that he's married for good—that he must do as others do. I do my best and tell him, but my very presence only reminds him of his duties as a husband. For instance *(Interrupting herself)* Here I am telling you all this—well— *(With bitterness)* He likes to go out alone at night, without me. He knows me well enough to understand that his being away makes me very unhappy, and as a matter of form, of common courtesy, he asks me whether I should like to go with him. I try to reason with myself, and convince myself that he doesn't mean what he says, but I can't help feeling sincerely happy when once in a while I do accept his invitation. But the moment we leave the house I see my mistake. Then he pretends to be in high spirits, but I know all the time he is merely acting a part; and when we come home again he lets drop without fail some hint about his having lost his liberty, that he took me out in a moment of weakness, that he really wanted to be alone.

Then I am most unhappy; I'm in torment for hours and hours. I wonder where he can be, and then I fear he won't come back at all. When the door opens, when I hear him come in, I'm so happy that I pay no attention to what he tells me. But I made a solemn promise with myself never to give the slightest indication of jealousy. My face is always tranquil, and what I say to him never betrays what I feel. I never knowingly betray myself, but his taking way, his tenderness, soon make me confess every fear; then he turns round and using my own confessions as weapons, shows me how wrong I am to be so afraid and suspicious. And when sometimes I say nothing to him, even when he tries to make me confess, he punishes me most severely by telling me stories of his affairs, narrow escapes, and all his temptations. He once told me about an old mistress of his, whom he had just seen, a very clever woman, who was never jealous! Or else he comes in so late that I have to be glad, for if he came in later, it would have been all night! He tells me he had some splendid opportunity, and had to give it up! A thousand things like that! He seems to delight in making me suspect and doubt him!

That's my life; as for my happiness, it exists from day to day. *(With an air of revolt)* If I only had the right to be unhappy!

But I must always wear a smile, I must be happy, not only in his presence, officially, but to the very depths of my soul! So that he may deceive me without the slightest feeling of remorse! It is his pleasure!

(She bursts into tears.)
Isn't my suffering a reproach to him? No matter how cynical, how blasé a man may be, isn't it his duty, his sacred duty to say to himself, "I have found a good and true woman in this world of deception; she is a woman who adores me, who is only too ready to invent any excuse for me! She bears my name and honors it; no matter what I do, she is always true, of that I am positive. I am always foremost in her thoughts, and I shall be her only love." When a man can say all that, Monsieur, isn't that real, true happiness?

NINETEENTH-CENTURY GERMAN

219.

MARION RECALLS HER PASSAGE FROM IGNORANCE TO SEXUAL AWAKENING (YT)

(1835) GEORG BÜCHNER, *DANTON'S DEATH*,
TR. CARL MUELLER, ACT I, SC. 5

[See, in Men's vols., the entries on Danton] Danton, after a bout with drawing-room politics that gives him a headache, escapes, and retires to a quiet brothel where he and the whore Marion are set up in one of the establishment's rooms. From the other rooms, friends, girls, drift in, drift out, chat, and move on. Pervasive sense of ease.

Marion is disinclined. Danton is inclined, but defers to her disinclination, giving her room for reverie. Sitting at his feet, leaning back, she lets flow true meaning, honest talk, quiet confessional: her mother's solicitously keeping her ignorant about sex; her sense of separation from her own body; her awakened but not understood feelings regarding a young suicide; her learning to know herself as "a sea that swallows down everything and sinks deeper and deeper into itself"; her knowing herself now as "only one thing, an unbroken yearning and grasping." Because of her sexuality, so alive, so passionate, so overtaking, her activities kill her mother, making her pariah to the respectable. But her lust, she concludes, is really prayer. "The person who enjoys the most, prays the most."

The unvarnished reality of her recitation isn't heard too clearly by Danton, who is only looking at her incredible beauty, not listening. Marion understands the overtaking of *his* sexuality perfectly. "Danton," she says, "your lips have eyes."

In the context of Hugo's, opera's, and melodrama's contemporaneous stage fictions, Buchner's truth is stunning.

MARION

My mother was a clever woman; she always told me that purity was the loveliest of virtues. When people would come to our house and begin talking about certain things, she always sent me out of the room; and when I asked her what they meant, she said I should be ashamed asking such questions; then when she gave me books to read I almost always had to leave out certain pages. But I could read as much of the Bible as I wanted because everything there was holy. Still there were parts of it that I never understood. I didn't want to ask anybody, so I brooded over them myself. Then the spring came; there was something happening all around me in which I had no share. I was in an atmosphere all my own, and it almost stifled me. I looked at my body; at times it seemed that there were two of me, and then they would melt again into one. About this time a young man came to the house. He was very beautiful and often talked to me about silly things. I didn't know exactly what they meant, but I had to laugh. My mother made him come often, and that pleased us both. Finally we didn't see why we shouldn't as soon lie next to one another between two sheets as sit beside one another on two chairs. I enjoyed that much more than his conversation and couldn't understand why they wanted me to be content with the smaller pleasures rather than the larger one. We did it secretly. And so it went on. But I became like the sea that swallows down everything and sinks deeper and deeper into itself. The only fact that existed for me was my opposite, all men melted into one body. It was my nature, what choice did I have? Finally he noticed. He came one morning and kissed me as though he wanted to suffocate me; his arms wound around my neck, I was terribly afraid. Then he let go of me and laughed and said that he had almost done a foolish thing; that I should keep my dress and wear it, that it would wear out soon enough by itself, and that he didn't want to spoil my fun for me too soon, because it was all I had. Then he went away; again I didn't know what he meant. That evening I sat at the window; I'm very sensitive, and the only hold I have on my surroundings is through what I feel; I sank into the waves of the sunset. A crowd of people came down the street then, children running ahead of them and women looking out of their windows. I looked down: they were carrying him past in a basket, the moon was reflected on his pale forehead, his hair was wet—he had drowned himself. All I could do was cry.—It was the only time that my life ever stopped. Other people have Sundays and weekdays, they work six days and pray on the seventh; once every year on their birthdays they become sentimental and every year they think about the New Year. I don't understand that at all: I know nothing of such breaks in time, of change. I am always only one thing, an unbroken longing and grasping, a flame, a stream. My mother died of grief. People were always pointing at me because of it. That's stupid. There's only one thing that matters, whether it's our bodies, or holy pictures, or flowers, or children's toys. It's all the same feeling: the person who enjoys the most, prays the most.

NINETEENTH-CENTURY ENGLISH

220.

JANE, DESPERATE TO UNBURDEN HER BROTHER OF HIS SECRET TORMENT, DEMANDS HIS COMPLIANCE (ot)

(N.D.) JOANNA BAILLIE, *DE MONFORT*, ACT II, SC. 2

"It is attempted," Joanna Baillie explains about her plays, "to delineate the stronger passions of the mind, each passion being the subject of a tragedy or comedy." The inspiration for this notion was Shakespeare: *Macbeth* delineates ambition, *Othello* jealousy, etc. And her own *De Monfort*, hate. It's her compelling idea that the strongest character is driven by the strongest passion, which makes for the most compelling play, but in Baillie's play, the hate in Monfort is not so much delineated as noted; De Monfort is darkly silent, perpetually morose, moved to unaccountable outbursts, but his moving passion remains, until late in the play, an enigma. It is his loving, devoted sister Jane who spends an inordinate amount of time trying to dig the secret out of him, but her efforts go for nothing; we learn late from the victim of his hate, Rezenvelt, that when they were children, the wealthy Monfort held his fellow schoolmate in casual contempt until his fortunes outdistanced Monfort's, and envy (and possibly low chagrin) promoted the violent emotion that eventually caused Monfort to murder his one-time friend.

Jane, by far the more accessible character of the two, imitates the role of Portia in her efforts to get the secret of impending assassination out of Brutus. Unlike Portia's, the privilege she claims is not the right of status of the noble Roman matron, but "the humbler station" of "a true entrusted friend" and "the soother of those griefs I must not know." Content with so humble and so effacing a role until she becomes frightened by the obsessiveness of his obdurate silence, she throws over the gentle appeal of sisterly devotion, and changes her tune: "I do command thee," and proceeds to urge him on to the strenuous effort of a psychological/moral divestiture: "Repel the hideous foe... Thou canst, thou may'st, thou wilt." Jane is clearly a precursor of the theory, as she puts it, that unshrouding "the sad infirmities of nature," exculpating that one "hideous foe" that's lodged in there, will release once again the nobility of soul within her brother. And she plans many and persistent therapeutic sessions to accomplish his cure: "We shall not part till I have turn'd thy soul." Banishing the Devil was gradually supplanted, as the century wore on, by the banishment of obsessive neurotic reactions. For Jane, early in the century, they're still one.

JANE

What say'st thou, Monfort? Oh! what words are these?
They have awaked my soul to dreadful thoughts.
I do beseech thee, speak!

> (He shakes his head, and turns from
> her; she follows him.)

By the affection thou didst ever bear me!
By the dear memory of our infant days!
By kindred living ties, ay, and by those
Who sleep i' the tomb, and cannot call to thee,
I do conjure thee, speak !

> (He waves her off with his hand, and
> covers his face with the other, still
> turning from her.)

Ha! wilt thou not?
(Assuming dignity.) Then, if affection, most unwearied love,
Tried early, long, and never wanting found
O'er generous man, hath more authority,
More rightful power than crown and sceptre give,
I do command thee.

> (He throws himself into a chair, greatly
> agitated.)

De Monfort, do not thus resist my love.
Here, I entreat thee, on my bended knees. (Kneeling)
Alas! my brother!
Unknit thy brows, and spread those wrath-clench'd hands:
Some sprite accursed within thy bosom, mates
To work thy ruin. Strive with it, my brother!

Strive bravely with it;—drive it from thy breast:
'Tis the degrader of a noble heart;
Curse it, and bid it part.
I've held my warfare throughout a troubled world,
And bourne with steady mind my share of ill;
For then, the helpmate of my toil wert thou.
But now the wane of life comes darkly on,
And hideous passion tears thee from my heart,
Blasting thy worth.—I cannot strive with this.
Call up thy noble spirit;
Rouse all the gen'rous energy of virtue;
And with the strength of heaven-endued man,
Repel the hideous foe. Be great—be valiant!
O, if thou couldst! E'en shrouded as thou art
In all the sad infirmities of nature,
What a most noble creature woudst thou be!
Thou canst, thou may'st, thou wilt.
We shall not part till I have turn'd thy soul.

Come to my closet! Free from all intrusion,
I'll school thee there; and thou again shalt be
My willing pupil, and my gen'rous friend;
The noble Monfort I have loved so long,
And must not, will not lose.

221.

ALHADRA RECALLS HER TORTURE AT THE HANDS OF THE INQUISITOR (OT)

(1813) SAMUEL TAYLOR COLERIDGE, *REMORSE*, ACT I, SC. 2

The substance if not the style of Coleridge's *Remorse* has an almost
uncomfortably contemporary relevance. It deals with the ethical
problem that attends the tortures and murders of warring oppressors
("war crimes") and the retribution against them that is morally justified. Coleridge is of course staring at the inhumanities of his own
time, the inhumanities that attended the Revolution in France, the
Napoleonic adventures that followed, and the retributions exacted by
victims and conquerors both during and after the days of infamy. But

the context in which the whole question of the inhumanity of humans is viewed is complex, and intentionally unresolved at play's end.

The play's action is happening during the last days of the civil wars fought by the Moors, who are being harrassed and driven out of Spain, and the Spanish forces of Philip II. Persecution of the Moors is raging, and Alhadra, the wife of a "Moresco" chief (i.e., a Christian Moor) suffered torture under the Inquisition—the Morsecos' true faith suspect—when she was captured.

Alhadra relives her time of torment when she recognizes her perseccutor, Ordonio, so bitterly hated by her for the horrors of her imprisonment, and longs, at once, for out-and-out retribution—for his assassination. She is confiding all this to a Christian woman, Terese, who is innocent of the knowledge of Ordonio's role in the Inquisition, and is bewildered by Alhadra's assertion that "Christians never pardon—'tis their faith." Herself a Moresco, Alhadra's learned the tenets of her faith in the Inquisition's cells. "Great evils," she concludes, "ask great passions to address them," and her passion for revenge is ready. But her plea now is for Isidore, her husband, who is in the Inquisition's custody. Alhadra is terrified that he, weak in stamina, won't survive.

ALHADRA

Hah! there he goes! a bitter curse go with him,
A scathing curse!
You hate him, don't you, lady?
These fell inquisitors! these sons of blood!
As I came on, his face so maddened me,
That ever and anon I clutched my dagger
And half unsheathed it—
And as he walked along the narrow path
Close by the mountain's edge, my soul grew eager;
'Twas with hard toil I made myself remember
That his Familiars held my babes and husband.
To have leapt upon him with a tiger's plunge,
And hurl'd him down the rugged precipice,
O, it had been most sweet!
O gentle lady!
You have no skill to guess my many wrongs,
Many and strange! Besides, I am a Christian,
And Christians never pardon—'tis their faith!
I know that man; 'tis well he knows not me.

Five years ago (and he was the prime agent),
Five years ago the holy brethren seized me.
My crime? I was a Moresco!
They cast me, then a young and nursing mother,
Into a dungeon of their prison house,
Where was no bed, no fire, no ray of light,
No touch, no sound of comfort! The black air,
It was a toil to breathe it! when the door,
Slow opening at the appointed hour, disclosed
One human countenance, the lamp's red flame
Cowered as it entered, and at once sank down.
Oh miserable! by that lamp to see
My infant quarrelling with the coarse hard bread
Brought daily; for the little wretch was sickly—
My rage had dried away its natural food.
In darkness I remained—the dull bell counting,
Which haply told me, that the all-cheering sun
Was rising on our garden. When I dozed,
My infant's moanings mingled with my slumbers
And waked me.—If you were a mother, lady,
I should scarce dare to tell you, that its noises
And peevish cries so fretted on my brain
That I have struck the innocent babe in anger.
What was it then to suffer? 'Tis most right
That such as you should hear it.—Know you not,
What nature makes you mourn, she bids you heal?
Great evils ask great passions to redress them,
And whirlwinds fitliest scatter pestilence.
I was at length released.
Yes, at length
I saw the blessed arch of the whole heaven!
'Twas the first time my infant smiled. No more—
For if I dwell upon that moment, Lady,
A trance comes on which makes me o'er again
All I then was—my knees hang loose and drag,
And my lip falls with such an idiot laugh,
That you would start and shudder!

222.

ALHADRA REVENGES HER HUSBAND'S MURDER (OT)

(1813) Samuel Taylor Coleridge, *Remorse*, Act V, Sc. 1

[Continues No. 221, above] Counter to Alhadra's story is Alvar's, Ordonio's brother. (After Schiller's *The Robbers* [see entries on Franz and Karl Moor in Men's vols.], twin brothers—one honorable, the other vicious—became fixtures of Romantic drama, used for contrasting moral outlooks—sometimes crudely, but here, as in *The Robbers*, paradoxically.) Alvar's wrongs at the hands of Ordonio are as blatant as Ordino's wrongs against Alhadra: Ordonio has killed Isidore, and he also imagines he has killed his brother. Alvar, who lives by the most truly Christian of codes, in final confrontation with his brother, elicits from him a depth of remorse that Ordonio confesses is worse than the pains of Hell. But in the same moment, Alhadra executes vengeance on Ordonio by assassinating him (with a troop of Morescos with her in guerrilla battle array), for which Ordonio is profoundly grateful. The proximity of opposites is a *leit-motif* shaping the thought of the entire play, and displays in the final speech of Alhadra's half the statement of the play's carefully balanced, carefully paradoxical non-resolution. Alhadra's is the authentic cry, and the authentic resolve, of the true revolutionary, and she accomplishes true retributive justice; Alvar is Mandela to her Robespierre.

ALHADRA

My husband murdered! Murdered most foully!
Why did'st thou leave his children?
Demon, thou should'st have sent thy dogs of hell
To lap their blood. Then, then I might have hardened
My soul in misery, and have had comfort.
I would have stood far off, quiet though dark,
And bade the race of men raise up a mourning
For a deep horror of desolation,
Too great to be one soul's particular lot!
Brother of Zagri! let me lean upon thee.
The time is not yet come for woman's anguish,
I have not seen his blood—Within an hour
Those little ones will crowd around and ask me,

Where is our father? I shall curse thee then!
Wert thou in heaven, my curse would pluck thee thence!
Rescue?
Rescue?—and Isidore's spirit unavenged?
—The deed be mine!

(Suddenly stabs Ordonio)
Now take my life!
I thank thee, Heaven! thou hast ordained it wisely,
That still extremes bring their own cure. That point
In misery, which makes the oppressed Man
Regardless of his own life, makes him too
Lord of the Oppressor's—Knew I a hundred men
Despairing, but not palsied by despair,
This arm should shake the kingdoms of the world;
The deep foundations of iniquity
Should sink away, earth groaning from beneath them;
The strongholds of the cruel men should fall,
Their temples and their mountainous towers should fall;
Till desolation seemed a beautiful thing,
And all that were and had the spirit of life,
Sang a new song to her who had gone forth,
Conquering and still to conquer!

223.

LUCRETIA IS BEWILDERED BY HER DAUGHTER'S UNEXPLAINED SIGNS OF FEAR (OT)

(1819) PERCY BYSSHE SHELLEY, *THE CENCI*, ACT II

[Quoting from Men's vols.: "Cenci Cries Curses on Beatrice and Prays for Her Destruction":] "Nowhere but in de Sade is the untrammeled appetite for the absolute of evil more fully accomplished than in Count Cenci. In the course of the play, he violates most of the taboos endemic to civilized life.... After his multiple crimes, done both before the play begins, and within it (the murder of his two sons, the torment of his wife, the rape of his daughter), he overwhelms the hopelessly patient submissiveness of his wife and daughter, and even the greed of the corrupt Papacy from whom he 'buys impunity with gold.'"

A bit earlier in his career of crime, his daughter Beatrice and her mother, Lucretia, exploiting their last hope, have sent a bill of particulars to the misnamed Pope Clement, suing for protection and for the punishment of Cenci. Their letter is returned unopened. At the same time that Lucretia receives the letter, her daughter suddenly appears, runs through the room with a look of terror, runs out again, and returns more composed but still trembling. Her father has just made clear to her that he's prepared to rape her that night.

Lucretia, usually so cowed by her husband's savagery that she tempers even her complaints, is now startled by her daughter's "unaccustomed" look of fear. Beatrice's courage and willingness to stand up to Cenci had been her only protection; the suggestion that her daughter might find solace in marriage is as much an expression of her fear of being abandoned as it is hope for Beatrice's future happiness. Beatrice, without revealing her father's newest outrage, immediately swears loyalty to her mother, but just as immediately, Cenci comes storming in, and removes the last shred of courage from his daughter's posture toward him. For the two women, their doom is now assured.

LUCRETIA

So, daughter, our last hope has failed; ah me,
How pale you look! you tremble, and you stand
Wrapped in some fixed and fearful meditation,
As if one thought were over strong for you:
Your eyes have a chill glare; O, dearest child!
Are you gone mad? If not, pray speak to me.
You talked of something that your father did
After that dreadful feast? Could it be worse
Than when he smiled, and cried, My sons are dead!
And every one looked in his neighbour's face
To see if others were as white as he?
At the first word he spoke I felt the blood
Rush to my heart, and fell into a trance;
And when it passed I sat all weak and wild;
Whilst you alone stood up, and with strong words
Checked his unnatural pride; and I could see
The devil was rebuked that lives in him.
Until this hour thus have you ever stood

Between us and your father's moody wrath
Like a protecting presence: your firm mind
Has been our only refuge and defence
What can have thus subdued it? What can now
Have given you that cold melancholy look,
Succeeding to your unaccustomed fear?
What did your father do or say to you?
He stayed not after that accursed feast
One moment in your chamber.
Nay, Beatrice; have courage, my sweet girl.
If any one despairs it should be I
Who loved him once, and now must live with him
Till God in pity call for him or me.
For you may, like your sister, find some husband,
And smile, years hence, with children round your knees;
Whilst I, then dead, and all this hideous coil,
Shall be remembered only as a dream.

224.

BEATRICE, CONDEMNED TO DEATH, BIDS FAREWELL TO HER BROTHER (YT)

(1819) PERCY BYSSHE SHELLEY, *THE CENCI*, ACT V

"Plead with blind lightning, or the deaf sea, not with man." Beatrice has reason to suppose so. Count Cenci, her father, has murdered two sons, tormented his wife without mercy, and raped her, his daughter Beatrice, but has barely worn out the patience of the Papacy, which bothers to exercise few if any restraints over its Italian nobility. Neither Beatrice nor her mother have any recourse to justice beyond Cenci's, and having no longer any strength to bear the Count's lunatic cruelties, plot and succeed in murdering him.

It isn't Cenci's cruelties alone that horrify Beatrice or Shelley, but the pleasure that the abandoned cruelty of power takes in tormenting its victims and exhibiting pleasurable indifference toward their suffering. But in striking for redress, victims like Beatrice and her mother do not have the immunity of victimizers; for them there's an easily activated justice; they're condemned, and face their legal execution.

"Worse than the bitterness of death, is hope." As in much of traditional tragedy, Beatrice stares at a fact: The world's justice is quixotic and removed, and clinging to the slender hope for its redemption adds only sharper pain. To avoid it, to assent to its despair, "Rock me to the sleep," she begs, "from which none awake."

But in the tradition of the tragic heroines of Jacobean tragedy, Beatrice as person transcends Beatrice as story agent; they practice, all the great ones, a deliberate disconnect between their terminal circumstance and their accumulation of desperate experience. With great calm, with great charity toward those who stay behind, with great concern for immediate domesticities, as though cheating death of its weight (The Duchess of Malfi's "Look thou giv'st my boy syrup for his cold, And let my girl say her prayers"); Beatrice's "bind up this hair... and yours I see is coming down," they defy the invasion of person by the situation and role to which they're confined in their last moments.

BEATRICE

Worse than the bitterness of death, is hope:
It is the only ill which can find place
Upon the giddy, sharp and narrow hour
Tottering beneath us. Plead with the swift frost
That it should spare the eldest flower of spring:
Plead with awakening earthquake, o'er whose couch
Even now a city stands, strong, fair, and free;
Now stench and blackness yawn, like death. Oh, plead
With famine, or wind-walking Pestilence,
Blind lightning, or the deaf sea, not with man!
Cruel, cold, formal man; righteous in words,
In deeds a Cain. No, Mother, we must die:
Since such is the reward of innocent lives;
Such the alleviation of worst wrongs.
And whilst our murderers live, and hard, cold men,
Smiling and slow, walk through a world of tears
To death as to life's sleep; 'twere just the grave
Were some strange joy for us. Come, obscure Death,
And wind me in thine all-embracing arms!
Like a fond mother hide me in thy bosom,
And rock me to the sleep from which none wake.
Live ye, who live, subject to one another
As we were once.

Farewell, my tender brother. Think

Of our sad fate with gentleness, as now:
And let mild, pitying thoughts lighten for thee
Thy sorrow's load. Err not in harsh despair,
But tears and patience. One thing more, my child:
For thine own sake be constant to the love
Thou bearest us; and to the faith that I,
Though wrapped in a strange cloud of crime and shame,
Lived ever holy and unstained. And though
Ill tongues shall wound me, and our common name
Be as a mark stamped on thine innocent brow
For men to point at as they pass, do thou
Forbear, and never think a thought unkind
Of those, who perhaps love thee in their graves.
So mayest thou die as I do; fear and pain
Being subdued.
Give yourself no unnecessary pain,
My dear Lord Cardinal. Here, Mother, tie
My girdle for me, and bind up this hair
In any simple knot; ay, that does well.
And yours I see is coming down. How often
Have we done this for one another; now
We shall not do it anymore. My Lord,
We are quite ready. Well, 'tis very well.

CAIN: the first son of Adam and Eve, who murdered his brother Abel.

225.

AMELIA DEBATES HER UNCERTAINTY: LOVING HER CAPTAIN OR SPARING HER UNCLE (YT)

(1828) EDWARD FITZBALL, *THE INCHCAPE BELL,
OR THE DUMB SAILOR BOY*, ACT I, SC. 2

Amelia's quandary is not deep, and by play's end is easily solved: her uncle, Sir John Trevanly, is after some years still mourning the loss of his wife and son, and her heart cannot bear to burden the old man with her accepting a lover, Captain Taffrail, whom her uncle has not yet explicitly sanctioned. This is very much a red herring in the plot of this fairly primitive melodrama whose interest lies elsewhere. A "nautical" melodrama combines with an earlier fashion in "Gothic" melodrama to excite spectators with a gloomy castle and its legacy of unsolved disappearances and murders, a clutch of ships at the town dock with their pirates and sailors and smugglers, a storm at sea, and a staged shipwreck for its "sensation" finish.

To excite whom? The play was written specifically for the Surrey Theatre, an East Side house near the Thames that played to an audience of sailors, local carpenters, shipwrights, and tradesmen who saw better than they heard. Dialogue, as in most early melodrama, had to carry its own weight over the confusion and din of the far more exciting visuals of the spectacle's stage life, and had to make its points with exceptionally emphatic and thoroughly overexplained statement. Amelia, quiet though her scene is, shows in her text how meaning was much simplified, much overvoiced, and heavily underscored, this done with care lest spectators miss a single wrinkle of plot point or background information. Acting as teaching, point by point; the posture of the Amelia "presenter" is focused more directly on the spectator, and talks more explicitly into his ear than into her interlocutor's onstage, or in monologue, to herself. That "character" and "emotion" are broad goes without saying; the skill of presentation lies in painting those with no matter how broad a brush while spelling out with perfect clarity the abc of meaning.

The Inchcape Bell belongs to the subgenre of melodrama called "burletta," meaning "melodrama with songs." Like the drunken sailors and smugglers, Amelia has her "signature" song, relating roughly to bringing cheer to her morose uncle.

> *(Enter Amelia with caution, regarding*
> *Sir John as he gazes at the picture of his*
> *wife and son)*

AMELIA

My uncle! my dear, loved, unhappy uncle!

> *(He starts—she throws herself into his*
> *arms.)*

Oh, sir! if you love me, why continue to yield yourself to this despondency! Your health, your life, is rapidly declining beneath accumulating sorrow. I knew, I was sure, your return to this melancholy scene of early misery must increase the gloom which too fully occupies your heart: for your poor Amelia's sake, I entreat you, dear sir, study to abandon these too vain regrets. Tears; ah! come with me, dear uncle, I'll take my harp, and sing to you; you know that always consoles you.

(Sir John hurries out, R)

Ah, woe is me! If my hand were not already promised to another, how could I add to the sufferings of my uncle, by acceding to a union, which, as yet, his voice has not sanctioned. Not marry Captain Taffrail, not see him? How can I? Long ere I beheld Captain Taffrail, my uncle had promised my hand to another, and has he not kindly consented to leave me to my own choice, on condition that I accede to the suit of no one till the completion of a year? That year will soon have expired, and how dishonourable, undutiful in me, not to keep my word with my uncle. If Captain Taffrail truly loves me, as he professes, the present delay will but enable him, by his patience, to prove that affection.

Heigho! I'm afraid, by these palpitations, that my tenderness on Taffrail's account is even more deeply rooted than I believed; but my uncle—yonder he sits, so sad, so mournful, *(Looking off, R)* I must not forget him. Ah! how assuasive is the voice of those we love!

SONG—AMELIA

Let us wander through the meadows,
Where the water-lilies bloom,
And the honey-bee is drinking
From the cups of golden broom.
In my bow'r full of beauty,
While the tear is in your eye,
I'll take my harp, and sing the song
Of happy days gone by.

Let us wander through the forest,
Under leaf and under bough,
Where the merry birds are singing,
And the briar-roses blow.
In my bow'r, &c.

(Exit, L)

226.

JULIE, DISTRAUGHT AND TERRIFIED, RUSHES TO TELL RICHELIEU OF HER ATTEMPTED SEDUCTION BY THE KING, AND OF THE COMPLICITY OF HER OWN HUSBAND (YT)

(1839) EDWARD BULWER, *RICHELIEU, OR THE CONSPIRACY*, ACT III, SC. 1

Plots and counterplots, spies and double agents, a slew of conspirators betraying and compromising one another—this is the substance of Bulwer's *Richelieu*. But shining through all this with a penetrating realization of who, what and where spies and counterspies are operating, is the splendidly knowing Richelieu, the crafty Cardinal and Prime Minister of Louis XIII's France, who nods and smiles at each new item of intelligence brought to his attention, knowing full well and in advance how far the new item of news will carry either in his favor, or fall short, or damage.

A pawn in all this is Julie, an orphan (by 1839, standard for young virtue) but also the ward of Richelieu, under whose protection she—sometimes knowing it, sometimes not—thrives. A slender thread in the maze of conspiracies is her story. She is desired by the King himself, and both she and Richelieu are determined to keep her away from royal defilement. One way is to marry her to a brave stalwart—the Chevalier de Mauprat—at once. Done. But into his ear is poured, by the faithless Baradas, a false story of her willing compliance to the King's attentions, and later there is poured into her ear, another false tale of her new husband's complicity in her seduction. She is summoned to the palace; commanded, she goes; that night, the King—.

But by 1839, febrile heroines endangered by seduction no longer quaked before their seducers. Julie, armed with virtue, repulses and shames the King. Still, as she reports here to Richelieu, there was worse to come: The treacherous Baradas himself attempts her, not with seduction, but with lies: the "god," her husband, she hears, is complicit with the King. The distraught Julie finds her way to the

Queen, who helps her escape the palace, and here she is, at Richelieu's feet, trembling with postponed terror.

Several strains combine here to provide a new and, for burgeoning middle-class audiences, a somewhat more acceptable texture for basic melodrama: there's the structure of the well-made play—a letter revealed at the end holds the key to the plot's unscrambling; the lower-class crudities of early melodrama are displaced by the silken maneuvers of royal courtiers; the complex weave of plot is closer to chess than to brawl; and most particularly, the reassuring closure shows a rebellion put down, a King renovated, and a Nation restored. The theater of comfortable gamesmanship and wittily overcome dangers and restored stabilities sits well with a class that asks of its amusements only plump comfort, easy wit, and political reassurance.

(Enter Julie)

JULIE
Cardinal! My father!

(Falls at his feet. He raises her.)
I am safe; and with thee!
Why did I love him, clinging to a breast
That knows no shelter? Listen—late at noon—
—The marriage day, ev'n then no more a lover,
He left me coldly. Well, I sought my chamber
To weep and wonder, but to hope and dream.
Sudden a mandate from the King—to attend
Forthwith his pleasure at the Louvre.
He frown'd and chid; proclaim'd the bond unlawful:
Bade me not quit my chamber in the palace,
And there at night—alone—this night—all still—
He sought my presence—dared—thou read'st the heart,
Read mine! I cannot speak it!
Humbled and abash'd,
He from the chamber crept—this mighty Louis;
Crept like a baffled felon! Yielded! Ah, no!
More royalty in woman's honest heart
Than dwells within the crowned majesty
And sceptred anger of a hundred kings!

Then came a sharper trial!
At the King's suit the Count de Baradas
Sought me to soothe, to fawn, to flatter; he let fall

Dark hints of treachery, and stung at last
By my disdain, the dim and glimmering sense
Of his cloak'd words broke into bolder light,
And then—ah, then my haughty spirit fail'd me!
Then I was weak—wept—oh, such bitter tears!
For (turn thy face aside, and let me whisper
The horror to thine ear) then did I learn
That he—that Adrien—that my husband—knew
The King's polluting suit, and deemed it honour!
Then glared upon me all the hideous truth,
Mystery of looks—words—all unravell'd, and
I saw the impostor, where I had loved the god!

To the despair he caused
The courtier left me; but amid the chaos
Darted one guiding ray—to 'scape—to fly—
Reach Adrien, learn the worst; 'twas then near midnight:
Trembling I left my chamber, sought the queen,
Fell at her feet, reveal'd the unholy peril,
Implored her aid to flee our joint disgrace.
Moved, she embraced and soothed me; nay, preserved;
Her word sufficed to unlock the palace gates:
I hasten'd home, but home was desolate—
No Adrien there! Fearing the worst, I fled
To thee, directed hither.
Oh, in one hour what years of anguish crowd!

LOUVRE: the royal palace in Paris.

227.

LADY GAY RECOUNTS HER BRILLIANT HORSEWOMANSHIP AT THE HUNT (OC)

(1841) DION BOUCICAULT, *LONDON ASSURANCE*, ACT III

Working to recover the tone of Restoration and eighteenth-century "laughing comedy," contrasting witty town and humdrum country, clever youth and outfoxed age, profligate libertine and outmaneuvering lady, Boucicault manages, while staying within the bounds of

Victorian moral sensibility, to somewhat anticipate the comic assurance of Wilde's comedies a half-century later.

The lady who outmaneuvers the libertine is Lady Gay Spanker, the brilliantly commanding force who rules over her willing husband to their mutual pleasure and comfort. The "country" the Restoration sneered at triumphs in *London Assurance* with its idyllic respectability over the vestigial libertinage of the town's would-be seducer, the sixtyish Sir Harcourt Courtly. Unlike her Restoration counterpart, Lady Gay's mind is not at all on the game of seduction, but on the wholly occupying center of her life: horses. She and her class will be remembered in 1913 in Shaw's *Heartbreak House* in Lady Utterword's aristocratic nostalgia for once grand and rural Horseback Hall.

Lady Gay comes onto her guests in the morning room at Oak Hall fully equipped in riding habit, greets her young guest Grace and her father Max with a welcoming morning kiss for each, notices her new guest Sir Harcourt Courtly, and at a moderately inviting cue from him, gets quickly onto the subject of the hunt. In the center of her own morning room, she's at once lost in the recollection and the joyful recitation of the adventure of her last outing, when in a field of sixteen horsemen, she outrode them all and won the steeplechase.

LADY GAY

Ha! ha! Well Governor, how are ye? I have been down five times, climbing up your stairs in my long clothes. How are you, Grace, dear? *(Kisses her)* There, don't fidget, Max. And there—*(Kisses him)* there's one for you. Oh, gracious, I didn't see you had visitors. You mustn't think anything of the liberties I take with my old papa here—bless him! I am so glad you have come, Sir Harcourt. Now we shall be able to make a decent figure at the heels of a hunt.

Does my ladyship hunt? Ha, I say, Governor, I rather flatter myself that I do hunt! Why, Sir Harcourt, one might as well live without laughing as without hunting. Man was fashioned expressly to fit a horse. Are not hedges and ditches created for leaps? Of course! And I look upon foxes to be one of the most blessed dispensations of a benign Providence.

Ah! Sir Harcourt, had you been here a month ago, you would have witnessed the most glorious run that ever swept over merry England's green cheek. There were sixty horses in the field, all mettle to the bone: the start was a picture—away we

went in a cloud—pell-mell—helter-skelter—the fools first, as
usual, using themselves up—we soon passed them—first your
Kitty, then my Blueskin, and Craven's colt last. Then came the
tug—Kitty skimmed the walls—Blueskin flew over the
fences—the Colt neck and neck, and half a mile to run—at
last the Colt baulked a leap and went wild. Kitty and I had it
all to ourselves—she was three lengths ahead, as we breasted
the last wall, six feet, if an inch, and a ditch on the other side.
Now, for the first time, I gave Blueskin his head—ha! ha!—
Away he flew like a thunderbolt—over went the filly—I over
the same spot, leaving Kitty in the ditch—walked the steeple
eight miles in thirty minutes, and scarcely turned a hair.

TUG: here, competitive struggle. BAULKED: missed. BREASTED: met, or advanced
boldly.

228.

MABEL'S BELIEF: A WOMAN'S SINGLE ACT OF CHOICE IN LIFE: THE CHOICE OF A HUSBAND (YT)

(1842) J. WESTLAND MARSTON, *THE PATRICIAN'S DAUGHTER*,
ACT I, SC. 1

Like women of gentility in Trollope's Victorian novels, Lady Mabel
maneuvers for *place* within understood parameters. Her goal is of
long standing, and only now is it wormed out of her in response to
direct challenge. Her ambition is the same as a prideful man's in
Victorian aristocracy—for praise, for prominence, for glory, culmi-
nating in a lifetime of deeply satisfied, well-earned self-congratula-
tion. Where is she to find this repletion, given the parameters for
women? Only in reflected glory, and Lady Mabel has the sagacity to
figure out, as Trollope's and Henry James' women frequently did, the
precise moment and precise act when the stab for that *place* can be
made: in choosing a husband.

Her assumption that she *has* a choice in itself reflects the almost
unique condition of fiction's aristocratic women. Their rank and
wealth set them apart from the common herd of women in nine-

teenth-century fiction, who still labored fretfully under the constraints of a frowning divinity. Along with her pride in her independence goes a partially unconscious cruelty—the cruelty defined by her lower-class suitor Mordaunt, and against which he rails in his eloquent speech of accusation [see, in Men's vols.: "Mordaunt Accuses Mabel of the Deepest Crime"]. But to the degree that she's casually cruel to suitors below her, she's reverential to the image of the being who will elevate her—leave her, that is to say, in that state of repletion. But what is that image?

He is to be "high-born," possessing the inner "light" of nobility (which, parsed, means old, well-connected family), a courageous warrior (high-ranking commission), an eloquent orator for the populace and a persuasive politician (a seat in Parliament), possess a cornucopia of charity (unbounded wealth), and win not just national but international fame (a Marlborough, a Cromwell or a Wellington). And for herself, she gains the infinite satisfaction of knowing that she had, in that one moment of independent choice given to woman, hitched her wagon to the right star.

MABEL

Although reason makes not love,
Love may consist with reason; am I right?
Now, if you grant me audience, I will
Possess you of my secret thoughts, till now
Nursed in the solitude of my own heart.
He whom my will shall for its king elect
Must bring me something more than that I have;
Women who marry seldom act but once;
Their lot is, ere they wed, obedience
Unto a father; thenceforth to a husband;
But in the *one* election which they make,
Choice of a mate for life and death, and heaven,
They may be said to act. The man they wed
Is as the living record of the deed,
Their one momentous deed. If he be base,
It veils their deed with shame; if he be great,
Encircles it with glory; and if good,
Haloes it with religion. Wouldst thou know
Whom I would have to be *my* husband, sire?
In brief terms I will sketch him. He shall be
High born; handsome, I'd rather, but at least
With features lit up by the sacred light
Which marks the elect band of noble men,

Whose history is the world's; and whose high names,
Linked close with empires, sound their synonyms;
With eye that quails not in the war; with voice
That thrills the popular ear, and o'erawes senates;
And of a wide, ceaseless benevolence,
Bounded but by the walls of the great world;
And O, whene'er affection breathed his name,
Or mind did homage to it, should my heart
Rush back to the bright hour when first I chose him,
Saying it was *my act*!

229.

MRS. CRANK IMAGINES WITH HORROR THAT SHE HAS DISCOVERED HER HUSBAND'S INFIDELITY (OC)

(1846) JOSEPH STIRLING COYNE, *DID YOU EVER SEND YOUR WIFE TO CAMBERWELL?*, ONE ACT

They were called "screamers," the one-act farces used for filler in the shows at the Adelphi, which otherwise featured flat-out melodramas. Their written style was similar to that of the "mellers"—every move, every turn of thought, every point in plot was accompanied by explicit footnoting in the dialogue, and every line was addressed so to speak face-forward, whether spoken solo or to another actor. The audience's presence was wholly acknowledged and wholly embraced; the acknowledgement went both ways: the yelling, the laughing, the screaming, the applauding, were what pushed the continuity along. Without them, the screamer was a silent non-event—a Keystone Kop comedy unreeling grainily on TV.

The text of Coyne's one-act is standard but funny, and plays with the precision of a Feydeau farce: the timed exits and entrances—missing one another by a hair's breadth—the couple in the wrong apartment, the wrong woman in bed, the right wife returning, the baby tossed behind the chest and believed squashed, the rich old aunt finding the baby and taking it, the four all arriving at the same time, the explanations, the baby finally turning up, the confusion over.

Before Mrs. Crank's scene below, her husband comes into the flat to meet his new neighbor, goes off, and leaves his hat. Mrs. Crank, directed to the wrong flat, sees her husband's hat and a woman's hat, screams, faints, leaves baby, hat, umbrella, and cloak, and rushes off for vengeance. First confusion, the beginning of the pile.

(Mrs. Crank enters in travelling dress; she carries an infant in her arms, and an umbrella in her hand.)

MRS. CRANK

So, a pretty chase I have had of it, after that runaway husband of mine. However I have traced him out at last—I can't be mistaken. The guard of the coach knows Crank as well as he knows the statty at Charing Cross—and he told me confidentially that he was living up atop of the house here. So I've travelled all the way from Stoke Poges to catch my old fox at his tricks—for I'm sure it's no good he can be after, to desert his innocent babe—and his virtuous wife that any man might be proud of.

(Sees Crank's hat on table)
Oh, I knew I couldn't be mistaken, here's his hat, and his name "Isaac Crank" inside it. Soh! Soh! He's pretty comfortable here too—well I suppose a wife has a right to make herself at home in her husband's chamber. So I'll just put baby to bed—bless the dear little fellow, he's fallen asleep in my arms—he's the living picture of his unnatural father, he is!

(Kisses the child, which she places in bed and throws her cloak over him)
And now I'll sit down and rest myself, for I'm tired to death.

(Sees a woman's cap on the chair and utters a scream of horror)
Oh! What's this? A cap—a cap—a woman's cap! Oh Crank, you old reprobate—I see it all now—real lace, too—and his lawful wife obliged to put up with bobbinet—that's an aggravation no woman couldn't stand, and I won't stand it— real lace!

(Tearing the cap to shreds)
There, there, and there! Oh dear, I'm a wretched insulted woman. I don't care what becomes of me now. I'll put an end to myself—I'll throw myself into the river—real lace! Oh I

could forgive anything but that. Where is the villain? I'll leave
my death on him, and have him hanged for it I will.

> *(Rushes out and in her exit snatches a
> plate from the table and dashes it on the
> floor)*

STATTY: statue. BOBBINET: a machine-made lacelike covering.

230.

MRS. HAWK PERSUADES SIR HARRY TO RENOUNCE HIS AND HER HUSBAND'S CRIMINAL SCHEME (oc)

(1851) GEORGE HENRY LEWES, *THE GAME OF SPECULATION*, ACT III

The Game of Speculation, "a sort of *Volpone* of the financial markets,"
is a nineteenth-century prevision of the stock market games of the
1980s and '90s, with the difference being that the play's speculating
anti-hero, Hawk, would now be happily sequestered in the Cayman
Islands and not require rescue by the *deus ex machina,* Sparrow, his
old business partner, returned a multimillionaire from India. Unlike
Bulwer-Lytton's *Money,* the play is about nothing but money. Its plot
tracks nothing but the frenzied speculations of the bankrupt Hawk,
who staves off his army of creditors with the balletic legerdemain of a
born swindler. The moment comes in the third act—as is *de rigeur* for
the well-made-play formula—for Hawk to launch his most daring
and most immoral trick, by which he and his pyramid of speculations will either sink or swim. The scheme: to disguise Sir Harry
Lester, his daughter's wealthy suitor (who as it turns out is as close to
bankruptcy as Hawk himself), as the returned Sparrow, to recover the
appearance of credit Hawk so desperately and immediately needs to
avoid the bench (prison). The scheme is so inordinately shocking to
Mrs. Hawk, the perfectly virtuous and hand-wringing wife who until
this moment has clung to the illusion of her husband as, deep down,
a man of honor, that she confronts the suitor, and mustering all the
authority of virtue, argues the young man out of this devilish ruse. In

the passage below, she succeeds with him—and puts her husband in the greatest possible danger for the sake of truth and honor. The reversal at play's end is punctuated by the real Sparrow arriving, to the astonishment of Hawk—who is the only one in the cast who remains (until the last moment) unconvinced that the real miracle has taken over from his shoddy fraud.

MRS. HAWK

I beg your pardon, Sir Harry.—No, you will not stir a step! I know all. You and my husband have been plotting schemes that will do very well in a comedy. I have employed one that is still older, and, as I think, better. I tell you I know all. The part my husband wishes you to play is a disgraceful one—give it up. I know to whom I am speaking. It is only a few hours I have had the pleasure of knowing you; and yet I *do* know you. One day was sufficient for me to judge you; and while my husband was seeking, perhaps, for the amount of folly in your breast, which he might turn to his purpose, I discerned that your heart was in the right place, and concealed honourable feelings which might save you. Yes, sir, save you—you and my husband—you are going to ruin each other. Do not you understand that debts dishonour no one, when they are avowed? We can but work to pay them. You have before you your whole life; and you have too much intelligence, if not too much heart, to wish to disgrace that life for ever, by a scheme which justice would repudiate, if not punish.

My husband shall return your bills to you, sir; I will undertake to see it done. We will be satisfied with your word, and you will pay them when you have honourably made your fortune. That will be rather long, but we will have patience. Now, Sir Harry, go—seek my husband, and persuade him to renounce this scheme, which you can do more easily, now that he will no longer have your assistance. There—in that room you will find writing materials. Remain there until I come to take your letter—I will give it to him myself.

(Lester exits)
I have succeeded. Oh, that I may now succeed with my husband!

231.

EMILIE, MEETING HER EX-LOVER, INSISTENTLY DEMANDS THE RETURN OF HER LETTERS (YT)

(1852) DION BOUCICAULT, *THE CORSICAN BROTHERS*, ACT II, SC. 2

By the mid-nineteenth century, the unhappy wives of upper-middle-class gentlemen in upper-middle-class melodrama had learned a solemn and a daunting lesson: that the sinfulness that in the past religion visited on the violation of marriage vows and still did was as nothing compared to the damnation visited on by upper-middle-class society's opprobrium. It wasn't perdition that restrained yearning wives from the "fatal misstep" that haunted the sentimental drama of the eighteenth century, but social ostracism. Scandal replaced hell as the terror beyond terror. "Death rather than that," shudders Hedda Gabler when she is offered the choice between secret adultery on the one hand, and suffering her name to be implicated in scandal on the other. Death, she concludes, is better than either choice. For married Emilie, in the passage below, merely to be seen talking privately with a young man in a secluded corner at a masked ball signifies that she could be "ruined" by "the tongue of slander." And in Boucicault's melodrama, the *coup de theatre* explodes at the moment when, subsequent to this scene, Emilie enters a late-night bachelor's supper party on the arm of Renaud—and but for her swift rescue she enjoys at the hands of a man of honor, who instantly removes her from this polluting environment, her "ruin" would indeed have been complete and forever.

Women of even moderate social station, in the "refined" melodrama of the latter half of the century, all lived in fear of the perpetual glare of "the world" tracking and judging their every decision and every move. Its ever-prying eyes considerably diminished the older and more familiar glare of the ever-prying eyes from above.

Emilie doesn't know it, but she is being tricked into supposing that this dastardly Renaud, once her lover long before her marriage, will return her letters; she's determined to have them back lest "the world" might construe indiscretion in them. But his promise is only a ruse to compromise her for the sake of winning a bet. Emilie has only the intention of recovering her letters and severing all ties with

Renaud; but the very act of meeting with him is already fraught with the danger of her seeming to be compromised.

*(The lobby of the Opera. Enter Emilie
and Chateau-Renaud)*

EMILIE

You requested my presence here; I am come, although at the risk of my motives being misinterpreted by you and by the world. Once seen, the tongue of slander would assail me; if known, I am ruined.

I have obeyed the conditions you insisted on; now keep your promise and restore to me those letters. You will return them? Give them to me at once, and let me go.

I have given you the right to think me wavering—fickle—nay, contemptible. I will not deny that you possessed my early love. My first affections, as you know, were yours; my father saw and crushed our hopes at once. The fate of my poor sister, the miserable marriage of Louise, was ever present to his mind. A marriage which lost him a daughter—me a sister. Unhappy girl, where is she now? Perhaps deserted, struggling with misery and want. Some cause, of which I am ignorant, taught his distempered mind to see in you a copy of my sister's husband. To snatch me from the fate he so much dreaded, he obliged me to accept the hand of the Admiral de L'Esparre. The disparity of our years, our total want of sympathy, rendered it impossible for me to love, although I respect and honour him. It is now a sacred duty I owe to my husband, as well as myself, to claim from you the evidences of our plighted troth.

Be not deluded by a thought so vain, so false, as to suppose I can again receive you with the feelings that inspired those letters: cease to claim possession of a heart which, with all its sufferings, all its anguish, belongs now to another; such sentiments are unworthy of you, and their avowal tends to degrade us both.

Those letters have been seen by others, and thus through the thoughtlessness of vanity, you assist to wound the honour you are bound to guard. It matters not. Sir, in reliance on your promise to restore them here, I have consented most reluctantly to meet you, and for the last time; it may be I have already compromised my position. You may no longer love, but you shall at least respect me. I bid you restore to me the only relics of our unhappy attachment, now that its very mention is a crime.

232.

LADY AUDLEY DETERMINES TO PRESERVE THE SECRET OF HER BIGAMY (OT)

(1863) COLIN HENRY HAZLEWOOD, *LADY AUDLEY'S SECRET*, ACT I, SC. 1

Even in the domestic interiors of the realistic plays of the later nineteenth century, playwrights hesitated to give up the ease and efficiency of the soliloquy and the aside. These devices were clear, they were truthful, and for the spectator, they were the absolute guarantee of accurate information. Therefore they should be performed with pride, not with shame. The characteristic Elizabethan soliloquizers told us their motive, their feeling about that motive, and their ethical assumptions behind that motive. The characteristic French neo-classical soliloquizers told us about their dilemma, worked through it, and frequently emerged with an answer. But here Lady Audley goes back to the early classical practice of reciting useful preliminary plot information, converting third-person narrative into first-person confessional. Note: Artemis or Dionysus or Athene might well recite just such a soliloquy—and did—in classical tragedy, touching on all of Lady Audley's points of personal and immediate motive. These included the long-term motive that the immediate motive was to serve, the favorable aspects and the obstacles in the present situation, and the overall plan and immediate plan that followed from these motives, situations, and obstacles. There is one radical difference, though: The gods and goddesses in Greek tragedy, as well as the servants and slaves in Roman comedy, faced the audience directly when they recited their soliloquies of important initial plot information, and were neither coy nor embarrassed about violating the frame of their fictional place. Yet Lady Audley's enclosed stage frame makes her address to us, while pretending we're not there seem, awkward and even silly, and we have reason to wonder whether the fault lies in—that terrible word—valorizing the fictional place over the real place, the theater, or whether the reverse might yet be more honest and more useful.

Lady Audley, in fact, because of her generous and clear supply of face-front expository information, needs no more of it here, but the actor of her role should earn considerable applause for the feat of moving instantly from one mode of theatrical address to the other, when Lady Audley's first husband shows up at just the moment when she has most dread of his return.

LADY AUDLEY

It must be my aim to stand well with this young man; he is my husband's favourite, I know. I manage Sir Michael as I like, and if his nephew gains too firm a hold upon him, he may prove a dangerous rival in my path. I live now for ambition and interest, to mould the world and its votaries to my own end. Once I was fool enough to wed for love. Now I have married for wealth. What a change from the wife of George Talboys to the wife of Sir Michael Audley! My fool of a first husband thinks me dead. Oh excellent scheme, oh cunning device, how well you have served me.

*(George enters at back, and comes down
silently to her side.)*
Where can he be now? Still in India no doubt. He is mourning my death perhaps—ha, ha! Why, I have only just begun to live—to taste the sweets of wealth and power. If I am dead to George Talboys, he is dead to me. Yes, I am well rid of him, and on this earth we meet no more.
(Turning with a shriek) George Talboys!

(Aside)
I am lost! But be prudent.

(To George)
George Talboys! Understand me! You left me in poverty and dependence—you promised to write from India. And not one letter reached my hands; I thought myself deserted, and determined to make reprisals on you; I changed my name; I entered the family of a gentleman as governess to his daughters; became the patient drudge for a miserable stipend, that I might carry my point—that point was to gain Sir Michael Audley's affections; I did so, I devoted all my energies, all my cunning, to that end! and now I have gained the

summit of my ambition, do you think I will be cast down by you, George Talboys? No, I will conquer you or I will die! With what means? With the power of gold. Listen to me. I have fought too hard for my position to yield it up tamely. Take every jewel, every penny I have and leave me! henceforth I can be nothing to you, nor you to me. Our first meeting was a mistake, it was the ardent passion of a boy and girl, which time has proved to have been ill advised on either side—I am no longer the weak confiding girl you first knew me—no, I am a resolute woman—and where I cannot remove an obstacle I will crush it. Yes—and fight you to the death!

(Starting—aside)
"Death! death!" Aye that is the word—that is the only way of escape.

(Aloud)
I defy you—scorn you—spurn you for a vindictive fool. Go to Sir Michael, if you will—denounce me, do—and I will swear to him that you are a liar—a madman—he will believe me before you. I gained his heart, his soul, his unbounded confidence, and before there is the felon's dock for me, there shall be the maniac's cell for you. Ah, ha! What think you now?

233.

THE MARCHIONESS EXHORTS HER SON TO EMULATE HIS FOREBEARS IN WINNING GLORY ON THE BATTLEFIELD (OT)

(1867) Thomas William Robertson, *Caste*, Act II

George D'Alroy, a scion of wealth and title, and his friend Captain Hawtree, are on the verge of going off to India with their regiment to fight the Sepoy rebellion, and D'Alroy is bidding farewell to Esther, whom he's secretly married. She is, like her sister Polly, a mere ballet dancer but—as the ethic of what was called the "cup-and-saucer" genre of socially responsible plays like *Caste* demanded—love has moved him to overlook small differences. Not so his mother, the Marchioness. A dragon in the upper reaches of the aristocracy, she lives by code, and she arrives—surprising her son, who must hide the two girls from Mother—to offer advice and benediction for his journey to India and glory.

By the time of Robertson's *Caste*, the problem of class misalliance had long been stereotypical (one remembers, in England, Dekker's sixteenth-century *Shoemaker's Holiday*, or Steele's eighteenth-century *Conscious Lovers*, and even plays as classically remote as Menander's in fourth-century BC, Athens), but its revival in earnest Victorian drama was certainly attributable to a restored rigidity of class consciousness among an aristocracy nostalgic for absolute political power. *Caste* is a mild taunt against this anachronism of caste, hardly competing with the thesis plays of Dumas and Augier that had been targeting, with considerably more sophistication, the same anomaly in French society (but from the opposite point of view, showing the reprehensible invasions of the *declasse* into the upper classes, as opposed to the English showing the reprehensible snobbishness of the upper classes in obstructing such an invasion).

The subjects of the Marchioness's sermon are three, Robertson mocking their anachronism: the indispensible nobility of heritage, or "blood"; chivalric honor on the battlefield; and the *noblesse oblige* a gentleman owes to the underclass victims of his sexual sport, as distinct from the piety he owes to the virginal Lady of his marital choice.

Hawtree, out of courtesy to the Marchioness before her interview with her son, retires, and the Marchioness takes advantage of his absence to make a slurring comment on the misalliance Hawtree himself and his bride's family will be guilty of in his impending marriage. Her observation becomes a convenient cue for her sermon.

MARCHIONESS

I'm not sorry that he's gone, for I wanted to talk to you alone.
Strange that a woman of such good birth as the Countess
should encourage the attention of Captain Hawtree for her
daughter Florence.

(*During these lines D'Alroy conceals
Polly's hat and umbrella under the
table.*)
Lady Clardonax was one of the old Carberrys of Hampshire—
not the Norfolk Carberrys, but the direct line. And Mr.

Hawtree's grandfather was in trade—He's a very nice person, but parvenu, as one may see by his languor and his swagger. My boy *(Kissing his forehead)* I am sure, will never make a misalliance. He is a D'Alroy, and by his mother's side Plantagenista. The source of our life stream is royal.

The Marquis, you must know, is paralysed now. I left him at Spa with three physicians. He is always paralysed at this time of the year; it is in the family. The paralysis is not personal, but hereditary. I came over to see my steward; got to town last night.

It's so long since I've seen you. *(Leans back in chair)* You're looking very well, and I daresay when mounted are quite a "beau cavalier." And so, my boy *(Playing with his hair)*, you are going abroad for the first time on active service. And now, my dear boy, before you go I want to give you some advice; and you mustn't despise it because I'm an old woman. We old women know a great deal more than people give us credit for. You are a soldier—so was your father—so was his father—so was mine—so was our royal founder; we were born to lead! The common people expect it from us. It is our duty.

When my boy fights—and you will fight—he is sure to distinguish himself. It is his nature to—*(Toys with his hair)*—he cannot forget his birth. And when you meet these Asiatic ruffians, who have dared to revolt, and to outrage humanity, you will strike as your ancestor Sir Galtier of Chevrault struck at Poictiers. *(Changing tone of voice as if remembering)* Froissart mentions it thus:—"Sir Galtier, with his four squires, was in the front, in that battell, and there did marvels in arms. And Sir Galtier rode up to the Prince; and sayd to him—"Sir, take your horse and ryde forth, this journey is yours. God is this daye in your handes. Gette us to the French Kynge's batayle. I think verily by his valyantesse, he woll not fly. Advance banner in the name of God and of Saynt George!" And Sir Galtier galloped forward to see his Kynge's victory, and meet his own death."

There is another subject about which I should have spoken to you before this; but an absurd prudery forbade me. I may never see you more. I am old—and you—are going into battle—*(Kissing his forehead with emotion)* We may not meet again on this earth. I do not fear your conduct, my George, with men; but I know the temptations that beset a youth who is well born. But a true soldier, a true gentleman, should not only be without fear, but without reproach. It is easier to fight a furious man than to forgo the conquest of a love-sick girl. A thousand Sepoys slain in battle cannot redeem the honour of a man who has betrayed the confidence of a trusting woman. Think, George, what dishonour—what stain upon your manhood—to hurl a girl to shame and degradation! And what excuse for it? That she is plebeian? A man of real honour will spare the woman who has confessed her love for him as he would give quarter to an enemy he had disarmed. *(Taking his hands)* Let my boy avoid the snares so artfully spread; and when he asks his mother to welcome the woman he has chosen for his wife, let me take her to my arms and plant a motherly kiss upon the white brow of a lady. *(Noise of fall heard within folding-doors. Rising)* What's that? I heard a cry.

> *(Folding-doors open; discovering Esther*
> *with Polly)*

Who are these *women*? George D'Alroy, these persons should have been sent away. How could you dare to risk your mother meeting women of their stamp?

PARVENU: an upstart; one who has risen to a position above his qualifications. ASIATIC RUFFIANS: the Sepoy Rebellion (1857–59), a revolt of the native soldiers (sepoy) in the British military service, which resulted in the transfer of the administration of India from the East India Company to the crown. POICTIERS: where the English fought against the French in 1356. FROISSART (1337–1410): French historian and poet; wrote his *Chronicles*, a history of his own time, over a period of twelve years beginning in 1374. To mock her devotion to ancient family prowess won on medieval battlefields, the Marchioness's quotation is written in the text of its original English translation. BATTELL: battle. BATAYLE: battle. VALYANTESSE: valor. WOLL: will. SAINT GEORGE: patron saint of England.

234.

CAROLINE, WEEPING, GREETS HER FRIEND WITH THE TALE OF HER BROKEN HEART AND HER SUIT FOR DAMAGES (YC)

(1875) WILLIAM SCHWENCK GILBERT, *TOM COBB*, ACT I

Gilbert's advice on the playing of farce should be written in stone. "It should be played with the most perfect earnestness and gravity throughout ... the characters, one and all, should appear to believe, throughout, in the perfect sincerity of their words and actions." And further, "the actors should rely for the fun of their parts on the most improbable things being done in the most earnest manner by *persons of everyday life*." His stage directions, on the other hand, should be written on water: Caroline, he writes, has "a gushing, poetical demeanor" and at her entrance, before she speaks, "she pauses melo-dramatically." The actor who follows the latter suggestion is on the way to erasing laughter. Caroline is in fact "a romantic young lady," and has a "gushing poetical demeanor" and pauses at her entrances "melodramatically," but neither she nor the actor should appear to know it, nor should they appear to signal that she is nothing else.

Caroline, in the tempered cynicism of mid-Victorian satire and farce, reflects the suspicion that the ardently romantic young ladies of the period have their sights set on the real main chance: money. It's an ancient suspicion in comedy, but the contrast between the lady's romantic ardor and her material yearnings is only partially the source of her comedy. Its greater source is in the ardent attack with which she treats with equally breathless passion all her subjects and all her interests. The serpent of sorrow that treads her underfoot, the poet-soldier whom she still loves, the frothings of his brain and the tele-graph rates to India, the solicitors on his track and the five thousand pounds owing to her heart-wreck, the taking off of her bonnet and her longing to see her friend Matilda's new clothes after ten years' deprivation from that pleasure, are all equally venerated in the moment of her attention to each. You have to imagine Carol Burnett.

(Enter Caroline, in great agitation. She

*is a romantic-looking young lady, with
long curls and gushing, poetical
demeanour. She pauses
melodramatically.)*

CAROLINE

Matilda! Don't ye know me? I came to town yesterday; and
though ten long weary years have flown since last we met, I
could not pass my dear old friend's abode without one effort
to awake those slumbering chords that, struck in unison, ever
found ready echoes in our sister hearts.

How well—how very well you're looking—and heavens, how
lovely!

Matilda! A maiden's heart should be as free as the summer sun
itself; and it's sad when, in youth's heyday, its trilling gladness
has been trodden underfoot by the iron-shod heel of a
serpent. Swear that, come what may, no torture shall ever
induce you to reveal the secret I am going to confide to you.

Will you believe me when I tell you that—I have loved? And
that I have been loved in return? He was a poet-soldier,
fighting the Paynim foe in India's burning clime—a glorious
songster, who swept the lute with one hand while he sabred
the foe with the other! He was a major-general! I never saw
him. I never saw his face; but—I have seen his soul! What's his
soul like? Like the frenzied passion of the antelope! Like the
wild fire of the tiger-lily! Like the pale earnestness of some
lovesick thunder-cloud that longs to grasp the fleeting
lightning in his outstretched arms!

He poured it into the columns of the *Weybridge Watchman,*
the local paper of the town that gave him birth. Dainty little
poems, the dew of his sweet soul, the tender frothings of his
soldier brain. In them I read him, and in them I loved him! I
wrote to him for his autograph—he sent it. I sent him my
photograph, and directly he saw it he proposed in terms that
cloyed me with the sweet surfeit of their choice exuberance,
imploring me at the same time to reply by telegraph. Then,
maiden-like, I longed to toy and dally with his love. But
Anglo-Indian telegraphic rates are high; so, much against my
maiden will, I answered in one word—that one word, yes!

Alas, he is faithless! We corresponded for a year, and then his letters ceased; and now, for eighteen months, no crumb nor crust of comfort has appeased my parched and thirsting soul! Fortunately my solicitor has all his letters. We have advertised for him right and left. Twenty men of law are on his track, and my brother Bulstrode, an attorney's clerk, carries a writ about him night and day. Thus my heart-springs are laid bare that every dolt may gibe at them—the whole county rings with my mishap—its gloomy details are on every bumpkin's tongue! This—this is my secret. Swear that you will never reveal it! The huckstering men of law appraise my heart-wreck at five thousand pounds. I have come to spend a long, long day. I'm going to take my bonnet off. *(Solemnly)* Dear Matilda, we have not met for many many years, and I long—I cannot tell you, Matilda, how earnestly I long—to see all your new things!

(Exeunt together, arms round waists)

PAYNIM: Mohammedan.

235.

ELEANOR OF AQUITAINE OFFERS A CHOICE TO HER RIVAL: DEATH BY POISON OR MARRIAGE WITH A MAN SHE HATES (OT)

(1879) ALFRED, LORD TENNYSON, *BECKET*, ACT IV, SC. 2

It took a while for Eleanor of Aquitaine, who was also Queen of England, to discover the romantic "bower," that is, the estate where her husband Henry II kept secure his mistress Rosamond, whom he loved at least as much as he hated Eleanor. After bearing Henry five sons and three daughters, their marriage soured into indifference and then plain hatred. Eleanor, the tigerish protector of her sons, supported them even in rebellion against their father, but this led him to keep her in "honorable confinement," that is, in accommodating imprisonment away from his royal seat until his death.

It's here that romantic legend takes over from history. The story of Eleanor murdering her rival with a bowl of poison is certainly fantasy, but it was told and retold many times before Tennyson, and by him as well. But told by him with a difference. Since *Becket* is essentially about the confrontation between Henry and Thomas à Becket, which ended with Becket's martyrdom, the incident of Eleanor and Rosamond is attached to the main tale only by a thread, and with novel additions. In *Becket,* Eleanor is led to the "bower" by Geoffrey, the innocent small son of Rosamond, while he supposes they are playing a game, and is followed by Fitzurse, the "judas-lover," the betrayer, the enemy of Henry, and the detestation of Rosamond. Stalking Rosamond at last to her hidden retreat, Eleanor offers her the choice of marriage with Fitzurse or death. Her motive in foisting Fitzurse on Rosamond is her fear that a marriage of the King and mistress would declare Eleanor's marriage void, and her children bastards. Either decision of Rosamond's would relieve Eleanor of that likelihood. But seeing the cross she gave Henry hanging around Rosamond's neck wakes again her jealousy.

But Eleanor's passion is not merely for murder out of jealousy or even policy; it's also for the pleasure of the game. Her humor is black; her wit overrides her deadly purpose; her amusement in making fun of, making a joke of, the desperation of her rival surmounts her emotion, until the moment when she is ready to strike with her upraised dagger. But Tennyson's invention stops her: Becket arrives on the instant, grabs her hand in midair, and prevents the murder on stage that history never sanctioned. But nothing defines Eleanor so much as the ease, the grace, the implicit forgiveness of bad manners in Becket for holding on to her arm for so long and almost breaking it, and the gentleness—on the surface—of the warning that he has done himself a bad turn by "spoiling the farce" of Fitzurse's mischievous marriage and spoiling her own plot as well.

On first arrival, Eleanor confronts Rosamond, who is shocked and frightened. For good reason: Eleanor holds a vial of poison and a knife.

ELEANOR OF AQUITAINE

The Judas-lover of our passion play
Hath trick'd us hither.
Ay, as the bears love honey.
How say'st thou, sweetheart?
Wilt thou go with him? he will marry thee.

Here! the poison wilt set thee free of him!

(Eleanor offers the vial.)
Will not have it?
Then this other,
The wiser choice, because my sleeping-draught
May bloat thy beauty out of shape, and make
Thy body loathsome even to thy child;
While this but leaves thee with a broken heart,
A doll-face blanch'd and bloodless, over which
If pretty Geoffrey do not break his own,
It must be broken for him.
That bosom never
Heaved under the King's hand with such true passion
As at this loveless knife that stirs the riot,
Which it will quench in blood! Slave, if he love thee,
Thy life is worth the wrestle for it. Arise,
And dash thyself against me that I may slay thee!
The worm! shall I let her go? But ha! what's here?
By very God, the cross I gave the King!
His village darling in some lewd caress
Has wheedled it off the King's neck to her own.
By thy leave, beauty. Ay, the same! I warrant
Thou hast sworn on this my cross a hundred times
Never to leave him—and that merits death,
False oath on holy cross—for thou must leave him
To-day, but not quite yet. My good Fitzurse,
The running down the chase is kindlier sport
Even than the death. Who knows but that thy lover
May plead so pitifully, that I may spare thee?
Come hither, man; stand there. (To Rosamund) Take thy one chance;
Catch at the last straw. Kneel to thy lord Fitzurse:
Crouch even because thou hatest him; fawn upon him
For thy life and thy son's.
(Raising the dagger) This in thy bosom, fool,
And after in thy bastard's!

(Enter Becket from behind. Catches hold
of her arm.

The dagger falls; they stare at one
another. After a pause)
My lord, we know you proud of your fine hand,
But having now admired it long enough,

We find that it is mightier than it seems—
At least mine own is frailer; you are laming it.

Might not your courtesy stoop to hand my dagger to me?
But crowns must bow when mitres sit so high.
Well—well—too costly to be left or lost.

> *(Picks up the dagger)*

I had it from an Arab soldan, who,
When I was there at Antioch, marvell'd at
Our unfamiliar beauties of the west;
But wonder'd more at my much constancy
To the monk-king, Louis, our former burden,
From whom, as being too kin, you know, my lord,
God's grace and Holy Church deliver'd us.
I think, time given, I could have talk'd him out of
His ten wives into one. Look at the hilt.
What excellent workmanship! In our poor west
We cannot do it so well.

My honest lord, you are known
Thro' all the courts of Christendom as one
That mars a cause with over violence.
You have wrong'd Fitzurse. I speak not of myself.
We thought to scare this minion of the King
Back from her churchless commerce with the King
To the fond arms of her first love, Fitzurse,
Who swore to marry her. You have spoilt the farce.

236.

MARY, TO SPARE HER FATHER KNOWLEDGE OF HER SHAME, DECIDES TO DISAPPEAR (YT)

(1889) HENRY ARTHUR JONES, *THE MIDDLEMAN*, ACT II

Mary's father, who adores her, has just undergone a test: his daughter has reminded him of another Mary whose father, as she puts it, "seems quite aged—quite broken—since—Mary—," to which her father replies, "Ah, no wonder! It would have killed me if my daughter—" And when she reminds him that that Mary is dead, he responds, "It's a mercy her shame is hidden in the grave." From this test, Mary takes her cue. She too is in the other Mary's condition, and not to put her father through that other father's grief, she decides in this passage to disappear altogether, to be as though dead.

As in Pinero's *The Second Mrs. Tanqueray* [see, in Men's vols.: "Aubrey Tanqueray Alerts His Friends: His New Wife May Not Meet with Their Set's Approval"], forbidden subjects can be talked about freely in polite British melodrama, but only if they are not mentioned. Mary and her father observe the same civility, and doing so, share with Pinero and Henry James a peculiarly late nineteenth-century British novelty in dramatic dialogue: hiatus freely practiced and freely understood. It is the necessary sign of decent breeding, to observe that hiatus and to understand its meaning at once. Within the range of this tight-jawed discipline, emotional commotion of whatever intensity, by the same understanding, is discreetly hidden. Its revelation in a crowd constitutes outrageous indiscretion—like throwing up at dinner, or bleeding on the carpet. Mary conscientiously takes her father's lesson—invisibly to him—to heart, and only when alone, allows the wells of emotion underneath to slip through.

MARY

Goodbye, my dear father! God bless you! Goodbye.

> (*The moment the door is closed, she
> bursts into a flood of tears, and stands
> mechanically repeating his words.*)

"It would have killed me if my daughter—" "It's a mercy her
shame is hidden—is hidden in the grave." "Death is a
thousand times better." (*Suddenly*) You shall think me dead. I
shall go away. You shall hear that I have died in a strange
country. And it will be true, for from this time forth, I shall be
dead to you. Yes, Mary Blenkarn, your child who never
guessed what evil was, is dead. This isn't me! No, I am dead,
and this is all you shall ever know of me. In a few months you
shall learn that I have died—there will be no disgrace for you
in that, and you shall never know how sinful and unhappy I
have been. How can I save you from troubling about my
leaving you? I'll write—there's a pen and ink.

I have thought of everything. If they follow me, they shall

think I have taken the express to London. Yes, that will be the surest plan of getting away. Forgive me for deceiving you, father. This will soften my departure—and when the news comes that I am dead, you must not grieve for me, father, I'm not worth it.

(Kisses letter, then places it on table, goes)

237.

THE DUCHESS OF BERWICK APPRISES LADY WINDERMERE OF HER HUSBAND'S SCANDAL (oc)

(1892) OSCAR WILDE, *LADY WINDERMERE'S FAN*, ACT I

In those episodes of *Lady Windermere's Fan* that are fraught with drama, Wilde abandons display of wit altogether, and emulates the emotionally overwrought standards of Victorian melodrama. Although they are in the same play, they're in different worlds from the alternate scenes that undercut with cynical license the very assumptions on which the melodramatic scenes rest. For instance, the piety with which the play's melodrama holds the sacred ties of mother love; the sin that engulfs a wife who flees husband, home, and offspring; the abiding, lifelong shame and torment of conscience of living with that sin; the horror of virtue being forced to mingle with, even welcome to her home, a woman of fallen virtue; the yawning gap between the true love of a husband and the defiling love of an abducting seducer—the shock and pain with which these bulwarks of melodrama's stock in trade are reverenced, are in each and every instance deftly mocked with memorable Wildean paradox, on total holiday from the different world sharing the space of the same play.

By some magic, they fit, and the tearful values hold their sober own even in those moments when they're being most cleverly dislodged. Oddly, they do so because their inherent contradiction accurately mirrors the mix of convictions at the turn of the century—the iconoclasm that was laughing off Victorian sanctities, and the reverence with which they were not merely still tolerated but still deeply internalized. For the cultivated gentleman and lady of the nineties, both were concurrently held, the one mitigating the other.

There's also an alternate genius at work in Wilde's dialogue: combining that reverence and irreverence in almost the same breath. It lies in his placing in the mouths of characters like the Duchess of Berwick straightforward plot-matter that is carefully suffocated by the delightfully meaningless. Meaningless, that is, in terms of its relevance to the strict matter at hand. But these barnacles of irrelevance suspended from the soberly necessary plot-talk are, as has long been recognized, the essence of his plays' charm, meaning, and value.

Take, for example, the Duchess of Berwick's functional plot-labor in conveying to Lady Windermere the initiating circumstance of the play's action—that Lord Windermere is having, it seems, an affair. It isn't merely the dither of the Duchess that produces her farrago of nonsequiturs in the midst of her pointedly on-course exposition, but Wilde's technique of explaining to us at the same time the social world in which Lady Windermere's dilemma is to be seen and understood. Is her quandary serious? Yes, nothing is more serious than scandal, the ultimate ostracizer, social death. Is it not at all serious? Again, yes, with a bit of wifely legerdemain, it's easily correctible, no one will really care, and everyone will agree not to notice.

The Duchess has arrived with her blank daughter Agatha just as Lord Darlington, the cynic who has been making overtures to Lady Windermere, is departing. She's filled with news.

DUCHESS

What a charming wicked creature! I like him so much. I'm quite delighted he's gone! How sweet you're looking! Where do you get your gowns? And now I must tell you how sorry I am for you, dear Margaret.

(Crosses to the sofa and sits down with
Lady Windermere)

Agatha, darling! Will you go and look over the photograph album that I see there? Dear girl! She is so fond of photographs of Switzerland. Such a pure taste, I think. But I really am so sorry for you, Margaret, on account of that horrid woman. She dresses so well, too, which makes it much worse, sets such a dreadful example. Augustus—you know, my disreputable brother—such a trial to us all—well, Augustus is completely infatuated about her. It is quite scandalous, for she is absolutely inadmissible into society. Many a woman has a past, but I am told that she has at least a dozen, and they all fit. About Mrs. Erlynne. Agatha, darling! Will you go out on the terrace and look at the sunset? Sweet girl! So devoted to sunsets! Shows such refinement of feeling, does it not? After all, there is nothing like Nature, is there? I assure you we're all so distressed about it. Only last night at dear Lady Jansen's every one was saying how extraordinary it was that, of all men in London, Windermere should behave in such a way. He goes to see her continually, and stops for hours at a time, and while he is there she is not at home to any one. Not that many ladies call on her, dear, but she has a great many disreputable men friends—my own brother particularly, as I told you—and that is what makes it so dreadful about Windermere. We looked upon *him* as being such a model husband, but I am afraid there is no doubt about it. My dear nieces—you know the Saville girls, don't you?—such nice domestic creatures—plain, dreadfully plain,—but so good—well, they're always at the window doing fancy work, and making ugly things for the poor, which I think so useful of them in these dreadful socialistic days, and this terrible woman has taken a house in Curzon Street, right opposite them—such a respectable street, too! I don't know what we're coming to! And they tell me that Windermere goes there four and five times a week—they *see* him. They can't help it—and although they never talk scandal, they—well, of course—they remark on it to every one. And the worst of it all is that I have been told that this woman has got a great deal of money out of somebody, for it seems that she came to London six months ago without anything at all to speak of, and now she has this charming house in Mayfair, drives her ponies in the Park every afternoon and all—well, all—since she has known poor dear Windermere.

It's quite true, my dear. The whole of London knows it. That is why I felt it was better to come and talk to you, and advise you to take Windermere away at once to Homburg or to Aix, where he'll have something to amuse him, and where you can watch him all day long. I assure you, my dear, that on several occasions after I was first married, I had to pretend to be very ill, and was obliged to drink the most unpleasant mineral waters, merely to get Berwick out of town. He was so extremely susceptible. Though I am bound to say he never gave away any large sums of money to anybody. He is far too high-principled for that!

Are all men bad? Oh, all of them, my dear, all of them, without any exception. And they never grow any better. Men become old, but they never become good. It was only Berwick's brutal and incessant threats of suicide that made me accept him at all, and before the year was out, he was running after all kinds of petticoats, every colour, every shape, every material. In fact, before the honeymoon was over, I caught him winking at my maid, a most pretty, respectable girl. I dismissed her at once without a character.—No, I remember I passed her on to my sister; poor dear Sir George is so short-sighted, I thought it wouldn't matter. But it did, though—it was most unfortunate.

(Rises)

And now, my dear child, I must go, as we are dining out. And mind you don't take this little aberration of Windermere's too much to heart. Just take him abroad, and he'll come back to you aright.

HOMBURG, AIX: resorts in the Alps situated in the vicinity of mineral water springs.

238.

LADY WINDERMERE REGRETS HER "FATAL MISSTEP," BUT QUICKLY CHANGES HER MIND (YC)

(1892) OSCAR WILDE, *LADY WINDERMERE'S FAN*, ACT III

[Continues No. 238, above] Lady Windermere is in a terrible quandary. Believing her husband to have fallen into a sinful liaison with a Mrs. Erlynne, a woman of abandoned reputation, she's taken the fatal step of leaving her home when Mrs. Erlynne is received by her husband, and has fled to the home of Lord Darlington, who that night professes his love for her. Lady Windermere, like Hester in *A Woman of No Importance*, is one of Wilde's extraordinarily naive Puritans who are doomed to learn a hard lesson: that no one is more ignorant of the true nature of virtue than the virtuous who are still untried.

But while waiting for Lord Darlington to appear, frightened and confused, she decides to hurry back home before she is compromised. Instead of Lord Darlington, it is Mrs. Erlynne who appears, and Lady Windermere, assuming she was sent as emissary by her husband, angrily determines to stay in Lord Darlington's care.

Famous misunderstanding, famous obligatory scene. Mrs. Erlynne, unknown to Lady Windermere, is actually her mother who twenty years before fled to a lover, leaving much the same farewell note for her husband. With the crumpled note in her hand (still unseen by Lord Windermere), Mrs. Erlynne has come to intercept her daughter's fatal misstep, and without revealing her identity, to bring her home before her absence is detected. Lady Windermere's angry, haughty, insulting rejection of Mrs. Erlynne's help forces Mrs. Erlynne to appeal to her daughter in a speech even more laden with the trappings of melodrama than Lady Windermere's own. By the time she wins her consent, all the gentlemen of the evening's reception from which Lady Windermere fled are about to arrive for a nightcap (and for one of Wilde's most famous and wittiest scenes) while the ladies hide. Lady Windermere does eventually escape unseen, but at the cost of Mrs. Erlynne's voluntary exposure to the shame of discovery in her daughter's place.

At scene's opening, Lady Windermere, alone, stands near the unlit fireplace in Lord Darlington's unfamiliar rooms, fretting, cold.

LADY WINDERMERE

Why doesn't he come? This waiting is horrible. He should be here. Why is he not here, to wake with passionate words some fire within me? I am cold—cold as a loveless thing. Arthur must have read my letter by this time. If he cared for me, he would have come after me, would have taken me back by force. But he doesn't care. He's entrammelled by this woman—fascinated by her—dominated by her. If a woman wants to hold a man, she has merely to appeal to what is worst in him. We make gods of men and they leave us. Others make brutes of them and they fawn and are faithful. How hideous life is!... Oh, it was mad of me to come here! And yet, which is the worst, I wonder, to be at the mercy of a man who loves one, or the wife of a man who in one's own house dishonors one? What woman knows? What woman in the whole world? But will he love me always, this man to whom I am giving my whole life? What do I bring him? Lips that have lost the note of joy, eyes that are blinded by tears, chill hands and icy heart. I bring him nothing. I must go back—no; I can't go back! That fatal letter. No! Lord Darlington leaves England tomorrow. I will go with him—I have no choice. *(Sits down for a few moments. Then starts up and puts on her cloak)* No, no, I will go back, let Arthur do with me what he pleases. I can't wait here. It has been madness my coming. I must go at once. As for Lord Darlington.—Oh! *(Hides her face in her hands)*

(Enter Mrs. Erlynne)

(Lady Windermere throws off her cloak and flings it on the sofa.)

Mrs. Erlynne—if you had not come here, I would have gone back. But now that I see you, I feel that nothing in the whole world would induce me to live under the same roof as Lord Windermere. You fill me with horror. There is something about you that stirs the wildest—rage within me. And I know why you are here. My husband sent you to lure me back that I might serve as a blind to whatever relations exist between you and him. Go back to my husband, Mrs. Erlynne. He belongs to you and not to me. I suppose he is afraid of a scandal. Men are such cowards. They outrage every law of the world, and are afraid of the world's tongue. But he had better prepare himself. He shall have a scandal. He shall have the worst scandal there has been in London in years. He shall see his name in every vile paper, mine on every hideous placard. Yes! He shall. Had he come himself, I admit I would have gone back to the life of degradation you and he had prepared for me—I was going back—but to stay himself at home, and to send you as his messenger—oh! it was infamous—infamous.

239.

MRS. ERLYNNE PLEADS WITH LADY WINDERMERE TO RETURN TO HUSBAND AND HOME (oc)

(1892) Oscar Wilde, *Lady Windermere's Fan*, Act III

[Continues No. 238, above] The classic speech of persuasion, the most strenuous rhetorical as well as emotional moment in Wilde's drama, is given to Mrs. Erlynne. She must urge Lady Windermere to step back from the precipice of moral doom, the precipice from which there is no return. All the rhetoric in the play is decidedly well-bred, but Mrs. Erlynne's aria at this moment has, in addition to breeding, the formidable undertaking of accomplishing within a single outburst the total reversal of Lady Windermere's sworn intent—to leave her husband forever. It's a certainty—since breeding was, for performances of the play in the nineties, at par for both well-bred play and well-bred playgoer—that the reception of Mrs. Erlynne's tirade was critical not only for the truth of its sentiments, but as much for the panache of its delivery. The speech is equivalent to opera aria, its notes, its progressions, calculated not only rhetorically but musically. In addition to its task of persuading Lady Windermere is the performer's task—as in opera—of accomplishing its technical feats, at the same time as persuading the spectator of the reality of emotion underlying a bravura performance. But its reality is theatrical "reality" through and through, not the reality underlying, for example, the musical/rhetorical calculations of Shaw's similar arias.

MRS. ERLYNNE

Oh! why do you disbelieve everything I tell you? What object do you think I have in coming here, except to save you from utter ruin, to save you from the consequence of a hideous mistake? Lady Windermere, before Heaven your husband is guiltless of all offence towards you! And I—I tell you that had it ever occurred to me that such a monstrous suspicion would have entered your mind, I would have died rather than have crossed your life or his—oh! died, gladly died!

(Moves away to sofa, R)
Believe what you choose about me. I am not worth a moment's sorrow. But don't spoil your beautiful young life on my account! You don't know what may be in store for you, unless you leave this house at once. You don't know what it is to fall into the pit, to be despised, mocked, abandoned, sneered at—to be an outcast! to find the door shut against one, to have to creep in by hideous byways, afraid every moment lest the mask should be stripped from one's face, and all the while to hear the laughter, the horrible laughter of the world, a thing more tragic than all the tears the world has ever shed. You don't know what it is. One pays for one's sin, and then one pays again, and all one's life one pays. You must never know that.—As for me, if suffering be an expiation, then at this moment I have expiated all my faults, whatever

they have been; for to-night you have made a heart in one who had it not, made it and broken it. But let that pass. I may have wrecked my own life, but I will not let you wreck yours. You—why, you are a mere girl, you would be lost. You haven't got the kind of brains that enables a woman to get back. You have neither the wit nor the courage. You couldn't stand dishonour! No! Go back, Lady Windermere, to the husband who loves you, whom you love. You have a child, Lady Windermere. Go back to that child who even now, in pain or in joy, may be calling to you.

(Lady Windermere rises.)

God gave you that child. He will require from you that you make his life fine, that you watch over him. What answer will you make to God if his life is ruined through you? Back to your house, Lady Windermere—your husband loves you! He has never swerved for a moment from the love he bears you. But even if he had a thousand loves, you must stay with your child. If he was harsh to you, you must stay with your child. If he ill-treated you, you must stay with your child. If he abandoned you, your place is with your child.

240.

MRS. ERLYNNE REFUSES TO REVEAL HER IDENTITY TO HER DAUGHTER (oc)

(1892) OSCAR WILDE, *LADY WINDERMERE'S FAN*, ACT IV

From the level struck in Mrs. Erlynne's speech [in No. 239, above], there's a considerable drop in emotional temperature in her meeting the following day with Lord Windermere, when her talk is closer to the more usual Wildean vein of mutually neutralizing the reverence of deep feeling and the witty irreverence of no feeling. But in this instance, Mrs. Erlynne's deeper notes of feeling are not easily neutralized. While she is being subjected to Windermere's angry attack for her presumed indecency of the night before, she's silently taking pride in her rescue of his wife from that very attack. And his threat to reveal her secret to her daughter rouses Mrs. Erlynne to the highest level of wrath that is permissible in the role of the morally abandoned woman, a role in which Windermere has cast her. What she does not permit herself to reveal—on the one hand to Windermere, on the other to her daughter—constitutes her moral heroism, by which she rises in our esteem at play's end, and by which she converts the puritanism of Lady Windermere. But earnest meaning is in any case subverted not only by Mrs. Erlynne's determined recovery of her flippancy at play's end, but by the easy flippancy of Wilde's ending: Mrs. Erlynne is to marry a willingly duped, infatuated Lord Augustus.

MRS. ERLYNNE

(With a note of irony in her voice) I have come to bid good-bye to my dear daughter, of course. *(Her voice and manner become serious. In her accents as she talks there is a note of deep tragedy. For a moment she reveals herself.)* Oh, don't imagine I am going to have a pathetic scene with her, weep on her neck and tell her who I am, and all that kind of thing. I have no ambition to play the part of a mother. Only once in my life have I known a mother's feelings. That was last night. They were terrible—they made me suffer—they made me suffer too much. For twenty years, as you say, I have lived childless—I want to live childless still. *(Hiding her feelings with a trivial laugh.)* Besides, my dear Windermere, how on earth could I pose as a mother with a grown-up daughter? Margaret is twenty-one, and I have never admitted that I am more than twenty-nine, or thirty at the most. Twenty-nine when there are pink shades, thirty when there are not. So you see what difficulties it would involve. No, as far as I am concerned, let your wife cherish the memory of this dead, stainless mother. Why should I interfere with her illusions? I find it hard enough to keep my own. I lost one illusion last night. I thought I had no heart. I find I have, and a heart doesn't suit me, Windermere. Somehow it doesn't go with modern dress. It makes one look old. And it spoils one's career at critical moments.

I suppose, Windermere, you would like me to retire into a convent, or become a hospital nurse, or something of that kind, as people do in silly modern novels. That is stupid of you, Arthur, in real life we don't do such things—not as long as we have any good looks left, at any rate. No—what consoles one nowadays is not repentance, but pleasure. Repentance is quite out of date. And besides, if a woman repents, she has to go to a bad dressmaker, otherwise no one believes in her. And nothing in the world would induce me to do that. No; I am going to pass entirely out of your two lives. My coming into them has been a mistake—I discovered that last night.

You propose to tell her? If you do, I will make my name so infamous that it will mar every moment of her life. It will ruin her, and make her wretched. If you dare to tell her, there is no depth of degradation that I will not sink to, no pit of shame I will not enter. You shall not tell her—I forbid you.

If I said to you that I cared for her, perhaps loved her even—you would sneer at me, wouldn't you? You are right. What could I know of such feelings? Don't let us talk anymore about it—as for telling my daughter who I am, that I do not allow. It is my secret, it is not yours. I shall never tell her.

241.

HESTER, A YOUNG AMERICAN, DELIVERS A BRACING SERMON TO EFFETE ENGLISH ARISTOCRATS (YC)

(1893) OSCAR WILDE, *A WOMAN OF NO IMPORTANCE*, ACT I

"That silly Puritan girl," Lord Illingworth calls her. Hester, the young American heiress who is visiting England and is a guest at the moment at the estate of Hunstanton Chase, purses her lips at the talk of the idle English worldlings sharing her country weekend. With the conviction of a severe American product of virtue, whose father made his fortune in dry goods ("What are American dry goods?" one of the ladies asks Hester when the subject of her family's wealth is brought up; "American novels," someone explains), unable to bear their careless chatter, she chastises them with a sermon that would do honor to an earlier New England. But for all its unadulterated virtue, there's a stupidity inseparable from inflexible morality, and by play's end, like the puritanical Lady Windermere in Wilde's other thesis play, Hester's unknowing uprightness is thoroughly chastised, and she, after brushing against the moral complexity of real life (actually, a highly melodramatic amplification of real life), suffers her thorough re-education.

Before that eventuality, though, she takes her cue from the chatter of the English ladies, who bother to think only approximately about the rest of the world. Lady Caroline, for instance, to make conversation, remarks to Hester, "There are a great many things you haven't got in America, I am told, Miss Worsley. They say you have no ruins, and no curiosities." Mrs. Allonby is quick to correct that false impression: "What nonsense! They have their mothers and their manners." But Hester, catching this knife-edged condescension toward America, defends her nation:

HESTER

The English aristocracy supply us with our curiosities, Lady Caroline. They are sent over to us every summer, regularly, in the steamers, and propose to us the day after they land. As for ruins, we are trying to build up something that will last longer than brick or stone. We are trying to build up life, Lady Hunstanton, on a better, truer, purer basis than life rests on here. This sounds strange to you all, no doubt. How could it sound other than strange? You rich people in England, you don't know how you are living. How could you know? You shut out from your society the gentle and the good. You laugh at the simple and the pure. Living, as you all do, on others and by them, you sneer at self-sacrifice, and if you throw bread to the poor, it is merely to keep them quiet for a season. With all your pomp and wealth and art, you don't know how to live— you don't even know that. You love the beauty that you can see and touch and handle, the beauty that you can destroy, and do destroy, but of the unseen beauty of life, you know nothing. You have lost life's secret. Oh, your English society seems to me shallow, selfish, foolish. It has blinded its eyes, and stopped its ears. It lies like a leper in purple. It sits like a dead thing smeared with gold. It is all wrong, all wrong. Your Lord Henry Weston! I remember him, Lady Hunstanton. A man with a hideous smile and a hideous past. He is asked everywhere. No dinner-party is complete without him. What of those whose ruin is due to him? They are outcasts. They are nameless. If you met them in the street you would turn your head away. I don't complain of their punishment. Let all women who have sinned be punished. It is right that they should be punished, but don't let them be the only ones to suffer. If a man and woman have sinned, let them both go forth into the desert to love or loathe each other there. Let them both be branded. Set a mark, if you wish, on each, but don't punish the one and let the other go free. Don't have one law for men and another for women. You are unjust to women in England. And till you count what is shame in a woman to be infamy in a man, you will always be unjust, and Right, that pillar of fire, and Wrong, that pillar of cloud, will be made dim to your eyes, or be not seen at all, or if seen, not regarded.

I am afraid you think I spoke too strongly, Lady Hunstanton.

STEAMER: steamship.

242.

MRS. ALLONBY ENUMERATES THE IDEAL QUALITIES OF THE IDEAL MAN (oc)

(1893) OSCAR WILDE, *A WOMAN OF NO IMPORTANCE*, ACT II

Mrs. Allonby in her own mind is so perfectly placed at the center of the design of things that she thinks and behaves as though the rest of mankind is her supporting cast. She stipulates a principle of general satisfactions that fits so precisely her particular ones, that Wilde's wit's usual preference for the trivial over the weighty ceases in her to be paradox and becomes norm. "I dislike Mrs. Allonby. I dislike her more than I can say," harumphs the highly principled American philistine Hester, having instinctively spotted her opposite in only a day or two as one of the guests at the very English country retreat of Hunstanton Chase, where Mrs. Allonby is fitfully tolerated as though her anti-system made perfectly valid sense. The objection she makes to men as they are—as opposed to her dissertation (below) on men as they should be—defines her perfectly. "Man, poor, awkward, reliable, necessary man, belongs to a sex that has been rational for millions of years. He can't help himself. The History of Woman is very different. We have always been picturesque protests against the mere existence of common sense. We saw its dangers from the first." When she is asked what then is her conception of the Ideal Husband, she demurs. "There couldn't be such a thing. The institution is wrong."

Her interlocator settles for her definition of the Ideal Man "in his relation to *us.*"

And Mrs. Allonby obliges with a description of the creature who most perfectly complements, in each of his words and deeds, the woman like herself who is both fixedly and frivolously at the center of the design of things, a design that—from the point of view of "man, poor, awkward, reliable, rational man" who is given to common sense—has been deliberately and programmatically stood on its head. Mrs. Allonby is in an essential sense remote from frivolity. Like Millamant in the Restoration *The Way of the World,* [see No. 161, above], she is making the perfect counterdemand to—as Mirabell puts it—"the enlargement of the husband."

MRS. ALLONBY

The Ideal Man! Oh, the Ideal Man should talk to us as if we were goddesses, and treat us as if we were children. He should refuse all our serious requests, and gratify every one of our whims. He should encourage us to have caprices, and forbid us to have missions. He should always say much more than he means, and always mean much more than he says. He should never run down other pretty women. That would show he had no taste, or make one suspect that he had too much. No; he should be nice about them all, but say that somehow they don't attract him. If we ask him a question about anything, he should give us an answer all about ourselves. He should invariably praise us for whatever qualities he knows we haven't got. But he should be pitiless, quite pitiless, in reproaching us for the virtues that we have never dreamed of possessing. He should never believe that we know the use of useful things. That would be unforgivable. But he should shower on us everything we don't want. He should persistently compromise us in public, and treat us with absolute respect when we are alone. And yet he should be always ready to have a perfectly terrible scene, whenever we want one, and to become miserable, absolutely miserable, at a moment's notice, and to overwhelm us with just reproaches in less than twenty minutes, and to be positively violent at the end of half an hour, and to leave us for ever at a quarter to eight, when we have to go and dress for dinner. And when, after that, one has seen him for really the last time, and he has refused to take back the little things he has given one, and promised never to communicate with one again, or to write one any foolish letters, he should be perfectly broken-hearted, and telegraph to one all day long, and send one little notes every half-hour by a private hansom, and dine quite alone at the club, so that every one should know how unhappy he was. And after a whole dreadful week, during which one has gone about everywhere with one's husband, just to show how absolutely lonely one was, he may be given a third last parting, in the evening, and then, if his conduct has been quite irreproachable, and one has behaved really badly to him, he should be allowed to admit that he has been entirely in the wrong, and when he has admitted that, it becomes a woman's duty to forgive, and one can do it all over again from the beginning, with variations. His reward? Oh, infinite expectation. That is quite enough for him.

243.

MRS. WARREN ARGUES THE COMMON SENSE OF PROSTITUTION FOR A WOMAN'S SURVIVAL (OC)

(1893) BERNARD SHAW, MRS. WARREN'S PROFESSION, ACT II

As Shaw describes her, Mrs. Warren is a "formerly pretty, showily dressed ... rather spoilt and domineering, and decidedly vulgar, but on the whole, genial and fairly presentable blackguard of a woman." She's a successful prostitute and now owns a chain of brothels in England and Europe, and is proud of the respectable way in which she runs them. Her daughter Vivie was brought up in total ignorance of her mother's profession, was boarded out, then sent to school, then Newnam College, Cambridge, and has predictably grown into a university-degreed, goal-driven, puritanical snob. After her Cambridge graduation, mother and daughter are to meet almost for the first time—as one of Mrs. Warren's train of followers puts it, "to have their moment together." It turns out, again predictably, to be disastrous. Vivie begins at once to grill her mother about the facts of her life, and Mrs. Warren works hard at first to fake the authority of a mother, an authority Vivie won't allow. Pretension vanishes between them when Vivie asks bluntly, "Who was my father? Was it that revolting Crofts?"

(an overbearing vulgarian of Mrs. Warren's retinue whom Vivie had just met) and at Mrs. Warren's inadvertent response, "Oh no, I'm certain of that, at least," the judgmental coolness with which Vivie takes the implications of her response plainly horrifies her mother, who's by far the more conventionally sentimental of the two. But so insulted is she by her daughter's dispassionate dismissal of her, that she explodes, with bitter resentment—but also, with blunt honesty—into her long confessional. Despite all the pain she feels at her daughter's educated ruthlessness, she maintains in her justification the most straightforward, level-headed, commonsensical explanation of her entire life. She puts aside every moralistic pretension society has about prostitution, and talks facts as she knows them. Lest there be any question of the exact meaning of Mrs. Warren's passionate confession to her daughter, Shaw precisely sums it up in his Preface to the play:

"*Mrs. Warren's Profession* was written in 1894 to draw attention to the truth that prostitution is caused, not by female depravity and male licentiousness, but simply by underpaying, undervaluing, and overworking women so shamefully that the poorest of them are forced to resort to prostitution to keep body and soul together. Indeed all attractive unpropertied women lose money by being infallibly virtuous or contracting marriages that are not more or less venal. If on the large social scale we get what we call vice instead of what we call virtue it is simply because we are paying more for it. No normal woman would be a professional prostitute if she could better herself by being respectable, nor marry for money if she could afford to marry for love."

The only updating of Shaw's then startling but still penetrating argument of a century ago is the additional argument that prostitution itself may be regarded not as a vice but as an acceptable occupation, and that the onus Shaw put on it as a necessarily vicious choice need no longer have the same bearing.

Mrs. Warren

You! you've no heart. (*She suddenly breaks out vehemently in her natural tongue—the dialect of a woman of the people—with all her affectations of maternal authority and conventional manners gone, and an overwhelming inspiration of true conviction and scorn in her.*) Oh, I won't bear it: I won't put up with the injustice of it. What right have you to set yourself up above me like this? You boast of what you are to me—to me, who gave you the chance of being what you are. What chance had I? Shame you for a bad daughter and a stuck-up prude!

Do you think I was brought up like you—able to pick and choose my own way of life? Do you think I did what I did because I liked it, or thought it right, or wouldn't rather have gone to college and been a lady if I'd had the chance?

D'you know what your gran'mother was? No, you don't. I do. She called herself a widow and had a fried-fish shop down by the Mint, and kept herself and four daughters out of it. Two of us were sisters: that was me and Liz; and we were both good-looking and well made. The other two were only half sisters—undersized, ugly, starved-looking, honest poor creatures: they were the respectable ones. Well, what did they get by their respectability? I'll tell you. One of them worked in a whitelead factory twelve hours a day for nine shillings a week until she died of lead poisoning. She only expected to get her hands a little paralyzed; but she died. The other was always held up to us as a model because she married a Government laborer in the Deptford victualling yard, and kept his room and the three children neat and tidy on eighteen shillings a week—until he took to drink. That was worth being respectable for, wasn't it?

Liz had more spirit. We both went to a church school—that was part of the ladylike airs we gave ourselves to be superior to the children that knew nothing and went nowhere—and we stayed there until Liz went out one night and never came back. I know the schoolmistress thought I'd soon follow her example; for the clergyman was always warning me that Lizzie'd end by jumping off Waterloo Bridge. Poor fool: that was all he knew about it! But I was more afraid of the whitelead factory than I was of the river; and so would you have been in my place. That clergyman got me a situation as scullery maid in a temperance restaurant where they sent out for anything you liked. Then I was waitress; and then I went to the bar at Waterloo station—fourteen hours a day serving drinks and washing glasses for four shillings a week and my board. That was considered a great promotion for me. Well, one cold, wretched night, when I was so tired I could hardly keep myself awake, who should come up for a half of Scotch but Lizzie, in a long fur cloak, elegant and comfortable, with a lot of sovereigns in her purse.

She's living down at Winchester now—chaperones girls at the county ball, if you please. No river for Liz, thank you! When she saw I'd grown up good-looking she said to me across the bar: "What are you doing there, you little fool? wearing out your health and your appearance for other people's profit!" Liz was saving money then to take a house for herself in Brussels: and she though we two could save faster than one. So she lent me some money and gave me a start; and I saved steadily and first paid her back, and then went into business with her as her partner. Why shouldn't I have done it? The house in Brussels was real high class—a much better place for a woman to be in than the factory where Anne Jane got poisoned. None of our girls were ever treated as I was treated in the scullery of that temperance place, or at the Waterloo bar, or at home. It's far better than any other employment open to her. I always thought that oughtn't to be. It can't be right, Vivie, that there shouldn't be better opportunities for women. I stick to that: it's wrong. But it's so, right or wrong; and a girl must make the best of it. But, of course, it's not worth while for a lady. If you took to it you'd be a fool; but I should have been a fool if I'd taken to anything else.

Where would we be now if we'd minded the clergyman's foolishness? Scrubbing floors for one and sixpence a day and nothing to look forward to but the workhouse infirmary. Don't you be led astray by people who don't know the world, my girl. The only way for a woman to provide for herself decently is for her to be good to some man that can afford to be good to her. If she's in his own station of life, let her make him marry her; but if she's far beneath him she can't expect it—why should she? It wouldn't be for her own happiness. Ask any lady in London society that has daughters; and she'll tell you the same, except that I tell you straight and she'll tell you crooked. That's all the difference.

Ashamed? Well, of course, dearie, it's only good manners to be ashamed of it, it's expected from a woman. Women have to pretend to feel a great deal that they don't feel. Liz used to be angry with me for plumping out the truth about it. She used to say that when every woman could learn enough from what was going on in the world before her eyes, there was no need to talk about it to her. But then Liz was such a perfect lady! She had the true instinct of it; while I was always a bit of a vulgarian.

But I can't stand saying one thing when everyone knows I mean another. What's the use in such hypocrisy? If people arrange the world that way for women, there's no pretending that it's arranged the other way. I never was a bit ashamed really. I consider that I had a right to be proud that we managed everything so respectably, and never a word against us, and that the girls were so well taken of. Some of them did very well: one of them married an ambassador. But of course now I daren't talk about such things: whatever would they think of us! *(She yawns.)* Oh, dear! I do believe I'm getting sleepy after all.

> *(She stretches herself lazily, thoroughly relieved by her explosion, and placidly ready for her night's rest.)*

VICTUALLING YARD: a yard where victuals (food rations) were distributed. WATERLOO BRIDGE: in London over the river Thames. SITUATION AS A SCULLERY MAID: a position as a kitchen maid. WATERLOO: the provincial train station of London, as opposed to the central Victoria Station. SOVEREIGN: a gold coin valued at two pounds, eighteen shillings (almost five dollars), i.e., Lizzy was quite well-off. WINCHESTER: a cathedral town in the South of England.

244.

JULIA, IN A JEALOUS RAGE, BREAKS IN UPON HER LOVER'S RENDEVOUS WITH A RIVAL, AND ATTACKS (YC)

(1893) GEORGE BERNARD SHAW, *THE PHILANDERER*, ACT I

What is universally said of Shaw's characters is precisely false: that they're position papers, author's mouthpieces, and have no internal life beyond their rhetoric. What is in fact the case—and Julia in *The Philanderer* is supremely the demonstration of that case—is that in terms of worldly common sense and within the boundaries of ordinary logic, they condemn themselves out of their own mouths, spelling out their limitations, their stupidities, their severely narrowed visions, with considerable rhetorical panache. But the emotions and motives and beliefs behind their rhetorical postures are totally—sometimes, as in the case of Julia, painfully—realized. What is unique in Shaw is the degree to which his characters can articulate even the inarticulate—their desperations, their rages, their wounds to the soul. Instead of sputtering, they talk, and each states the plight of his or her particular skewed enlightenment out of their own class and kind and limitation and intellectual partiality. Each proves himself, and although all the characters in one of Shaw's stage gatherings may argue simultaneously in mutual contradiction, each in turn persuades, each in turn wins his case. How come? Because the marshalling of their evidence involves the dredging up of experience that has at bottom the truth of its rapture or its pain.

Julia, as test case: She's as irrational, as mad, as self-justifying, and as vicious as the woman with whom Shaw suffered a nine-year liaison of misery in his initiation into love's delights, and on whom Julia is wholly and accurately based. But that judgment is as nothing compared to the blinding suffering Julia is enduring, and moved entirely by the horror of that suffering, she struggles to overcome it, so that every gesture and every word she speaks is a feint in the direction of escape. Notice the directions of these feints: there are four. First, by ridding herself of her rival Grace, by slander, or murder if necessary; second, by pleading the helpless dependence of her love for Charteris, to which in all conscience he in decency must respond; third, by exposing him and disgracing him as a lying philanderer to her rival, who will consequently abandon him; and fourth, by winning him back to his genuine love of herself by reminding him of its depth, and of her willingness to pledge anything to reawaken that love. The contradiction of these actions is ridiculous, comic; their motivating impulse, though, is pain, which is hardly comic and hardly ridiculous.

The real, the fundamental question in Shaw is not merely whether the intellect or morality of his characters is justified, but whether their reality is justified. And as with all great comic writers, the absurdity of mind or manners of characters registers as real only to the degree that genuine experience and rich—best of all, tragic—emotion can be discerned behind their show.

Charteris and Grace Tranfield have been mouthing, half-seriously and with half-mock-bravado, the lover's ritual of do you really, don't you really, love me? How deeply? For how long? etc., when the trembling voice of Charteris' nemesis is heard in the hallway:

> (A violent double knock is heard
> without)

JULIA

Is Mr. Charteris here?

*(The door of the flat is opened without.
Charteris and Grace hastily get away
from each other.)*
Never mind: I will announce myself.

*(A beautiful, dark, tragic looking
woman in mantle and toque appears at
the door, raging)*
Oh, this is charming. I have interrupted a pretty tête-a-tête.
Oh, you villain!

*(She comes straight at Grace. Charteris
runs across behind the sofa and stops
her. She struggles furiously with him.
Julia, finding Charteris too strong for
her, gives up her attempt to get at
Grace, but strikes him in the face as she
frees herself.)*
What are you doing up here with that woman? You scoundrel!
But now listen to me, Leonard: you have driven me to
desperation; and I don't care what I do, or who hears me: I'll
not bear it. She shall not have my place with you.

No, no: I dont care: I will expose her true character before
everybody. You belong to me: you have no right to be here;
and she knows it. I am going to stay here—here—until I have
made you give her up.

Let her ring the bell if she dares. Let us see how this pure
virtuous creature will face the scandal of what I will declare
about her. Let us see how you will face it. I have nothing to
lose. Everybody knows how you have treated me: you have
boasted of your conquests, you poor pitiful vain creature: I am
the common talk of your acquaintances and hers. Oh, I have
calculated my advantage *(she tears off her mantle)*: I am a most
unhappy and injured woman; but I am not the fool you take
me to be. I am going to stay: see?

*(She flings the mantle on the round
table; puts her toque on it; and sits
down.)*

Now, Mrs Tranfield: theres the bell *(Pointing to the button beside the fireplace)*: why dont you ring?

> *(Grace, looking attentive at Charteris, does not move.)*

Ha! ha! I thought so. She shall know what you are, and how you have been in love with me: how it is not two days since you kissed me and told me that the future would be as happy as the past. *(Screaming at him)* You did: deny it if you dare.

> *(Julia, with a stifled cry of rage, rushes at Grace, who is crossing behind the sofa towards the door. Charteris seizes Julia, and prevents her from getting past the sofa. Grace goes out. Charteris, holding Julia fast, looks round to the door to see whether Grace is safely out of the room.)*

(Throwing herself at his feet) Oh, Leonard, dont be cruel. I'm too miserable to argue—to think. I only know I love you. You reproach me with not wanting to marry you. I would have married you at any time after I came to love you, if you had asked me. I will marry you now if you will. We could be so happy. You love me: I know you love me. I feel it. You say "My dear" to me: you have said it several times this evening. I know I have been wicked, odious, bad: I say nothing in defence of myself. But dont be hard on me. I was distracted by the thought of losing you. I cant face life without you, Leonard. I was happy when I met you: I had never loved any one: and if you had only let me alone, I could have gone on contentedly by myself. But I cant now. I must have you with me. Dont cast me off without a thought of all I have at stake. I could be a friend to you if you would only let me; if you would only tell me your plans; give me a share in your work; treat me as something more than the amusement of an idle hour. Oh, Leonard, Leonard, youve never given me a chance: indeed you havnt. I'll take pains; I'll read; I'll try to think; I'll conquer my jealousy; I'll—*(She breaks down, rocking her head desperately on his knees and writhing)* Oh, I'm mad: I'm mad: youll kill me if you desert me.

> *(Julia sobbing, he rises and tenderly lifts her with him)*

One word from you will make us happy for ever.

245.

PAULA TANQUERAY ENVISIONS THE HOPELESS FUTURE OF HER MARRIAGE (OT)

(1893) ARTHUR WING PINERO, *THE SECOND MRS. TANQUERAY*, ACT IV

[See, in Men's vols., the entry "Aubrey Tanqueray Alerts His Friends: His New Wife May Not Meet with Their Set's Approval"] There are two kinds of classless women in nineteenth-century drama, who, lifted by courageous but naive upper-class husbands over the ramparts of prejudice, suffered upper-class marriages: the perfect woman, and the tainted one. Esther in *Caste* [see No. 233, above] is perfect; Paula in *The Second Mrs. Tanqueray* is tainted, the woman with a past. Both in their marriages wear the crown of thorns of class prejudice. Esther, perfect, ultimately proves the fallacy of such prejudice; Paula, tainted, ultimately proves its fitness. Given these instances, either way the conclusion is comforting. The weight of argument visited on these "problem" plays, the anger and moral rectitude with which their "problem" was attacked, is in retrospect strikingly innocuous: their conclusion, given these instances, was foregone; both, the victim punished and the one rewarded, reaffirmed a morality that all classes happily shared.

But there are other strands in Pincro's study of Paula that touch reality more closely than this familiar public debate: that she's stifled, that she envisions a monotony of days that will in themselves come to nothing, that the memory of the revelation of her past will never leave her husband, and that when her attractiveness is gone, there'll be nothing left but that memory between them, and that, other than that end, she has no way out. Her vision of the boredom and the emptiness of the rest of her life is precisely in the vein, though not perhaps on the level of insight, of the heroines of his own time whose tragic ends Pinero is echoing: Anna Karenina, Emma Bovary, Hedda Gabler. Paula, in a smaller way, is of their company.

In the play's last act (the act, oddly, in which the "reality" of Paula's character was most heavily criticized) she's confronted, first, by the man from her past who had "ruined" her, then by her husband's daughter from his first marriage who detects the terrible "truth," then by her husband—who swallows hard and is determined to forgive and forget her past. Then—in almost direct imitation of the revelation that overwhelms Hedda Gabler and instigates her immediate decision to commit suicide—answering her husband's bravely meant "We'll make our calculations solely for the future, talk about the future, think about the future," Paula replies:

PAULA

I believe the future is only the past again, entered through another gate. You must see now that, do what we will, go where we will, you'll be continually reminded of—what I was. I see it. You'll do your best—oh, I know that—you're a good fellow. But circumstances will be too strong for you in the end, mark my words.

Of course I'm pretty now—I'm pretty still—and a pretty woman, whatever else she may be, is always—well, endurable. But even now I notice that the lines of my face are getting deeper; so are the hollows about my eyes. Yes, my face is covered with little shadows that usen't to be there. Oh, I know I'm "going off." I hate paint and dye and those messes, but, by-and-by, I shall drift the way of the others; I shan't be able to help myself. And then, some day—perhaps very suddenly, under a queer, fantastic light at night or in the glare of the morning—that horrid, irresistible truth that physical repulsion forces on men and women will come to you, and you'll sicken at me.

You'll see me then, at last, with other people's eyes; you'll see me just as your daughter does now, as all wholesome folks see women like me. And I shall have no weapon to fight with—not one serviceable little bit of prettiness left me to defend myself with! A worn-out creature—broken up, very likely, some time before I ought to be—my hair bright, my eyes dull, my body too thin or too stout, my cheeks raddled and ruddled—a ghost, a wreck, a caricature, a candle that gutters—call such an end what you like! Oh, Aubrey, what shall I be able to say to you then? And this is the future you talk about! I know it—I know it! (*She is still sitting, staring forward; she rocks herself to and fro as if in pain.*) Oh, Aubrey! Oh! Oh! Oh, and I wanted so much to sleep tonight!

CANDLE THAT GUTTERS: i.e., one that melts away.

246.

SALOME LASCIVIOUSLY WOOS THE PROPHET JOKANAAN (YT)

(1893) OSCAR WILDE, *SALOME*, ONE ACT

[See, in Men's vols., entries on Jokanaan and Herod] The rhythms of the perverse Salome's sensual wooing of the prophet Jokanaan are like tidal motions, rolling wave over wave in one direction, and then after his thundering rejections of this "daughter of Sodom's" "abomination," her rush of similes undoes her wooing with equally intense incantations of disgust. Then lusting for another feature of his inflaming and equally repelling voice and body, she intensifies her sensual longing, to be repelled again, and then with even greater intensity, is once again wooing. Language alone, the lasciviousness of unremitting ululations of sound, spills over into the simulation of sexual tremor, and Wilde's mode of speech here takes on a value and color unique to this play and to these lines.

John the Baptist (Wilde's Jokanaan) has so bitterly denounced Herodias, the wife of Herod Antipas of Palestine, for her abandoned promiscuity that at her request, Herod has ordered him executed. It's Herodias' daughter Salome who greets Jokanaan when he rises out of the cistern into which Herod has had him thrown. As she insinuates her temptation with more and more intensity, he thunders his anathemas with equal intensity.

(To echo the note in Men's vols.: "Jokanaan Cries Abomination on Herod, Herodias and Their Daughter Salome," what is missing, unfortunately, in reducing the text in this scene to monologue is the musical alternation of the major-key fulminations of Jokanaan and the minor-key wooing of the temptress. Truncating the cadenced duologue of the original, leaves only half—but a characteristically powerful half—of the original's so-to-speak musical score.)

SALOME

Jokanaan, I am amorous of thy body! Thy body is white like the lilies of a field that the mower hath never mowed. Thy body is white like the snows that lie on the mountains, like the snows that lie on the mountains of Judea, and come down into the valleys. The roses in the garden of the Queen of Arabia are not so white as thy body. Neither the roses in the garden of the Queen of Arabia, nor the feet of the dawn when they light on the leaves, nor the breast of the moon when she lies on the breast of the sea... There is nothing in the world so white as thy body. Let me touch thy body.

Thy body is hideous. It is like the body of a leper. It is like a plastered wall where vipers have crawled; like a plastered wall where the scorpions have made their nest. It is like a whitened sepulchre full of loathsome things. It is horrible, thy body is horrible. It is of thy hair that I am enamoured, Jokanaan. Thy hair is like clusters of grapes, like the clusters of black grapes that hang from the vine-trees of Edom in the land of the Edomites. Thy hair is like the cedars of Lebanon, like the great cedars of Lebanon that give their shade to the lions and to the robbers who would hide themselves by day. The long black nights, when the moon hides her face, when the stars are afraid, are not so black. The silence that dwells in the forest is not so black. There is nothing in the world so black as thy hair... Let me touch thy hair.

Thy hair is horrible. It is covered with mire and dust. It is like a crown of thorns which they have placed on thy head. It is like a knot of black serpents writhing round thy neck. I love not thy hair... It is thy mouth that I desire, Jokanaan. Thy mouth is like a band of scarlet on a tower of ivory. It is like a pomegranate cut with a knife of ivory. The pomegranate-flowers that blossom in the garden of Tyre, and are redder than roses, are not so red. The red blasts of trumpets, that herald the approach of kings, and make afraid the enemy, are not so red. Thy mouth is redder than the feet of those who tread the wine in the wine-press. Thy mouth is redder than the feet of the doves who haunt the temples and are fed by the priests. It is redder than the feet of him who cometh from a forest where he hath slain a lion, and seen gilded tigers. Thy mouth is like a branch of coral that fishers have found in the twilight of the sea, the coral that they keep for the kings...! It is like the vermilion that the Moabites find in the mines of Moab, the vermilion that the kings take from them. It is like the bow of the King of the Persians, that is painted with vermilion, and is tipped with coral. There is nothing in the world so red as thy mouth... Let me kiss thy mouth.

I will kiss thy mouth, Jokanaan. I will kiss thy mouth.

EDOM: Greek, a region between the Dead Sea and the Gulf of Aqaba, bordering ancient Palestine. **TYRE:** an ancient Phoenician seaport, one of the great cities of antiquity, famous for its navigators and traders. **MOAB:** the ancient kingdom east of the Dead Sea, now Jordan.

247.

CANDIDA CHOOSES BETWEEN HER POET LOVER AND HER PREACHER HUSBAND (OC)

(1894) BERNARD SHAW, *CANDIDA*, ACT III

Candida is only the first of Shaw's prescient women who, like Socrates' Diotima, speak out of a fund of wisdom it is not given to the rest of us, certainly not to men, to emulate. They know what men cannot know, they've reached a level of endurance and suffering that men inflict but do not share, they have a suprarational insight into being that men cannot encompass. If it is not demonstrably true, it is overwhelmingly moving. And it is expressed in a singular prose that can often transcend music.

It's the other side of the coin of the violent antifeminism that broke out in the intellectual and artistic community of the turn of the century, but shares with those writers and artists who expressed their hatred of women *sui generis*, an almost religious reverence for woman as the Mother of Us All. The paradox floats through the writings and stagings of the period, but it must be noted that Shaw did not share that ambivalence, or if he did, he got rid of it in his fictional male characters, who behave like pigs toward women.

Candida relates directly and inevitably to Ibsen's *Doll House*, and to what amounted for Shaw to an Ibsenian explosion in England, particularly as it related to "the woman question." The "question" was dealt with in extraordinarily naive ways by other "advanced" or at least semi-advanced playwrights, who had their Noras either slam the door at the end of their plays to signify their open views, or reconcile tearfully with Torvald to signify their upholding domestic sanctity. Shaw in *Candida* partitions the "question" as Ibsen himself did in *Love's Comedy* [see, in Men's vols., entries on the characters Straamand and Gulstad] in which the poet Falk is defeated for his love on the domestic battleground by the bourgeois Gulstad, who offers for domesticity the values precisely relevant to bourgeois life. In Shaw's parallel play, the poet Marchbanks is defeated because of his irrelevance to the arena in which his supposed battle for Candida and against her preacher husband Morell is being fought. But the opposition between the two men is put differently by Candida: It is not the soaring eagle of the poet against the mudhen of the business man, but the strength of the one as opposed to the frailty of the other. Candida is not the heroine of romance who exists in the mind of Marchbanks, but the sagacious mother of a brood of two. "I am to choose, am I?" she asks of the two whom she regards, in the context of their understanding of themselves and of her, as children. And in defining them to make her decision, she defines herself.

She asks each one to make his "bid." Marchbanks offers what the poet Shelley might offer: his "weakness, his desolation, his heart's need." ("That's a good bid, Eugene," she compliments him.) Deeply responsible Morell makes a strong man's offer: his strength, honesty, industry, authority.

CANDIDA

Now I know how to make my choice.

> *(She pauses and looks curiously from
> one to the other, as if weighing them.)*
> I give myself to the weaker of the two. Do you understand, Eugene? *(Smiling a little)* Let us sit and talk comfortably over it like three friends. *(To Morell)* Sit down, dear. *(Morell takes the chair from the fireside—the children's chair.)* Bring me that chair, Eugene. *(She indicates the easy chair. He fetches it silently, even with something like cold strength, and places it next to Morell, a little behind him. She sits down. He goes to the sofa and sits there, still silent and inscrutable. When they are all settled she begins, throwing a spell of quietness on them by her calm, sane, tender tone.)* You remember what you told me about yourself, Eugene: how nobody has cared for you since your old nurse died: how those clever, fashionable sisters and successful brothers of yours were your mother's and father's pets: how miserable you were at Eton: how your father is trying to starve you into returning to Oxford: how you have had to live without comfort or welcome or refuge, always lonely, and nearly always disliked and misunderstood, poor boy!

Now I want you to look at this other boy here—my boy—
spoiled from his cradle. We go once a fortnight to see his
parents. You should come with us, Eugene, and see the
pictures of the hero of that household. James as a baby! the
most wonderful of all babies. James holding his first school
prize, won at the ripe age of eight! James as the captain of his
eleven! James in his first frock coat! James under all sorts of
glorious circumstances! You know how strong he is, how
clever he is—how happy! *(With deepening gravity)* Ask James'
mother and his three sisters what it cost to save James the
trouble of doing anything but be strong and clever and happy.
Ask me what it costs to be James' mother and three sisters and
wife and mother to his children all in one. Ask Prossy and
Maria how troublesome the house is even when we have no
visitors to help us to slice the onions. Ask the tradesmen who
want to worry James and spoil his beautiful sermons who it is
that puts them off. When there is money to give, he gives it:
when there is money to refuse, I refuse it. I build a castle of
comfort and indulgence and love for him, and stand sentinel
always to keep little vulgar cares out. I make him master here,
though he does not know it, and could not tell you a moment
ago how it came to be so. *(With sweet irony)* And when he
thought I might go away with you, his only anxiety was what
should become of me! And to tempt me to stay he offered me
his strength for my defence, his industry for my livelihood, his
position for my dignity, his—*(Relenting)* Ah, I am mixing up
your beautiful sentences and spoiling them, am I not, darling?

Am I your mother and sisters to you, Eugene? One last word.
How old are you, Eugene? Eighteen! Will you, for my sake,
make a little poem out of the two sentences I am going to say
to you? And will you promise to repeat it to yourself whenever
you think of me? When I am thirty, she will be forty-five.
When I am sixty, she will be seventy-five. In a hundred years,
we shall be the same age.

ETON COLLEGE: in the south of England, though prestigious, cannot be compared to
Oxford.

248.

MRS. CHEVELEY ENGAGINGLY PROPOSES TO BLACKMAIL SIR ROBERT (OC)

(1895) OSCAR WILDE, *AN IDEAL HUSBAND*, ACT I

[Quoting, in Men's vols., from the entry: "Sir Robert Chiltern Confesses to the Youthful Crime That Has Given Him His Wealth and Position"] "The unscrupulous Mrs. Cheveley has found out the details of Sir Robert's long-concealed lapse of eighteen years ago, the insider-trading ploy that made his fortune, and plans to blackmail him into lending his name to an even more dishonorable scheme now." She is able to propose it with good cheer to a stunned Sir Robert because she has no morals and is perfectly sure of her ground. What makes her especially sure that Sir Robert has no option but to agree, is that "nowadays"—Oscar Wilde's favorite time frame for consigning every lapse from decency—there is the disadvantage that though "the world" (the financial world) remains as criminal as ever, "nowadays" scandal, which "used to lend charm" to ingenious swindlers, now crushes them. Mrs. Cheveley, aware that she is holding a loaded gun to his head, can afford to be cordial and generous in her advice. "I am your enemy. I admit it," she says, smiling kindly at him, and leaving him no way out.

MRS. CHEVELEY

(In her most nonchalant manner) My dear Sir Robert, you are a man of the world, and you have your price, I suppose. Everybody has nowadays. The drawback is that most people are so dreadfully expensive. I know I am. I hope you will be more reasonable in your terms.
I realize that I am talking to a man who laid the foundation of his fortune by selling to a Stock Exchange Speculator a Cabinet secret. I mean that I know the real origin of your wealth and your career, and I have got your letter, too. The letter you wrote to Baron Arnheim, when you were Lord Radley's secretary, telling the Baron to buy Suez Canal shares—a letter written three days before the Government announced its own purchase. You thought that letter had been destroyed. How foolish of you! It is in my possession. It was a swindle, Sir Robert. Let us call things by their proper names. It

makes everything simpler. And now I am going to sell you that letter, and the price I ask for it is your public support of the Argentine scheme. You made your own fortune out of one canal. You must help me and my friends to make our fortunes out of another!

Supposing you refuse—My dear Sir Robert, what then? You are ruined, that is all! Remember to what a point your Puritanism in England has brought you. In old days nobody pretended to be a bit better than his neighbours. In fact, to be a bit better than one's neighbour was considered excessively vulgar and middle-class. Nowadays, with our modern mania for morality, every one has to pose as a paragon of purity, incorruptibility, and all the other seven deadly virtues—and what is the result? You all go over like ninepins—one after the other. Not a year passes in England without somebody disappearing. Scandals used to lend charm, or at least interest, to a man—now they crush him. And yours is a very nasty scandal. You couldn't survive it. If it were known that as a young man, secretary to a great and important minister, you sold a Cabinet secret for a large sum of money, and that was the origin of your wealth and career, you would be hounded out of public life, you would disappear completely. And after all, Sir Robert, why should you sacrifice your entire future rather than deal diplomatically with your enemy? For the moment I am your enemy. I admit it! And I am much stronger than you are. The big battalions are on my side. You have a splendid position, but it is your splendid position that makes you so vulnerable. You can't defend it! And I am in attack.

Of course I have not talked morality to you. You must admit in fairness that I have spared you that. Years ago you did a clever, unscrupulous thing; it turned out a great success. You owe to it your fortune and position. And now you have got to pay for it. Sooner or later we have all to pay for what we do. You have to pay now. Before I leave you to-night, you have got to promise me to suppress your report, and to speak in the House in favour of this scheme. You must make it possible. You are going to make it possible.

Sir Robert, you know what your English newspapers are like. Suppose that when I leave this house I drive down to some newspaper office, and give them this scandal and the proofs of it. Think of their loathsome joy, of the delight they would have in dragging you down, of the mud and mire they would plunge you in. Think of the hypocrite with his greasy smile penning his leading article, and arranging the foulness of the public placard.

NINEPINS: bowling.

249.

MABEL CHILTERN COMPLAINS ABOUT TOMMY'S MANNER OF PROPOSING: TOO OFTEN, OUT OF DATE, AND IN BAD STYLE (YC)

(1895) OSCAR WILDE, *AN IDEAL HUSBAND*, ACT II

There's no Tommy in the cast of characters. His only function is to give Mabel Chiltern a subject to dwell on while she's waiting for a proposal, to come in the last act, from another character, Lord Goring, in whom her interest is genuine. Nor does she have any other function in the play; she is a character with literally nothing to do until the plot's brief attention turns, for a very brief moment, and very late, to her. Wilde, given her relative pointlessness, is free to improvise character, subject and style, and since her conventional role in comedy would be: young lady who is wooed, he makes the burden of her chatter her indifference to wooing, and her charm, her inattention to her charm. But he means her to be the quintessence of charm; this is how he imagines her: she is "a perfect example," he tells us on her arrival, "of the English type of prettiness, the apple-blossom type. She has all the fragrance and the freedom of a flower.... She has the fascinating tyranny of youth, and the astonishing courage of innocence." Wilde's revenge on such fragrant, youthful liberty would have come had he lived to write more such comedies after *An Ideal Husband*, when he would have aged her into the supporting cast of elderly titled matrons who gather in his plays for ideally unfocused conversation, in which they comment on everything serious with indifferent nonchalance and everything trivial with grave opinion.

It is the Lord Goring in whom she is interested who has just walked out, not noticing, apparently, her interest, and when Mabel turns to her hostess Lady Chiltern, she turns also to her old joke about Tommy's proposals, but does so this time with a small touch of asperity—hardly at inoffensive Tommy; more at the departed Lord Goring.

MABEL CHILTERN

Well, Tommy has proposed to me again. Tommy really does nothing but propose to me. He proposed to me last night in the music-room, when I was quite unprotected, as there was an elaborate trio going on. I didn't dare to make the smallest repartee, I need hardly tell you. If I had, it would have stopped the music at once. Musical people are so absurdly unreasonable. They always want one to be perfectly dumb at the very moment when one is longing to be absolutely deaf. Then he proposed to me in broad daylight this morning, in front of that dreadful statue of Achilles. Really, the things that go on in front of that work of art are quite appalling. The police should interfere. At luncheon I saw by the glare in his eye that he was going to propose again, and I just managed to check him in time by assuring him that I was a bimetallist. Fortunately I don't know what bimetallism means. And I don't believe anybody else does either. But the observation crushed Tommy for ten minutes. He looked quite shocked. And then Tommy is so annoying in the way he proposes. If he proposed at the top of his voice, I should not mind so much. That might produce some effect on the public. But he does it in a horrid confidential way. When Tommy wants to be romantic he talks to one just like a doctor. I am very fond of Tommy, but his methods of proposing are quite out of date. I wish, Gertrude, you would speak to him, and tell him that once a week is quite often enough to propose to any one, and that it should always be done in a manner that attracts some attention.

TWENTIETH-CENTURY ENGLISH

250.

MAJOR BARBARA, DISCOVERING THE TRUE SECRET FOR SAVING SOULS, REDEDICATES HER LIFE (YC)

(1905) BERNARD SHAW, *MAJOR BARBARA*, ACT IV

Major Barbara, the zealous missionary of the Salvation Army, suffers a paralyzing revelation: The Army's good deeds, its soup kitchens, its saving of benighted souls, depends for its economic well-being on a devil's bargain with drunkenness and murder.

The beer baron Bodger, the munitions manufacturer Undershaft (Major Barbara's own father) and their like—presumably the Army's targeted enemies—are the very ones who underwrite the Army's ventures and keep its game alive. When Barbara discovers this shaming truth and the Army's willingness to tolerate that tainted revenue, she turns in her uniform, and nurses despair.

But Undershaft has made a pact with his daughter. "If I go to see you in your Salvation Shelter, will you come the day after to see me in my cannon works?" His visit to the Shelter, and the happy greed with which the Army's general takes his check, is what drives Barbara from her mission. But her visit to her father's cannon works transforms her. Undershaft's factory, it turns out, is a model community exhibiting capitalism's fairest face: its largesse, its prosperity, its benignity. And so far has it gone along the path of guaranteeing secure and decent well-being that it resembles the early twentieth century's vision of the utopia of Socialism. That Undershaft manufactures the machinery of war clearly invites Barbara's revulsion. But he counters her revulsion with a challenge: "Dare you make war on war?" His products, he explains, can be used for agriculture, for example, for good as well as for murder: not they but human intent gives them the face of good or of evil.

With Barbara during her visit is her fiancé, Adolphus Cusins (Dolly), a classicist (like Shaw's friend Gilbert Murray) and a street orator (like Shaw himself) who offers street-corner lectures on Euripides—to few heeders. He, like Barbara, overcomes his own revulsion at Undershaft's proud Machiavellianism, and learns the lessons she learns: Without Undershafts, there is no life of the intellect, and—as Barbara discovers here—no sustainable life of the soul. It is not a devil's but a divine bargain: the mutual embrace of a trinity—body, mind, and soul.

There may be a bit of slippage in Shaw's reasoning, and too easily accommodating a marriage of the three entities at play's end, but *Major Barbara*'s and Shaw's commitment to a mutual embrace of the pragmatic ideal of social justice and the mystical ideal of the soul's perpetual flight toward self-transcendence has rarely, even in his own plays, been so movingly spoken as in Barbara's reconciling speech here, in which she gathers together all the play's thematic strands in a kind of paean to the great idealistic hopes of the early twentieth century, the very hopes Shaw himself was to see, twenty years later, destroyed after the First World War [see, in Men's vols.: "Shaw... Mourns the Unhinging of Western Civilization's Values..."].

Barbara

Oh, if only I could get away from you and from father and from it all! if I could have the wings of a dove and fly away to heaven! And leave you, and all the other naughty mischievous children of men. But I cant. I was happy in the Salvation Army for a moment. I escaped from the world into a paradise of enthusiasm and prayer and soul saving; but the moment our money ran short, it all came back to Bodger: it was he who saved our people: he, and the Prince of Darkness, my papa. Undershaft and Bodger: their hands stretch everywhere: when we feed a starving fellow creature, it is with their bread, because there is no other bread; when we tend the sick, it is in the hospitals they endow; if we turn from the churches they build, we must kneel on the stones of the streets they pave. As long as that lasts, there is no getting away from them. Turning our backs on Bodger and Undershaft is turning our backs on life.

If I were middle-class I should turn my back on my father's business; and we should both live in an artistic drawing room, with you reading the reviews in one corner, and I in the other at the piano, playing Schumann: both very superior persons, and neither of us a bit of use. Sooner than that, I would sweep out the guncotton shed, or be one of Bodger's barmaids. Do you know what would have happened if you had refused papa's offer? I should have given you up and married the man who accepted it. After all, my dear old mother has more sense than any of you. I felt like her when I saw this place—felt that I must have it—that never, never, never could I let it go; only she thought it was the houses and the kitchen ranges and the linen and china, when it was really all the human souls to be saved: not weak souls in starved bodies, sobbing with gratitude for a scrap of bread and treacle, but fullfed, quarrelsome, snobbish, uppish creatures, all standing on their little rights and dignities, and thinking that my father ought to be greatly obliged to them for making so much money for him—and so he ought. That is where salvation is really wanted. My father shall never throw it in my teeth again that my converts were bribed with bread. *(She is transfigured.)* I have got rid of the bribe of bread. I have got rid of the bribe of heaven. Let God's work be done for its own sake: the work he had to create us to do because it cannot be done except by living men and women. When I die, let him be in my debt, not I in his; and let me forgive him as becomes a woman of my rank.

(Seizing him with both hands)
Oh, did you think my courage would never come back? did you believe that I was a deserter? that I, who have stood in the streets, and taken my people to my heart, and talked of the holiest and greatest things with them, could ever turn back and chatter foolishly to fashionable people about nothing in a drawing room? Never, never, never, never: Major Barbara will die with the colors. Oh! and I have my dear little Dolly boy still; and he has found me my place and my work. Glory Hallelujah!

251.

MRS. GEORGE, IN TRANCE, SPEAKS
ORACULARLY OF WOMAN'S PLIGHT (oc)

(1908) BERNARD SHAW, *GETTING MARRIED*,
FULL-LENGTH PLAY IN A SINGLE ACT

A group gathers in the capacious kitchen of the Bishop of Chelsea's twelfth-century Norman house over the question of marriage. Two young people in their midst are planning to venture, and the more elderly try to find common ground for rationally verifying their step. (It does them little good; in the end, the young ones, before the group comes to any resolution, have gone off and gotten married any old how.) But among the argumentative inquirers into the question comes a Mrs. George, the Mayoress and the wife of the town's coal merchant, "a triumphant, pampered, wilful, intensely alive woman," Shaw reports, "who has always been rich among poor people." But she also unfortunately wears on her face the ravages of too many tormenting life experiences, and while chatting with the Bishop and his Sexton, Soames, she unaccountably has a faint convulsion, is saved by the Bishop from falling, hears music where there is none, sees great light which they do not, and Soames the Sexton, suddenly inspired to prophesy, begins to intone, but does it badly: "There was a certain woman, the wife of a coal merchant, which had been a great sinner"—at which point, Mrs. George interrupts him, and with her eyes wide open, "You prophesy falsely, Anthony: never in my life have I done anything that was not ordained for me." And quieting a bit, she speaks directly to them, but as though her thoughts are coming from another place within her.

That place is, of course, the place of prophecy familiar to the daughters of Pytho, the Delphic oracle, and what emerges from Mrs. George in her trance mode is a wisdom and a sorrow that transcends all "discussion plays," as this one is called, all rational discourse. She is the second of Shaw's great women of visionary sagacity—following Candida, and preceding *Back to Methusaleh's* Lilith. But the woman who speaks her supernal prophecy has little to do, on the face of it, with the Mrs. George who, when she emerges from her state of trance, is delighted and intrigued by her strange ability, marvels at it, and shows herself, oddly, hardly equal to its possession.

Ive been myself. Ive not been afraid of myself. And at last I
have escaped from myself, and am become a voice for them
that are afraid to speak, and a cry for the hearts that break in
silence. I have earned the right to speak. I have dared: I have
gone through: I have not fallen withered in the fire: I have
come at last out beyond, to the back of Godspeed. *(With
intensely sad reproach)* When you loved me I gave you the
whole sun and stars to play with. I gave you eternity in a single
moment, strength of the mountains in one clasp of your arms;
and the volume of all the seas in one impulse of your souls. A
moment only; but was it not enough? Were you not paid then
for all the rest of your struggle on earth? Must I mend your
clothes and sweep your floors as well? Was it not enough? I
paid the price without bargaining: I bore the children without
flinching: was that a reason for heaping fresh burdens on me?
I carried the child in my arms: must I carry the father too?
When I opened the gates of paradise, were you blind? was it
nothing to you? When all the stars sang in your ears and all
the winds swept you into the heart of heaven, were you deaf?
were you dull? was I no more to you than a bone to a dog?
Was it not enough? We spent eternity together; and you ask
me for a little lifetime more. We possessed all the universe
together; and you ask me to give you my scanty wages as well.
I have given you the greatest of all things; and you ask me to
give you little things. I gave you your own soul: you ask me for
my body as a plaything. Was it not enough? Was it not
enough? It was enough for me. When you spoke to my soul
years ago from your pulpit, you opened the doors of my
salvation to me; and now they stand open for ever. It was
enough. I have asked you for nothing since: I ask you for
nothing now. I have lived: it is enough. I have had my wages;
and I am ready for my work. I thank you and bless you and
leave you. You are happier in that than I am; for when I do for
men what you did for me, I have no thanks, and no blessing: I
am their prey; and there is no rest from their loving and no
mercy from their loathing. *(Troubled)* You are dragging me
back to myself. You are tormenting me with your evil dreams
of saints and devils and—what was it?—*(Striving to fathom it)*
the pythoness—the pythoness—*(Giving it up)* I dont
understand. I am a woman: a human creature like yourselves.
Will you not take me as I am?

(Waking) What was that? *(She is mortified.)* I beg your pardon.

(With great energy, becoming quite herself again) What the
goodness gracious has been happening? *(Delighted)* My
second sight! Oh, how I have prayed that it might come to me.
And now it has come. How stunning! You may believe every
word I said: I cant remember it now; but it was something
that was just bursting to be said; and so it laid hold of me and
said itself. Thats how it is, you see.

PYTHONESS: a woman with the power of divination, such as the priestess of Apollo at
Delphi.

252.

MRS. GRACEDEW RESPONDS TO THE BEAUTY AND GRANDEUR OF AN OLD HOUSE (oc)

(1909) HENRY JAMES, *THE HIGH BID*, ACT I

Gaev, in Chekhov's *The Cherry Orchard*, would have understood Mrs.
Gracedew: her love of the thing that survives—his two-hundred-
year-old cupboard, her newly discovered old English mansion. When
she first appears in Act I, she's rummaging through the old house for
the first time, discovering it with delight, not fully understanding her
delight in it but nevertheless experiencing it with peculiar thrill. She's
an American, a very rich one from Missoura Top, and her first
impulse is to take back its old servant and plant him in that America
that is still manufacturing its own past. She will, through this initial
outburst and throughout the rest of the play, gradually discover her
whole mission and its whole, for her, almost mystical meaning.

The American invasion of Europe and particularly of England,
and that same invasion in reverse, was being chronicled by Henry
James at the turn of the century in his novels and his plays, sometimes with subtle, sometimes with obvious, observations of the life of
that interchange. In *The High Bid*, the observation is not subtle, but
decidedly passionate; Mrs. Gracedew is replicating James' own journey to what he deeply felt was the heart of the old civilization, and her
discovery goes far beyond the love of neglected or decaying bricks

and mortar: it was the benediction the past held for those who were transformed into its votaries.

An old house up for sale is not the most compelling or poetic image of the fruit of that benediction, but it is for Mrs. Gracedew. At first, she intuits it almost comically—and decidedly patronizingly—in Chivers, the old servant who, a bit like Firs in Chekhov's play, is "dilapidated, much darned and repaired ... [with] a universal gentleness and sadness." Transported by the look of the house and the old servant, she addresses both of them as one, not in confusion but in an inevitable merging; one, for her, is the other. Both together are her enthusiastic, but only initial, discovery.

> (*The high, clear vocal sound that heralds the appearance at the top of the stairs of the wonderful figure of the visiting lady; who, having taken possession of the place above, prepares, with the high pitch of her interest, gaily to descend. Enter Mrs. Gracedew from the gallery, speaking as she comes down.*)

MRS. GRACEDEW

> (*On the stairs*)

Housekeeper! Butler! Old family servant! (*With beautiful laughter and rustling garments; as if approaching amid an escort and with music*) Did you think I got snapped down in an old box like that poor girl—what's-her-name? the one who was poking round *too*—in the celebrated poem? (*Her manner to him all on the basis of a relation, the frankest and easiest, already formed by what has happened between them before he gave her the range*) You dear, delightful man, why didn't you *tell* me? That you're so perfectly—perfect! (*As if she had almost been swindled*) You're ever so much better than anyone has ever said. Why, in the name of all that's lovely has nobody ever said *anything*—as nobody for that matter, with all the fun there is, *does* seem ever to say anything! (*Then, as to tell him all about the place he seems, poor dear, really to understand so little*) You're everything in the world you *ought* to be and not the shade of anything you *oughtn't*! No, no—don't try! That's *just* your *charm.* (*She explains with her free benevolence*) I try—I have to; but you do *nothing.* Here you simply *are.* You can't help it.

*(Mrs. Gracedew who has been speaking of the house itself,
applies her delight to his image as well)* Yes, you too, you
positive old *picture. (Perfectly familiar in her appreciation)* I've
seen the old masters, but you're the old master! "The good and
faithful *servant*"—Rembrandt van *Rhyn*. With three Baedeker
stars. *That's* what you are. *(His humility doesn't check her)* The
house is a vision of beauty and *you're* just worthy of the house,
I can't say *more* for you!

Yet I haven't come here to suffer in *silence,* you know, to suffer,
I mean, from envy, or rage, or despair. *(Full of movement and
of sincerity of interest, observing, almost measuring, everything
in the place, she takes notes, while she gossips, jots down signs for
her own use in a small book of memoranda that she carries)* You
almost kill me; however, I take some killing! *(Then again, to
explain herself to his perpetual amaze)* I mean you're so fatally
right and so deadly *complete,* that if I wasn't an angel I could
scarcely *bear* it; with every fascinating feature I had already
heard of and thought I was *prepared* for, and ever so many
others that, strange to say, I *hadn't* and *wasn't,* and that you
just spring right at me like a series of things going off; a sort of
what-do-you-call-it, eh? A royal *salute,* a hundred *guns!*

Before I left America, I had got you by *heart,* from books,
prints, photographs; I had you in my pocket when I came; so,
you see, as soon as you were so good as to give me my head
and let me loose, I knew my way *about.* You're all her, every
inch of you, and now at last *(With decision)* I can do what I
want!

And what might *that* be? Why, take you right *back* with me, to
Missoura Top. *(Leaping, delighted at the idea)* You'd *come,* as
the old family servant? Then *do,* you nice real thing, it's just
what I'm dying for; an old family servant! You're somebody
else's, yes, but everything over here is somebody else's, and I
want, too, a second-hand one, in good order; all ready *made,*
as *you* are, but not too much done up. You're the best I've
struck yet, and I wish I could have you *packed*—put up in
paper and *bran*—as I shall have my old *pot* there.

(She whisks about, remembering, recovering, eager) Don't let me
forget my precious pot!

*(Struck more than with anythng else by the beauty of Chiver's
compunction)* The way you *take* it it's too sweet, you're too

quaint really to *live*! *(She keeps it up to cheer him.)* You're just the very *type*! That's all I *want* of you now—to *be* the very type. It's what you *are*, you poor dear thing, for you can't *help* it; and it's what everything and everyone else are, over here: so that you had just better all make up your minds to it and not try to *shirk* it. There was a type in the *train* with me, the "awfully nice girl" of all the English novels, the "simple maiden in her flower" of—*who* is it? your great *poet*. *She* couldn't help it either; in fact I wouldn't have *let* her! *(With which, starting, she remembers)* By the way, she was coming right *here*. Has she come?

GOT SNAPPED DOWN... CELEBRATED POEM: *Ginevra* by Samuel Rogers (in *Poems*, London 1836): Ginevra, missing on her wedding day, was discovered years later in a chest, in which she had, apparently, locked herself as a prank. REMBRANDT VAN RHYN: probably, his painting *The Good Samaritan*. BAEDEKER: the famous travelers' guidebook.

253.
MRS. GRACEDEW WOOS CAPTAIN YULE TO TAKE ON HIS PROPER DESTINY (OC)

(1909) HENRY JAMES, *THE HIGH BID*, ACT II

[Continues No. 252, above] Mrs. Gracedew's talk, as cryptic as it is lucid, is gradually moving toward its object. "This, your ancestral home, *is* the temple." Her praise of it, and her urgency for its meaning to be understood, is directed at Captain Yule, its owner. "It's such an honor... for anything to have been *spared* from the wreck of time." (Here, the plot intrudes.) The young man has just inherited the house. Technically, it's his, but the mortgage (this is not the first plot in James that in outline is pretty shameless) is held by a nefarious Prodmore, who designs to make the house his own. More of an obstacle than Mr. Prodmore is the commitment of the young man to radical politics, not to the house. It's Mrs. Gracedew's labor to win Captain Yule to his proper destiny, which is to take command of his treasure. Like its ministering angel, she woos the Captain to that destiny, and does so in large part through the speech below.

Apart from the bare bones of the underlying plot, the text of Mrs.

Gracedew's exhortation to the young man avoids as much as possible stating bluntly the bare bones of her message. Unadorned, and head-on, it's merely a partisan appeal to the most conservative posture in turn-of-the-century British politics, in which radical socialism on the one hand and commercial vulgarity on the other, both of which James could hardly bear to countenance, were endangering, naturally, the entrenched old aristocracy whose cause he sighed for and mourned. His upstart vulgarian Prodmore is not too remote in function from Chekhov's upstart vulgarian Lopakhin, and the danger to James' mansion is not too remote from the danger to Chekhov's cherry orchard. But the financial miracle that Madame Ranevskaya waits for in vain comes to the young Captain in the obligatory scene: Mrs. Gracedew buys off the mortgage, and gives the house to Yule "in trust" to keep alive the "beauty" it represents.

It's hardly fair, though, to diminish the play for the nature of the politics that peeps through its plot. It's the nature of its dramatic discourse that constitutes its significant value. Note the weave of the adjustments Mrs. Gracedew makes from one sentence, or phrase, or word, to another. The quick play of mind, the inner urgencies that control it, the suggestions she finds in other faces, the intuition she has of their moment's feeling or thought, plays all through her dialogue, constituting a kind of dramatic discourse that almost defies accurately detailed transcription to stage performance. What James was aiming for in drama was a density of discourse that would equal the psychological density of his novels' characters. That so much of the freight has to be borne by stage directions is an indication of the wide margin that exists between his attempt and usual dramatic practice. Whatever one's admiration might be for the play's substance, the dare of the technique, and its consequent challenge to the actor, invite the hope that one day—yet to happen—a play of James' will be fully realized in performance.

Yule has been arguing with Mrs. Gracedew for his radical politics; for him, "the beauty of old show-houses and the glory of old show-families" have considerably less value than "the thousands of people in England who can show no houses at all, and I dont feel it utterly shameful to share their fate." It's not, to be sure, the most ringing declaration of commitment to "poor humanity," but Mrs. Gracedew is alert to its appeal, and counters:

> *(Roused but unwilling to lose ground
> and moved to use, with a sad and
> beautiful headshake, an eloquence at
> least equal to his own)*

We share the poor fate of humanity whatever we do and we do much to help and console when we've something precious to *show. (Then warming, with all charm, to her work)* What on earth is more precious than what the ages have slowly *wrought? (Specious, ingenious)* They've trusted us—the brave centuries!—to *keep* it; to do something, in our turn, for them. *(Then in earnest, tender, pleading possession of her idea)* It's such a virtue, in anything, to have lasted; it's such an honour, for anything, to have lasted; it's such an honour, for anything, to have been *spared. (After which, for the very climax of her plea for charity)* To all strugglers, from the wreck of time, hold out a pitying hand!

(Shedding his irony; holding up her head; speaking with the highest competence) We're making a past at Missoura Top as fast as ever we *can,* and *(With a sharp smile and hand-gesture of warning)* I should like to see you lay your hand on an hour of the one we've made! *(Then with her always prompt and easy humour)* It's a tight fit, as yet, I *grant,* and *(All ingenious)* that's just why I like, in *yours,* to find room, don't you see, to turn round. *(Then as knowing and able to say just what she thus intensely and appreciatively means)* You're *in* it, over here, and you can't get *out. (Hence lucidly concluding)* So just make the *best* of that and treat it all as part of the fun! If there be aches—there may be—you're here to *soothe* them; and if there be draught—there indeed *must* be!—you're here to stop them up.

(Then intenser) And do you know what I'm here for? If I've come so far and so straight I've almost wondered myself. I've felt with a kind of *passion,* but now I see *why* I've felt. *(Having moved about the hall with the excitement of this perception and separated from him at last by a distance across which he follows her discovery with a visible suspense, she brings out her vivid statement)* I'm here for an act of salvation. I'm here to avert a wrong. *(She glows, she fairly shines, face to face across the distance.)*

(Coming nearer while she sociably and subtly argues)

You'll be one for *mine*, I can see you by that *hearth*. Why do you make such a fuss about changing your politics? *(Then with a flare of gay emphasis)* If you'd come to Missoura Top too you'd change them quick enough! *(But seeing further still and striking harder, she rises again to bright eloquence with the force of her plea)* What do politics amount to compared with religions? Parties and programmes come and go, but a duty like this *abides. (Driving it home, pressing him closer, bringing it out)* There's nothing you can break with that would be like breaking *here*. The very words are ugly and cruel, as much sacrilege as if you had been trusted with the key of the temple. This, your ancestral home, *is* the temple! *(Very high and confident)* Don't *profane* it! Keep up the old altar *kindly,* you can't raise a new one as *good. (Reasoning, explaining, with her fine, almost feverish plausibility)* You *must* have beauty in your life, don't you see, that's the only way to make sure of it for the lives of others. Keep leaving it to *them,* to all the poor others, and heaven only knows what will *become* of it! Does it take one of *us* to feel that, to preach you the *truth?* Then it's good, Captain Yule, we come right over; just to see, you know, what you may happen to be "up to." *(With her sense of proportion again, as always, playing into her sense of humour)* We know what we haven't *got,* worse luck, so that if you've happily got it you've got it also for *us.* You've got it in *trust,* you see, and oh we have an eye on you! You've had it so for *me,* all these dear days of my drinking it in, that, to be grateful, I've wanted regularly to do *something. (With the rich assumption, the high confidence, of having convinced him)* Tell me now I shall have *done* it, I shall have kept you at your *post!*

254.

HYPATIA UNBURDENS HERSELF OF HER LONGING TO, AS SHE PUTS IT, "BE AN ACTIVE VERB" (YC)

(1910) BERNARD SHAW, *MISALLIANCE*, ONE ACT

"I want to be an active verb," Hypatia cries, fed up with the imprisoning respectability to which her class (wealthy), her gender (female), her age (young), and her kind (yearning) have condemned her. Hypatia anticipates the restlessness of the young that followed the First World War, and Shaw anticipates, in portraying her, the loosening of the last restraints on the young that signaled the collapse of a whole host of vestigial genteelisms carried over from the Victorian century. Her energy and longing exceed her imagination; charged almost electrically though she is, she cannot yet imagine her escape.

Her frustrated yearning is contrasted to Lina Shchepanowska's rare accomplishments: a self-made, self-reliant, self-impelling, self-generating Polish aviatrix, a circus acrobat, a powerhouse of self-invented values, Lina has and knows no limits to the satisfaction of her desires for living. Hypatia is marooned in the marriage-proposal orbit of her gender and class, to be inevitably followed through the years by the withering-into-marriage-and-old-age orbit, and so, peering into the future, she sees the dead landscape of a lifetime of marriage-alliance, family-alliance, and female-world alliance staring back. Lina, on the other hand, when one of the young men, instead of proposing a love affair, proposes marriage, is infuriated by the insult: to give up life as she savors it ("I am brave; I am independent; I am unbought; I am all a woman ought to be") and to shrivel into a creature that "take[s] my bread from a man and make[s] him the master of my body and my soul," is a barbarism she reviles. (Never mind that she is the image of the female virago that haunted, lured, and frightened Shaw all his life.) She represents the absolute value against which the implicit failure and impotent yearning of respectably bred well-to-do young ladies is measured, and she is the measure as well of the round of romantic proposals and discreet affairs and discreetly overlapping amatory adventures that constitute the world of this wealthy, overreaching bourgeois set.

Hypatia, who hates the "talk talk talk" that is the life and soul of her family's world, condescends to talk herself, confidently and confessionally, to one of the very few men she trusts to listen and understand: Lord Summerhays, a noncommittal but wise old gentleman who is both out of the game and still sufficiently in it to have unbecomingly fallen in love with Hypatia a while ago and proposed to her, displacing the proposal of Bentley, his own son. Well over his indiscretion, he listens wisely and noncommittally to Hypatia's yearning and starvation.

HYPATIA

Thats part of the routine of life here: the very dullest part ot it. The young man who comes a-courting is as familiar an incident in my life as coffee for breakfast. Of course, he's too much of a gentleman to misbehave himself; and I'm too much of a lady to let him; and he's shy and sheepish: and I'm correct and selfpossessed; and at last, when I can bear it no longer, I either frighten him off or give him a chance of proposing, just to see how he'll do it, and refuse him because he does it in the same silly way as all the rest. You dont call that an event in one's life, do you? With you it was different. I should as soon have expected the North Pole to fall in love with me as you. You know I'm only a linen-draper's daughter when all's said. I was afraid of you: you, a great man! a lord! and older than my father. And then, what a situation it was! Just think of it! I was engaged to your son; and you knew nothing about it. He was afraid to tell you: he brought you down here because he thought if he could throw us together I could get round you because I was such a ripping girl. We arranged it all: he and I. We got Papa and Mamma and Johnny out of the way splendidly: and then Bentley took himself off, and left us— you and me!—to take a walk through the heather and admire the scenery of Hindhead. You never dreamt that it was all a plan: that what made me so nice was the way I was playing up to my destiny as the sweet girl that was to make your boy happy. And then! and then!

> *(She rises to dance and clap her hands*
> *in her glee)*

And then—ha, ha!—you proposed. You! A father! For your son's girl!

That was something happening at last with a vengeance. It was splendid. It was my first peep behind the scenes. If I'd been seventeen I should have fallen in love with you. Even as it is, I feel quite differently towards you from what I do towards other old men. So *(Offering her hand)* you may kiss my hand if that will be any fun for you.

We get on very well, I think. Nobody else ever called me a glorious young beast. I like that. Glorious young beast expresses exactly what I like to be. I'm fed up with nice things: with respectability, with propriety! When a woman has nothing to do, money and respectability mean that nothing is ever allowed to happen to her. I dont want to be good; and I dont want to be bad: I just dont want to be bothered about either good or bad: I want to be an active verb.

I want to be; I want to do; and I'm game to suffer if it costs that. But stick here doing nothing but being good and nice and ladylike I simply wont. Stay down here with us for a week; and I'll shew you what it means: shew it to you going on day after day, year after year, lifetime after lifetime. Girls withering into ladies. Ladies withering into old maids. Nursing old women. Running errands for old men. Good for nothing else at last. Oh, you cant imagine the fiendish selfishness of the old people and the maudlin sacrifice of the young. It's more unbearable than any poverty: more horrible than any regular-right-down wickedness. Oh, home! home! parents! family! duty! how I loathe them! How I'd like to see them all blown to bits! The poor escape. The wicked escape. Well, I cant be poor: we're rolling in money: it's no use pretending we're not. But I can be wicked; and I'm quite prepared to be.

Anyhow, I mean to make a fight for living. Living, instead of withering without even a gardener to snip you off when youre rotten.

255.

ELLIE DUNN DEFENDS HER "HARD AS NAILS" DETERMINATION TO MARRY MONEY AGAINST HESIONE'S SENTIMENTAL SQUEAMISHNESS (YC)

(1913–16) BERNARD SHAW, *HEARTBREAK HOUSE*, ACT II

Ellie's heart is broken, having succumbed at first to the illusions of Heartbreak House, where illusion reigns in all the forms normally taken for reality. By play's end, when the night sky is lit up and blazing with a magnificent display of bombs raining all around and even a bit on Heartbreak House itself—the play takes place in the English countryside during the First World War—much of its illusion is undone, or at least found out, by a few of its guests. Oddly, though, they're braced and eager for more challenging air raids to come.

Ellie is the first to make bracing discoveries. They feel at first like sorrows, but become, for her at least, stages of release. The first is the most painful. She's fallen in love with an amiable charlatan who happens to be, she discovers, the husband of the Mrs. Hushabye who's invited her to Heartbreak House. Rebounding from that revelation, she's more determined than ever to marry the Boss Mangan to whom she's been promised—the "capitalist" who's swindled her father but, unaccountably, still commands all her father's gratitude. It's the sentimental Mrs. Hushabye who's determined to steer her away from so grossly unromantic an alliance, but her efforts set the teeth on edge of the Ellie who's now resolutely weaning herself away from romantic fantasy, and turning, hard as nails, in the direction of marriage for money.

She already, hard as nails, has held Mangan to his promise of marriage against his own determination to squirm out of it, but in confronting him, so bewildered and nonplussed does he become that Ellie, with a peculiar magic she commands, not only soothes him with stroking, but succeeds in putting him into what appears to be a trance. Throughout her interview with Mrs. Hushabye, in which both women are equally blunt about their distaste for the object lying on the floor between them, Boss Mangan, not in a trance at all, is sufficiently awake to hear it all. When Ellie "wakes" him at last, she weathers his vituperation, holds to her determination, but is granted yet another "revelation"—a mystical marriage with the ancient Captain Shotover, the patriarch of Heartbreak House. But that revelation is intended—as Shotover puts it—for both of them to embrace the seventh degree of concentration, and is intended too, therefore, to pass our own understanding.

ELLIE

(Turning vigorously on Hesione the moment her father is out of the room) Hesione: what the devil do you mean by making mischief with my father about Mangan? Why dont you mind your own business? What is it to you whether I choose to marry Mangan or not? Oh yes! Every woman who hasnt any money is a matrimonial adventurer. It's easy for you to talk: you have never known what it is to want money; and you can pick up men as if they were daisies. I am poor and respectable. You were born to lead men by the nose: if you werent, Marcus would have waited for me, perhaps.

(Fiercely) Oh, dont slop and gush and be sentimental. Dont you see that unless I can be hard—as hard as nails—I shall go mad. I dont care a damn about your calling me names: do you think a woman in my situation can feel a few hard words?

I suppose you think youre being sympathetic. You are just foolish and stupid and selfish. You see me getting a smasher right in the face that kills a whole part of my life: the best part that can never come again; and you think you can help me over it by a little coaxing and kissing. When I want all the strength I can get to lean on: something iron, something stony, I dont care how cruel it is, you go all mushy and want to slobber over me. I'm not angry; I'm not unfriendly; but for God's sake do pull yourself together; and dont think that because youre on velvet and always have been, women who are in hell can take it as easily as you.

I must make the best of my ruined house. I shall get over it. You dont suppose I'm going to sit down and die of a broken heart, I hope, or be an old maid living on a pittance from the Sick and Indigent Roomkeepers' Association. But my heart is broken, all the same. What I mean by that is that I know that what has happened to me with Marcus will not happen to me ever again. In the world for me there is Marcus and a lot of other men of whom one is just the same as another. Well, if I cant have love, thats no reason why I should have poverty. If Mangan has nothing else, he has money.

A young man would have the right to expect love from me, and would perhaps leave me when he found I could not give it to him. Rich young men can get rid of their wives, you know, pretty cheaply. But this object, as you call him, can expect nothing more from me than I am prepared to give him. And I have more to give Boss Mangan than he has to give me: it is I who am buying him, and at a pretty good price too, I think. Women are better at that sort of bargain than men. I have taken the Boss' measure; and ten Boss Mangans shall not prevent me doing far more as I please as his wife than I have ever been able to do as a poor girl. *(Stooping to the recumbent figure)* Shall they, Boss? I think not.

> *(She passes on to the drawing-table, and leans against the end of it, facing the windows.)*

I shall not have to spend most of my time wondering how long my gloves will last, anyhow.

Let us wake the object. *(She begins stroking Mangan's head.)* Wake up, do you hear? You are to wake up at once. Wake up, wake up—

256.
ELIZA DOOLITTLE CREDITS HER TRANSFORMATION TO ITS TRUE MAKER (YC)

(1916) Bernard Shaw, *Pygmalion*, Act V

Pygmalion, when it was transformed into a brilliant but sentimental musical and violated every stricture Shaw put on the possible outcome of the combat between Eliza Doolittle and Professor Higgins, added to the stock of romantic fantasy Shaw spent his literary life demolishing. "People in all directions," Shaw wrote in a postscript to the text of the play, "have assumed, for no other reason than that [Eliza] became the heroine of a romance, that she must have married the hero of it. This is unbearable... because her little drama, if acted on such a thoughtless assumption, must be spoiled." Entirely spoiled, because the "little drama" has nothing to do with romantic reconciliation, and everything to do with transfiguration and its cost. Eliza, possessing now the speech of a lady and the look of a duchess, is in fact neither, but only a displaced flower girl, thoroughly declassed. "What's to become of me?" she wonders, and Shaw's postscript provides a sensible, down-to-earth, thoroughly unromantic solution for her: she's to marry her doting and incompetent Freddy and more or less support him. But there's one sense, and only one, in which her transfiguration has been truly accomplished—and she spells it out in this passage. Ignoring the presence of Professor Higgins, who is grinding his teeth in chagrin at her not agreeing to settle again into her para-"scullerymaid" role in his household, she addresses only the affable Colonel Pickering, Higgins' associate and Eliza's comforter, who actually lives by the codes of affability and courtesy prescribed for gentlemen, prescriptions that Higgins ignores and deplores. The code of the gentleman, and its pretensions concerning the lofty place of women in the firmament, may be fiction, but it does wonders for the social adornment of the lady. The answer to Eliza's question, "Who am I now?" is not internal but entirely external: her class identity is determined by the voluntary civilities offered to her. In this speech, she acknowledges that fact, and thanks the Colonel.

ELIZA

Do you know what began my real education? Your calling me Miss Doolittle that day when I first came to Wimpole Street. That was the beginning of self-respect for me. And there were a hundred little things you never noticed, because they came naturally to you. Things about standing up and taking off your hat and opening doors... Yes: things that showed you thought and felt about me as if I were something better than a scullerymaid if she had been let into the drawing room. You never took off your boots in the dining room when I was there. Higgins takes off his boots all over the place. I am not blaming him. It is his way, isn't it? But it made such a difference to me that you didnt do it. You see, really and truly, apart from the things anyone can pick up (the dressing and the proper way of speaking, and so on), the difference between a lady and a flower girl is not how she behaves, but how she's

treated. I shall always be a flower girl to Professor Higgins,
because he always treats me as a flower girl, and always will;
but I know I can be a lady to you, because you always treat me
as a lady, and always will. I should like you to call me Eliza
now, if you would. And I should like Professor Higgins to call
me Miss Doolittle.

257.

LILITH, LOOKING BACK FROM THE TIME "AS FAR AS THOUGHT CAN REACH," PRONOUNCES THE HUMAN JOURNEY WELL BEGUN (OC)

(1919–21) BERNARD SHAW, *BACK TO METHUSELAH*, PART V

Back to Methuselah is Shaw's "metabiological pentateuch," a five-
book bible and play constructed out of the "neo-Darwinian" notion
of "creative evolution," which supposes that evolution does not operate merely mechanically through the process of "natural selection,"
but through the voluntarism of its subjects, that is, that species (of
particular interest, mankind) "will" their transformations themselves, creating and nurturing their own progressive development.
Shaw, in the face of the devastating effect of the First World War on
his earlier idealisms, elaborated the inherent teleological longings of
that earlier socialism, Nietzscheanism, and romantic Shelleyism, into
an almost mystical doctrine combining the "mechanisms" of biolog-
ical evolution with the solace of the human will inherently striving
toward its own perfection.

In *Back to Methuselah*, each of the five plays, or books, represents
another stage in the development of the human species. The urgent
first job of that species is to get beyond the stage of stupidity and
veniality in which it currently flounders (or as Shaw puts it, to get
beyond the cultural and mental stage of "a taste for golf and cigars"),
to be accomplished when the normal life span of the species, "three
score and ten," is successfully exceeded. As the life span lengthens in
each of the plays, problems are not dissipated but transformed, but

each stage signifies a progress toward a transcendent perfection. But what is that ultimate perfection? Lilith, at the end of the "pentateuch," reappears to tell us. It is she who was the original source of human being, she who was bifurcated to create in Adam and Eve the two sexes, and she who has been nurturing, in the thousands of years' progress of that species, its progression.

The last play's time period is designated "as far as thought can reach." Even Lilith cannot see beyond that time. But given the momentary limit to her foretelling, she sums up her temporary balance sheet. Mankind has not only gotten beyond its taste for golf and cigars, it has reached the stage at which its enslaving materiality can conceivably be overcome altogether, and the species pass into a state of pure spirituality, "become all life and no matter." Should it occur, Lilith herself, the Life Force itself, would be surpassed and overcome. She has no fear should that occur; her fear is only for stagnation, that the species give up its striving for a beyond. And for Lilith, "it is enough that there is a beyond."

Shaw shares the cautious wisdom of all religions: the faith that can successfully arrive at its goal obliterates its reason for being, and therefore its value as sustenance. The mists beyond the perpetual beyond, sustain.

LILITH

They have accepted the burden of eternal life. They have taken the agony from birth; and their life does not fail them even in the hour of their destruction. Their breasts are without milk: their bowels are gone: the very shapes of them are only ornaments for their children to admire and caress without understanding. Is this enough; or shall I labor again? Shall I bring forth something that will sweep them away and make an end of them as they have swept away the beasts of the garden, and make an end of the crawling things and the flying things and of all them that refuse to live for ever? I had patience with them for many ages: they tried me very sorely. They did terrible things: they embraced death, and said that eternal life was a fable. I stood amazed at the malice and destructiveness of the things I had made: Mars blushed as he looked down on the shame of his sister planet: cruelty and hypocrisy became so hideous that the face of the earth was pitted with the graves of little children among which living skeletons crawled in search of horrible food. The pangs of another birth were already upon me when one man repented and lived three hundred years; and I waited to see what would come of that. And so much came of it that the horrors of that time seem now but an evil dream. They have redeemed themselves from their vileness, and turned away from their sins. Best of all, they are still not satisfied: the impulse I gave them in that day when I sundered myself in twain and launched Man and Woman on the earth still urges them: after passing a million goals they press on to the goal of redemption from the flesh, to the vortex freed from matter, to the whirlpool in pure intelligence that, when the world began, was a whirlpool in pure force. And though all that they have done seems but the first hour of the infinite work of creation, yet I will not supersede them until they have forded this last stream that lies between flesh and spirit, and disentangled their life from the matter that has always mocked it. I can wait: waiting and patience mean nothing to the eternal. I gave the woman the greatest of gifts: curiosity. By that her seed has been saved from my wrath; for I also am curious; and I have waited always to see what they will do tomorrow. Let them feed that appetite well for me. I say, let them dread, of all things, stagnation: for from the moment I, Lilith, lose hope and faith in them, they are doomed. In that hope and faith I have let them live for a moment; and in that moment I have spared them many times. But mightier creatures than they have killed hope and faith, and perished from the earth; and I may not spare them for ever. I am Lilith: I brought life into the whirlpool of force, and compelled my enemy, Matter, to obey a living soul. But in enslaving Life's enemy I made Life's master; for that is the end of all slavery; and now I shall see the slave set free and the enemy reconciled, the whirlpool become all life and no matter. And because these infants that call themselves ancients are reaching out towards that, I will have patience with them still; though I know well that when they attain it they shall become one with me and supersede me, and Lilith will be only a legend and a lay that has lost its meaning. Of Life only is there no end; and though of its million starry mansions many are empty and many still unbuilt, and though its vast domain is as yet unbearably desert, my seed shall one day fill it and master its matter to its uttermost confines. And for what may be beyond, the eyesight of Lilith is too short. It is enough that there is a beyond.

(She vanishes.)

258.

JOAN, BETRAYED BY THE COURT'S VERDICT, RECANTS HER CONFESSION (YT)

(1923) BERNARD SHAW, *SAINT JOAN*, SC. 6

"The devil has betrayed you, the church holds out its arms to you," urges Brother Martin Ladvenue, pressing hard for Joan of Arc to recant her "abominations" during her trial by the Inquisition. Among her abominations: listening to and being guided by her "voices," dressing in man's clothing and doing man's fighting. In fact, though, she is on trial, as Shaw has it, because of an odd alliance of political interests—the French Catholic Church on the side of Rome, the English enemy army, the Inquisition itself in its own right. And for each of them, Joan's victorious career on the battlefield is either religious, political, or military anathema.

At her trial, one champion for Joan among the Inquisition's accusers tries hard to save her soul—Ladvenue, and it is he who, with care and compassion, guides her to the "recantation of her errors." She allows, at last, that her voices were "of the devil," and signs the document of recantation. It will save her, she is promised, from the horror of being burned at the stake. But once spared that punishment, she is immediately sentenced, as the condition of her returning to the bosom of the Church, to life imprisonment, to which horror she responds with even greater fear and despair than to the other.

Shaw's Joan is entirely and unalterably a peasant girl, and throughout her miraculous career she remains in Shaw's play a peasant—her understanding, her worldly innocence, her superstitions, her technical ignorance of doctrine, and her extraordinary wisdom are determined entirely by that fact. It is that instinct of the peasant toward the ultimate value and pleasure of being alive that shakes Joan immediately out of the lethargy in which she consented to her confession, and toward which she was induced by the Inquisition's doctrinal jargon about sin and damnation ("she did not understand a word we were saying," the Grand Inquisitor confesses after the trial). Shocked by what she conceives to be the Court's blatant betrayal, enraged, she tears up her recantation, and condemning their counsel as "of the devil," and her own as of God, she dooms herself to the stake.

JOAN

(Rising in consternation and terrible anger) Perpetual imprisonment! Am I not then to be set free? Give me that writing.

(She rushes to the table; snatches the paper; and tears it into fragments.)

Light your fire: do you think I dread it as much as the life of a rat in a hole? My voices were right! Yes: they told me you were fools, and that I was not to listen to your fine words nor trust to your charity. You promised me my life; but you lied *(Indignant exclamations)*. You think that life is nothing but not being stone dead. It is not the bread and water I fear: I can live on bread: when have I asked for more? It is no hardship to drink water if the water be clean. Bread has no sorrow for me, and water no affliction. But to shut me from the light of the sky and the sight of the fields and flowers; to chain my feet so that I can never again ride with the soldiers nor climb the hills; to make me breathe foul damp darkness, and keep from me everything that brings me back to the love of God when your wickedness and foolishness tempt me to hate Him: all this is worse than the furnace in the Bible that was heated seven times. I could do without my warhorse; I could drag about in a skirt; I could let the banners and the trumpets and the knights and soldiers pass me and leave me behind as they leave the other women, if only I could still hear the wind in the trees, the larks in the sunshine, the young lambs crying through the healthy frost, and the blessed church bells that send my angel voices floating to me on the wind. But without these things I cannot live; and by your wanting to take them away from me, or from any human creature, I know that your counsel is of the devil, and that mine is of God.

259.

ANNA LIVIA BIDS FAREWELL (oc)

(1939) JAMES JOYCE, *FINNEGANS WAKE*, PART IV (PP. 627–628)

In the novel *Finnegans Wake,* "multiple meanings are present in every line; interlocking allusions to key words and phrases are woven like fugal themes into the pattern of the work.... Its mechanics resemble those of a dream, a dream which... compress[es] all periods of history... into a circular design." Anna Livia in the passage below—the last words of the book—completes that circular design. Her last words circle back to, and are completed by, the book's first sentence.

Anna Livia Plurabelle is the composite figure of woman: The wife of a Dublin pubkeeper, Humphrey Chimpden Earwicker, himself the universally composite figure whose "dream" is the substance of the book. She is by turns and simultaneously, among other incarnations, Eve, the Egyptian goddess Isis, Iseult of the legend of Tristan and Iseult, a cloud in heaven, a flowing stream. Above all, she is a river, the river Liffey that flows through Dublin. At the end of Joyce's novel that comprehends the universe of human experience within the shell of HCE's night's dream, Anna Livia, lying beside him, wakes, and in her reverie journeys through her life, from the little cloud which bursts and rains way up on the Wicklow Hills, to the woman-river heavy with age, sorrow, old experience, a muddy river emptying into the sea and returning to her father Neptune, God of the Sea, from whence she will, in a cyclic determinism, return to heaven, and once again "feel, then fall" to earth and its repetitious journey of endless days.

As day dawns, and her reverie continues, reality "lightens up and tightens down." Things become more what they are in the light of day, and she sees, from the perspective of an old woman worn with sorrow and disillusionment—"all my life I have *been lived* among them," she recognizes bitterly—she recognizes too that her husband (from his movement in bed) has already "turned" from her, she to be replaced in his longings by a "daughterwife from the hills again." She gives her blessing to this anticipated union, but it awakens in her the realization of the waste and loss she's suffered at the instance of— what she now sees as—the littleness, the smallness of the souls for which she's labored all her grown woman's life—"You're only a bumpkin." And she reverts, in compensatory recollection, to the happiest time of all—her adolescence, her pre-male loving time when, like an Amazon among Amazons, she played and thrilled in the sexual freedom of young, vigorous, warrior-like girls together. But her feeling of "loothing" for her life with husband and children again overwhelms her, and she determines—"for all their faults"—to pass out of their lives. And the disillusioned old woman goes back—in reverie? in reality?—to her "cold mad father"—(to Neptune? to mad old King Lear, as his young daughter Cordelia?)—but as the waves come rushing in "moananoaning," she's terrified, and throws herself into the arms of that trusted—(father Neptune? or husband, HCE?) But the "prongs" on Neptune's triton terrify her into recognizing the imminence of her end, and she cries out for a delay of "two more-mens more"—(two more moments of life? or two more men before the end?) But the water washes over her, and then, surrendering, she welcomes it—"ave" (hail) "laval" (cleansing wash). She notices then that all the leaves with which she/Eve has had to cover her nudity in deference to propriety and "sin" are washed away, but that the one that clings and still covers her vagina will stay to remind her of "lff" (life; the river Liffey, which was her life's journey's self). Then looking up at the beautiful morning sky, the great moment that corresponds to Molly Bloom's yea-saying (her "yes," the last word of *Ulysses),* occurs when Anna Livia utters her almost inadvertent benediction, her "yea-saying."

The old woman reverts to a small child, begging her father (a personal recollection of Joyce's similar prayer to his father) to carry her "like you done through the toy fair." But then, a moment of reversion: if he were to see appear—who? her husband? her first lover?—she would turn back from this sea-death, and fall on her knees before this beloved figure, only to—worship, or, wash up from the sea, back to dry land. "Yes, tid," she confirms to her "dad," the father to whom she's succumbing in this sea-merger, and assures him that that pious blessing she still hopes to see on the shore would turn her back from him to her first and deepest loyalty: him. No such earthly redemption occurs, and she/the river continues her journey, swishing past the riverside's growths. She sees gulls overhead, hears calls (theirs? or her father Neptune's to hurry?) and she answers she's coming, "End here" ("Am here," and "I'm ending the journey here"). But she turns back once more to her husband (in the guise of the progenitor of all, Finn) to "take" her once more, but gently. And to remember her "till thousendsthee" ("thousands of aeons?" or "till you send yourself, till you come back, to me"). "Lps"—a kiss. Then, final gesture: like Nora in *A Doll House* whose last gesture is her leaving the keys on the table when she leaves Torvald for her solitary journey from him, Anna Livia remembers that same practical detail, throws the keys all the way from the mouth of the river to the pub above which her husband is still sleeping, and with that done—"Given!"—she goes her way, alone, the last journey, she who was once loved, journeying now along the (the book's beginning) "riverrun past Eve and Adams, from swerve of shore to bend of bay..." (The "river" reconstituted, beginning again, courses its way through the Garden of Eden.)

Anna Livia's farewell has by much critical assent taken its place among the most beautiful passages in any genre in English literature.

Anna Livia

Yes, you're changing, sonhusband, and you're turning, I can feel you, for a daughterwife from the hills again. Imlamaya. And she is coming. Swimming in my hindmoist. Diveltaking on me tail. Just a whisk brisk sly spry spink spank sprint of a thing theresomere, saultering. Saltarella come to her own. I pity your oldself I was used to. Now a younger's there. Try not to part! Be happy, dear ones! May I be wrong! For she'll be sweet for you as I was sweet when I came down out of me mother. My great blue bedroom, the air so quiet, scarce a cloud. In peace and silence. I could have stayed up there for always only. It's something fails us. First we feel. Then we fall. And let her rain now if she likes. Gently or strongly as she likes. Anyway let her rain for my time is come. I done me best when I was let. Thinking always if I go all goes. A hundred cares, a tithe of troubles and is there one who understands me? One in a thousand of years of the nights? All me life I have been lived among them but now they are becoming lothed to me. And I am lothing their little warm tricks. And lothing their mean cosy turns. And all the greedy gushes out through their small souls. And all the lazy leaks down over their brash bodies. How small it's all! And me letting on to meself always. And lilting on all the time. I thought you were all glittering with the noblest of carriage. You're only a bumpkin. I thought you the great in all things, in guilt and in glory. You're but a puny. Home! My people were not their sort out beyond there so far as I can. For all the bold and bad and bleary they are blamed, the seahags. No! Nor for all our wild dances in all their wild din. I can seen meself among them, allaniuvia pulchrabelled. How she was handsome, the wild Amazia, when she would seize to my other breast! And what is she weird, haughty Niluna, that she will snatch from my ownest hair! For 'tis they are the stormies. Ho hang! Hang ho! And the clash of our cries till we spring to be free. Auravoles, they says, never heed of your name! But I'm loothing them that's here and all I lothe. Loonely in me loneness. For all their faults. I am passing out. O bitter ending! I'll slip away before they're up. They'll never see. Nor know. Nor miss me. And it's old and old it's sad and old it's sad and weary I go back to you, my cold father, my cold mad father, my cold mad feary father, till the near sight of the mere size of him, the moyles and

moyles of it, moananoaning, makes me seasilt saitsick and I
rush, my only, into your arms. I see them rising! Save me from
those therrble prongs! Two more. Onetwo moremens more.
So. Avelaval. My leaves have drifted from me. All. But one
clings still. I'll bear it on me. To remind me of. Lff! So soft this
morning, ours. Yes. Carry me along, taddy, like you done
through the toy fair! If I seen him bearing down on me now
under whitespread wings like he'd come from Arkangels, I sink
I'd die down over his feet, humbly dumbly only to washup.
Yes, tid. There's where. First. We pass through grass behush the
bush to. Whish! A gull. Gulls. Far calls. Coming, far! End here.
Us then. Finn, again! Take. Bussoftlhee, mememormee! Till
thousendsthee. Lps. The keys to. Given! A way a lone a last a
loved a long the

GLOSSARY OF GREEK
AND ROMAN NAMES

Aphrodite: (Greek mythology) goddess of love, daughter of Zeus

Apollo: (Greek mythology) god of the sun, healing, music, and prophecy; patron of the Oracle at Delphi; son of Zeus

Ares: (Greek mythology) god of war, son of Zeus and Hera, sometime paramour of Aphrodite

Argive: a native of ancient Argos; or, any Greek

Artemis: (Greek mythology) virgin goddess of the hunt, also identified with the moon; twin sister of Apollo

Ate: (Greek mythology) Avenger, goddess of rage and mischief; daughter of Eris (Strife) and Zeus. She personifies infatuation, with guilt its cause and evil its consequence.

Athena Pallas: (Greek mythology) warrior goddess, goddess of wisdom, the arts and sciences; patroness of Athens; daughter of Zeus

Bacchus: Roman equivalent of Dionysus

Charon: (Greek mythology) with his boat, he takes the souls of the dead across the river Lethe or Styx to Hades

Cypris: the island of Cyprus (or Cypris). Center for the worship of Aphrodite; hence, "the Cyprian"

Delphi: a town in northern Greece, site of the famous oracular shrine of Apollo (see Pytho)

Demeter: (Greek mythology) goddess of agriculture; sister of Zeus, mother of Persephone

Dionysus: (Greek mythology) god of wine; patron of drama in Athens; son of Zeus

Elysium: (Greek mythology) the equivalent of Heaven

Erynyes: see Furies

Furies: (Greek mythology) spirits of Divine Vengeance, especially transgressions that touch on the basis of human society. They punish violations of filial duty, the claims of kinship, rites of hospitality, murder, perjury, etc., eventually reconciled by Athena to Athenian law

Hades: (Greek mythology) god of the Underworld, where the souls of the dead go; brother of Zeus and Poseidon; also used as a name for the Underworld

Hecate: (Greek mythology) a confusing divinity, identified with the moon, Artemis, and Persephone, and invoked by sorcerers. She is the great sender of visions, of madness, and of sudden terror. Medea was her witch-priestess before falling in love with Jason.

Helios: Apollo

Hera: (Greek mythology) sister and wife of Zeus

Hermes: (Greek mythology) messenger of the gods and guide of souls departing to Hades

Hymen: (Greek mythology) god of marriage

Ilion: Greek name for ancient Troy

Ilium: Greek name for ancient Troy

Jove: see Jupiter

Jupiter: Roman equivalent of Zeus

Lethe: (Greek mythology) the river in Hades, from which the souls of the dead drank and became oblivious to their past lives. Then they were carried across by Charon in his boat.

Neptune: Roman equivalent of Poseidon

Orpheus: (Greek mythology) a Thracian philosopher, poet, and musician, who wins permission by his music to bring his wife back to earth from Hades

Pallas: Athena

Persephone: (Greek mythology) wife of Hades, queen of the underworld, daughter of Demeter

Phoebus: epithet for Apollo meaning purity, light

Phrygian: of Phrygia, an ancient country in Asia Minor, one of whose cities was Troy

Pluto: Roman equivalent of Hades

Poseidon: (Greek mythology) god of the sea; brother of Zeus and Hades

Pytho: ancient name for Delphi, Apollo's seat of prophecy. It is conducted by the prophetess Pythia seated on a tripod over the Oracle proper, which is a cleft in the ground in the innermost sanctuary, from which rose cold vapors that have the power of inducing the ecstasy that induces the priestess to have prophetic vision. Her responses are ambiguous, but though always true, give rise to misinterpretation.

Styx: see Lethe

Tartarus: (Greek mythology) the infernal depths of Hades

Zeus: (Greek mythology) chief of the gods, master of the lightning bolt

BIBLIOGRAPHY OF
MONOLOGUE SOURCES

Aeschylus, *Agamemnon*: Translated by Leon Katz (unpublished); alternate source: Aeschylus, *The Oresteia*. Translated by Ted Hughes. Farrar, Strauss & Giroux, 1999.

———, *Prometheus Bound*: Robert W. Corrigan, ed. *Classical Tragedy, Greek and Roman*. Applause Books, 1990.

Anonymous, *Arden of Feversham*: Martin White, ed. *Arden of Feversham*. New Mermaids, 1982.

Aretino, Pietro, *The Courtezan*: Samuel Putnam, editor and translator. *The Works of Aretino*. Covici-Friede, 1933.

———, *The Stablemaster*: Bruce Penman, ed. *Five Italian Renaissance Comedies*. Penguin, 1978.

Ariosto, Ludovico, *Lena; The Necromancer; The Pretenders*: Translated by Leon Katz (unpublished); alternate source: Edmond M. Beame and Leonard G. Sbrocchi, editors and translators. *The Comedies of Ariosto*. University of Chicago, 1975.

Aristophanes, *Lysistrata*: Translated by Leon Katz (unpublished); alternate source: Robert W. Corrigan. *Classical Comedy, Greek and Roman*. Applause, 1987. Translated by Donald Sutherland.

———, *Thesmaphoriazusae*: Translated by Leon Katz (unpublished); alternate source: Whitney J. Oates and Eugene O'Neill Jr., ed. *The Complete Greek Drama*. Modern Library, 1938.

Augier, Emile, *Olympe's Marriage*: Stephen S. Stanton, ed. *Camille and Other Plays*. Mermaid Dramabook, 1957.

Baillie, Joanna, *De Monfort*: Mrs. Incbald, ed. *The British Theatre* vol. 24. Longman, Hurst, Rees, Orme, 1808.

Balzac, Honoré de, *The Stepmother*: J. Walker McSpadden, ed. *The Works of Honoré de Balzac*. Avil Publishing, 1901.

Banks, John, *The Unhappy Favorite, or The Earl of Essex*: James Sutherland, ed. *Restoration Tragedies*. Oxford University, 1977.

Beaumont, Francis, and John Fletcher, *The Knight of the Burning Pestle; The Maid's Tragedy*: A.H. Nethercourt, Ch. R. Baskervill, and V.B. Heltzel, ed. *Elizabethan and Stuart Plays*. Holt, Rinehart & Winston, 1971.

———, *The Philaster*: C.F. Tucker Brooke and N.B. Paradise, ed. *English Drama 1580–1642*. D.C. Heath & Co., 1933.

Behn, Aphra: *The Feigned Courtesans; The Lucky Chance*: Aphra Behn. *The Rover and Other Plays*. Edited by Jane Spencer. Oxford University, 1995.

———, *Sir Patient Fancy*: Katharine M. Rogers, ed. *The Meridian Anthology of Restoration and Eighteen Century Plays by Women*. Meridian Press, 1994.

———, *The Young King*: Montague Summers, ed. *The Works of Aphra Behn*, vol. 2. William Heinemann, 1965.

Boucicault, Dion: *The Corsican Brothers; London Assurance*: A. Parkin, ed. *Selected Plays of Dion Boucicault*. Catholic University of America Press, 1987.

Bruno, Giordano, *Il Candelaio*: Eric Bentley, ed. *The Genius of the Italian Theater*. New American Library, 1964.

Büchner, Georg, *Danton's Death*: Georg Büchner. *Complete Plays and Prose*. Translated by Carl Richard Mueller. Hill & Wang, 1963.

Bulwer, Edward, *Richelieu*: M.R. Booth, ed. *English Plays of the XIX Century*, vol. 1. Clarendon, 1969.

Cervantes, Miguel de, *The Jealous Old Man, an Interlude*: Walter Starkie, editor and translator. *Eight Spanish Plays of the Golden Age*. The Modern Library, 1964.

Chapman, George, John Marston, and Ben Jonson, *Eastward, Ho!*: Brian Gibbons. *Elizabethan and Jacobean Comedies*. E. Benn, 1984.

Cibber, Colley, *The Careless Husband*: George Nettleton, ed. *British Dramatists from Dryden to Sheridan*. Houghton Mifflin Co., 1939.

———, *Love's Last Shift*: Douglas MacMillan and Howard M. Jones, ed. *Plays of the Restoration and Eighteenth Century*. Holt, Rinehart & Winston, 1966.

Coleridge, Samuel Taylor, *Remorse*: Gerald B. Kauvar and Gerald C. Sorensen. *Nineteenth-Century English Verse Drama*. Associated University Presses, 1973.

Colman, George, the Elder, *The Jealous Wife*: George Nettleton and Arthur Case, ed. *British Dramatists from Dryden to Sheridan*. Houghton & Mifflen, 1939.

Congreve, William: *The Double Dealer; The Way of the World*: Eric S. Rump, ed. *Comedies by William Congreve*. Penguin, 1985.

Corneille, Pierre, *Le Cid*: Paul Landis, ed. *Six Plays by Corneille and Racine*. Modern Library, 1931.

Corneille, Thomas, *Laodice*: Lacy Lockert, tr. *The Chief Rivals of Corneille and Racine*. The Vanderbuilt University, 1956.

Coyne, Joseph Stirling, *Did You Ever Send Your Wife to Camberwell?*: Michael R. Booth, ed. *The Lights o' London and Other Victorian Plays*. Clarendon Press, 1995.

Dekker, Thomas, *The Shoemaker's Holiday*: Brian Gibbons. *Elizabethan and Jacobean Comedies*. E. Benn, 1984.

Dryden, John, *All for Love*: James Sutherland, ed. *Restoration Tragedies*. Oxford University, 1977.

Dumas, Alexandre, *fils, Camille*: Stephen S. Stanton, ed. *Camille and Other Plays*. Mermaid Dramabook, 1957.

Dumas, Alexandre, *père, The Tower of Nesle*: Alexandre Dumas. *The Tower of Nesle*. Translated by Adam Gowans. Gowans and Gray, 1906.

Euripides, *Alcestis; Andromache; Electra; Ion*; Euripides. *Ten Plays by Euripides*. Translated by Moses Hadas and John McLean. Bantam, 1960.

———, *Bacchae; Iphigenia in Aulis*: Translated by Leon Katz (unpublished); alternate source: Euripides. *Ten Plays by Euripides*. Translated by Moses Hadas and John McLean. Bantam, 1960.

———, *Hecuba*: Euripides. *Hecuba*. Translated by Janet Lembke and Kenneth J. Reckford. Oxford University Press, 1991.

———, *Hippolytus*: Euripides. *Ten Plays by Euripides*. Translated by Moses Hadas and John McLean. Bantam, 1960; Dudley Fitts, ed. *Greek Plays in Modern Translation*. Dial Press, 1947.

———, *Medea*: Dudley Fitts, ed. *Greek Plays in Modern Translation*. Dial Press, 1947.

———, *The Phoenician Women*: Translated by Leon Katz (unpublished); alternate source: Whitney J. Oates and Eugene O'Neill, Jr., ed. *The Complete Greek Drama*. Modern Library, 1938. Translated by E.P. Coleridge.

———, *Rhesus*: Translated by Leon Katz (unpublished); alternate source: Whitney J.

Oates and Eugene O'Neill Jr., ed. *The Complete Greek Drama*. Modern Library, 1938.

————, *The Trojan Women*: Jean-Paul Sartre, ad. *Euripides' The Trojan Women*. Vintage Books, 1967. Translated by Ronald Duncan; Euripides. *Ten Plays by Euripides*. Translated by Moses Hadas and John McLean. Bantam, 1960; Gilbert Murray, editor and translator. *Five Plays of Euripides*. Oxford University Press, 1934.

Farquhar, George, *The Beaux' Stratagem*; *The Constant Couple*: George Farquhar. *The Recruiting Officer and Other Plays*. Edited by William Myers. Clarendon, 1995.

Fitzball, Edward, *The Inchcape Bell, or the Dumb Sailor Boy*: Michael R. Booth, ed. *The Lights o' London and Other Victorian Plays*. Clarendon Press, 1995.

Ford, John, *The Broken Heart*; *The Lover's Melancholy*; *Perkin Warbeck*: John Ford. *Five Plays*. Edited by Havelock Ellis. Mermaid Dramabook, 1957.

Gay, John, *The Beggar's Opera*: Douglas MacMillan and Howard M. Jones, ed. *Plays of the Restoration and Eighteenth Century*. Holt, Rinehart & Winston, 1966.

Gilbert, William Schwenck, *Tom Cobb*: Michael R. Booth, ed. *English Plays of the Nineteenth Century*, Vol. IV. Clarendon, 1973.

Greene, Robert, *Friar Bacon and Friar Bungay*: C.F. Tucker Brooke and N.B. Paradise, ed. *English Drama 1580–1642*. D.C. Heath & Co., 1933.

Hazlewood,Colin Henry, *Lady Audley's Secret*: George Rowell, ed. *Nineteenth Century Plays*. Oxford University, 1972.

Herondas, *The Jealous Woman* (Mime #5); *A Chat Between Friends* (Mime #6): Translated by Leon Katz (unpublished); alternate source: *The Mimes of Herondas*. Grey Fox Press, 1981. Translated by Guy Davenport.

Heywood, Thomas, *A Woman Killed with Kindness*: Kathleen E. McLuskie and David Bevington, ed. *Plays on Women*. Manchester University, 1999.

Hugo, Victor, *Mary Tudor*; *The Twin Brothers*: Victor Hugo. *Victor Hugo, Dramas*, vols. 1, 2, and 4. Anonymous translation. Dana Estes and Company, n.d.

————, *Ruy Blas*: Translated by Leon Katz (unpublished); alternate source: Helen A. Gaubert, ed. *Three Plays by Victor Hugo*. Washington Square Press, 1964. Translated by Camilla Crosland.

James, Henry, *The High Bid*: Leon Edel, ed. *The Complete Plays of Henry James*. J.B. Lippincott, 1949.

Jones, Henry Arthur, *The Middleman*: Michael R. Booth, ed. *The Lights o' London and Other Victorian Plays*. Clarendon Press, 1995.

Jonson, Ben, *The Alchemist*; *Bartholomew Fair*; *Epicoene, or the Silent Woman*; *Volpone*: J. Procter, ed. *The Selected Plays of Ben Jonson*. Cambridge University, 1989.

————, *Catiline's Conspiracy*: *The Complete Plays of Ben Jonson*, vol. 2. E.P. Dutton, 1946.

Joyce, James, *Finnegans Wake*: James Joyce. *Finnegans Wake*. Viking, 1939.

Kyd, Thomas, *Spanish Tragedy*: W. Tydemon, ed. *Two Tudor Tragedies*. Penguin, 1992.

Lee, Nathaniel, *The Princess of Cleves*: Michael Cordner and Ronald Clayton, ed. *Four Restoration Marriage Plays*. Clarendon, 1995.

————, *The Rival Queens, or the Death of Alexander the Great*: D. MacMillan and H.M. Jones, ed. *Plays of the Restoration and Eighteenth Century*. Holt, Rinehart and Winston, 1931.

Le Sage, Alain-René, *Turcaret*: *French Comedies of the XVIII Century*. George Routledge & Sons, n.d.

Lessing, Gottfried Ephraim, *Emilia Galotti*: Translated by Leon Katz (unpublished); alternate source: Peter Demetz, ed. *Gottfried Ephraim Lessing, Nathan the Wise,*

Minna von Barnhelm, and Other Plays and Writings. Continuum, 1991. Translated by Anna Johanna Gode von Aesch.

————, *Miss Sara Sampson*: Ernest Bell, editor and translator. *The Dramatic Works of G.E. Lessing*, vol. 1. George Bell & Sons, 1901.

Lewes, George Henry, *The Game of Speculation*: Michael R. Booth, ed. *The Lights o' London and Other Victorian Plays*. Clarendon Press, 1995.

Lillo, George, *Fatal Curiosity*: Wm H. McBurney, ed. *George Lillo, Fatal Curiosity*. University of Nebraska, 1966.

————, *The London Merchant*: Douglas MacMillan and Howard M. Jones, ed. *Plays of the Restoration and Eighteenth Century*. Holt, Rinehart & Winston, 1966.

Marlowe, Christopher, *Edward II*; *Tamburlaine*: Christopher Marlowe. *Dr. Faustus and Other Plays*. Oxford University, 1995.

————, *The Jew of Malta*: C.F. Tucker Brooke and N.B. Paradise, ed. *English Drama 1580–1642*. D.C. Heath & Co., 1933.

Marston, John, *The Dutch Courtesan*: John Marston. *The Dutch Courtesan*. Edited by M.L. Wine. University of Nebraska, 1965.

————, *The Malcontent*: Brian Gibbons. *Elizabethan and Jacobean Comedies*. E. Benn, 1984.

Marston, J. Westland, *The Patrician's Daughter*: J.O. Bailey, ed. *British Plays of the Nineteenth Century*. Odyssey, 1966.

Massinger, Philip, *A New Way to Pay Old Debts*: A.H. Nethercourt, Ch.R. Baskervill, and V.B. Heltzel, ed. *Stuart Plays*. Holt, Rinehart & Winston, 1971.

Menander, *The Arbitration*: Translated by Leon Katz (unpublished); alternate source: *Menander*. Wm. Heinemann, 1930. Translated by Francis G. Allinson.

Middleton, Thomas, and Thomas Dekker, *The Roaring Girl*: Kathleen E. McLuskie and David Bevington, ed. *Plays on Women*. Manchester University, 1999.

Middleton, Thomas, and William Rowley, *The Changeling*: A.H. Gomme, ed. *Jacobean Tragedies*. Oxford University, 1971.

Molière, *Dom Garcie de Navarre*; *George Dandin*; *Les Fourberies de Scapin*: *The Plays of Molière*. vol. 2. Translated by A.R. Waller. John Grant, 1907.

————, *Don Juan*; *Les Precieuses Ridicules*; Ian Maclean, Molière, *Don Juan and Other Plays*, Oxford University, 1989. Translated by George Gravely and Ian Maclean.

————, *The Learned Ladies*: Molière. *Comedies* vol. 2. Translated by Henry Baker and James Miller. Everyman's Library, 1948.

————, *The Misanthrope*: Molière. *Four Comedies*. Translated by Richard Wilbur. Harcort Brace, 1982,.

————, *Tartuffe*: Molière. *Molière's Tartuffe or The Impostor*, Translated by Christopher Hampton. Faber & Faber, 1984; Molière *The Plays of Molière*. vol. 2. Translated by A.R. Waller. John Grant, 1907.

Molina, Tirso de, *The Playboy of Seville*: Walter Starkie, editor and translator. *Eight Spanish Plays of the Golden Age*. The Modern Library, 1964.

Musset, Alfred de, *The Follies of Marianne*: *The Complete Writings of Alfred de Musset*, Vols. 3 and 4. National Library Company, 1905.

Otway, Thomas, *Don Carlos*; *Venice Preserv'd*: Havelock Ellis, ed. *Thomas Otway*. Mermaid Series, 1888.

Pinero, Arthur Wing, *The Second Mrs. Tanqueray*: George Rowell, ed. *Late Victorian Plays 1890–1914*. Oxford University, 1972.

Pix, Mary, *The Innocent Mistress*: Fidelis Morgan. *The Female Wits: Women Playwrights on the London Stage 1660–1720*. Virago, 1981.

Porto-Riche, Georges de, *Francoise' Luck*: *Four Plays of the Free Theater*. Syewart and Kidd, 1915.

Racine, Jean, *Andromache; Brittanicus; Phaedra*: Paul Landis, ed. *Six Plays by Corneille and Racine*. Modern Library, 1931.

Robertson, Thomas William, *Caste*: George Rowell, ed. *Nineteenth Century Plays*. Oxford University, 1972.

Rojas, Fernando de, *Celestina*: Eric Bentley, ed. *The Classic Theatre*, Vol. 3. Doubleday/Anchor, 1959.

Rowe, Nicholas, *The Fair Penitent*: Bonamy Dobree, ed. *Five Restoration Tragedies*. Oxford University Press, 1935.

———, *The Tragedy of Jane Shore*: George Nettleton and Arthur Case, ed. *British Dramatists from Dryden to Sheridan*. Houghton & Mifflen, 1939.

Sade, Marquis de, *Oxtiern*: *The Marquis de Sade: The 120 Days of Sodom and Other Writings*. Compiled and translated by Austryn Wainhouse and Richard Seaver. Grove Press, 1966.

———, *Philosophy in the Bedroom*: Marquis de Sade. *Justine, The Philosophy in the Bedroom, and Other Writings*. Translated by Austryn Wainhouse, Richard Seaver. Grove Press, 1966.

Schiller, Friedrich, *Intrigue and Love*: Friedrich Schiller. *Intrigue and Love*. Translated by Charles E. Passage. Ungar, 1971.

———, *Mary Stuart*: Walter Hinderer, ed. *Schiller, Wallenstein and Mary Stuart*. Continuum, 1991.

Seneca, *Agamemnon; Hercules Oetaeus; The Phoenician Women*: Translated by Leon Katz (unpublished); alternate source: *The Tragedies of Seneca*. Translated by Ella Isabel Harris. Oxford University Press, 1904.

———, *Medea*: Translated by Leon Katz (unpublished); alternate source: Philip Whaley Harsh, ed. *An Anthology of Roman Drama*. Rinehart, 1960.

———, *Phaedra*: Frank Justus Miller, editor and translator. *The Tragedies of Seneca*. University of Chicago, 1907.

———, *The Trojan Women; The Phoenician Women*: *The Tragedies of Seneca*. Translated by Ella Isabel Harris. Oxford University Press, 1904.

Shaw, Bernard, *Back to Methuselah; Candida; Getting Married; Heartbreak House; Major Barbara; Misalliance; Mrs. Warren's Profession; The Philanderer; Pygmalion; Saint Joan*: Bernard Shaw. *The Complete Plays*. Paul Hamlyn, 1965.

Shelley, Percy Bysshe, *The Cenci*: Percy Bysshe Shelley. *The Cenci*. Woodstock Books, 1999.

Sheridan, Richard Brinsley, *Pizarro*: John Hampden, ed. *The Plays of R.B. Sheridan*. Thomas Nelson & Sons, n.d.

———, *The Rivals*: Alexander W. Allison, Arthur J. Carr, and Arthur M. Eastman, ed. *Masterpieces of the Drama*. Macmillan, 1957.

———, *The School for Scandal*: Douglas MacMillan and Howard M. Jones, ed. *Plays of the Restoration and Eighteenth Century*. Holt, Rinehart & Winston, 1966.

Shirley, James, *The Cardinal*: C.F. Tucker Brooke and N.B. Paradise, ed. *English Drama 1580–1642*. D.C. Heath & Co., 1933.

Sophocles, *Ajax; Electra*: David Grene and Richard Lattimore, ed. *Sophocles*, vol. 2. University of Chicago, 1954.

———, *Antigone*: Sophocles. *Antigone*. Translated by Nicholas Rudall. Ivan R. Dee, 1998; Sophocles. *Oedipus the King and Antigone*. Translated and edited by Peter D. Arnott. Appleton-Century-Croft, 1960; David Grene and Richard Lattimore, ed. *Sophocles*, vol. 1. University of Chicago, 1954.

Steele, Richard, *The Conscious Lovers; The Funeral; The Tender Husband*: S.S. Kenny, ed. *The Plays of Richard Steele*. Clarendon, 1971.

Tennyson, Alfred, Lord, *Beckett*: Gerald B. Kauvar and Gerald C. Sorensen. *Nineteenth-Century English Verse Drama*. Associated University Presses, 1973.

Terence, *The Mother-in-Law*: Translated by Leon Katz (unpublished); alternate source: George Duckworth, ed. *Complete Roman Drama*. Random House, 1942.

Theocritus, *Idylls, 2,* "The Sorceress": Translated by Leon Katz (unpublished); alternate source: *The Idylls of Theocritus*. Translated by Robert Wells. Carcanet Press, 1988.

Thompson, Benjamin, *The Stranger*: Douglas MacMillan and Howard M. Jones, ed. *Plays of the Restoration and Eighteenth Century*. Holt, Rinehart & Winston, 1966.

Tourneur, Cyril, *The Atheist's Tragedy*: Sir John Churton Collins, ed. *The Plays and Poems of Cyril Tourneur*. New York Books for Libraries Press, 1972.

———, *The Revenger's Tragedy*: Cyril Tourneur. *The Revenger's Tragedy* Edited by Brian Gibbons. The New Mermaids, 1989.

Trotter, Catherine, *Love at a Loss*: Edna L. Steeves, ed. *The Plays of Mary Pix and Catharine Trotter*. Garland, 1982.

Vanbrugh, Sir John, *The Provok'd Wife*: *Twelve Famous Plays of the Restoration and the Eighteenth Century*. Modern Library, 1933.

———, *The Relapse*: D. Davison, ed. *Restoration Comedies*. Oxford University, 1970.

Vega, Lope de, *Acting is Believing*: Lope de Vega. *Acting Is Believing*. Translated by Michael D. McGaha. Trinity University Press, 1986.

———, *The Duchess of Amalfi's Steward*: Lope de Vega. *The Duchess of Amalfi's Steward*. Translated by Cynthia Rodriguez-Bodendyck. Dovehouse Canada, 1985.

———, *Fuente Ovejuna*: Eric Bentley, ed. *The Classic Theatre*, Vol. 3. Doubleday/Anchor, 1959.

———, *Peribanez and the Comendador de Ocana*: Lope de Vega. *Lope de Vega: Five Plays*. Edited by R.D.F. Pring-Mill. Translated by Jill Booty. Mermaid Dramabook, 1961.

Voltaire, *The Prodigal; Zaire*: *The Dramatic Works of Voltaire* vol. 5. E.R. DuMont, 1901.

Webster, John, *The Duchess of Malfi*: A.H. Nethercourt, Ch.R. Baskervill, and V.B. Heltzel, ed. *Stuart Plays*. Holt, Rinehart & Winston, 1971.

———, *The White Devil*: John Webster. *The White Devil*. Edited by Christina Luckyj. W.W. Norton, 1996.

Wilde, Oscar, *An Ideal Husband; Lady Windermere's Fan; Salome; A Woman of No Importance*: *Oscar Wilde, The Complete Works*. Barnes & Noble, 1994.

Wiseman, Jane, *Antiochus the King*: Jane Wiseman. *Antiochus the Great, or The Fatal Relapse*. W. Turner & R. Bassert, 1702.

Wycherley, William, *The Country Wife*: D. Davison, ed. *Restoration Comedies*. Oxford University, 1970.

———, *The Plain Dealer*: B. Gibbons, ed. *Five Restoration Comedies*. Bloch/New Mermaids, 1984.

COPYRIGHT INFORMATION